Restless

The life of a modern seeker, Sampath's questing mind can be sensed through his professional life at the California Institute of Integral Studies (CIIS), his questions range freely across new fields of knowledge, in the search for value and meaning.

Debashish Banerji, Haridas Chaudhuri
Professor of Indian Philosophies and Cultures, and
Doshi Professor of Asian Art, CIIS, San Francisco

This book offers one of those rare opportunities to get the inside story about world events that most of us know about only through pared down media reports. Because Sampath occupied a major role in the Indian Police Service, he was intimately involved in many of the incidents that shaped contemporary India: the Partition, the deaths of Rajiv and Indira Gandhi, the Tamil Tigers, the Naxalites, the Kashmiri Separatists and more. His clear writing tells a gripping story in vivid detail. And then, he brings his rich and complex history to the United States where he enters the world of higher education and cybercrime. Once again in his later chapters, we get the fresh perspective of someone from another world on matters that have become too familiar to us here. In addition, he gives us an insider's view of the ancient yoga tradition of which he is a practitioner. This book is such a rare blend of engaging and thrilling stories, combined with the thoughtful reflections of one who has seen so much of the world in turmoil.

Don Hanlon Johnson, professor of Somatics, CIIS, and
author, *Body, Spirit, and Democracy*

Like Walt Whitman, Sampath Ramanujan 'contains multitudes'—husband and father, cop, a student of Vedanta and J. Krishnamurti, somatist and Rolfing enthusiast, cybersecurity consultant and memoirist. This book is the story of India, of police work, of spiritual striving, and academic success. Read it for insight, inspiration and deep enjoyment.

Robert McDermott, president emeritus, professor, Department
and Chair, Philosophy, Cosmology and Consciousness, CIIS

Restless

Chronicles of a
POLICEMAN

V.R. SAMPATH

RUPA

Published by
Rupa Publications India Pvt. Ltd 2018
7/16, Ansari Road, Daryaganj
New Delhi 110002

Sales centres:
Allahabad Bengaluru Chennai
Hyderabad Jaipur Kathmandu
Kolkata Mumbai

ISBN: 978-93-5304-104-5

First impression 2018

10 9 8 7 6 5 4 3 2 1

The moral right of the author has been asserted.

Printed by Parksons Graphics Pvt.Ltd., Mumbai.

My life, thereby, this book, is dedicated to my parents,
V.V. Ramanujan and R. Kamala, who are no more.

Contents

Foreword

When I agreed to write a foreword for Sampath's book, I was under the impression that it would be yet another autobiography by someone, who after spending a quarter of a century as a member of the Indian Police Service, felt it was time for him to write his memoirs. I was, hence, quite unprepared for what the book contained. It is, indeed autobiographical, but as the book develops, one discerns that it is in part a philosophical dissertation that helps bring out another side of the author's personality. Leaving behind the mundane world of job security, which a job in government offered, as also the challenging environment of the corporate sector, he ventures subsequently to seek inner solace and understand the true meaning of life. The first six chapters of the book do follow a predictable script, but everything seems to change once he decides to leave India to carve out a new life in the US. His stint with the California Institute of Integral Studies and his master's in fine arts there, appear to have induced a fundamental change in his attitudes and outlook. Consequently, the second part of the book conveys an impression that the author was experimenting with life in more ways than one. There are no doubt interesting chapters on technology and related matters, as also on cybersecurity, apart from interesting vignettes on art and life, but there are also enough broad hints about the changes taking place in the author's personality. This becomes evident as we go through Part Two of his work, Exploration, Expansion and Integration. The author seems to become increasingly metaphysical in outlook, and dwells on religion, philosophy and spirituality. He expounds on Vaishnavism and Vishistadvaita at one level. At another, he talks of philosophers like G.I. Gurdjieff and their thoughts, attempting a leap of faith as far as religion and philosophy are concerned. The author acknowledges his brief brush with J. Krishnamurti, which possibly led him to seek ways and means to achieve self-fulfilment. For those who knew Sampath as a committed, though restless, police officer, the change in his personality cannot but be a surprise. The book is worth reading, especially for those who feel that one should not be content with following a single trajectory. Life needs to be lived to the fullest, and the mind set free to follow its spirit of search and enquiry. For those like me, who have followed a single career, we are left dissatisfied that we did not have the courage and strength of purpose that Sampath demonstrated to try something different. To achieve what Sampath mentions as his basic philosophy in life, 'tonnes of experience, an estate of consciousness and vast acres of mind' is something all of us would wish for.

M.K. Narayanan,
former national security advisor and
former governor of West Bengal
November 2017

Introduction

Much premium is placed on serving society. I agree, but I have a point of view here. While I don't advocate a selfish life, I don't believe in an entirely 'selfless' life too. Discovering the self—not the 'ego self' but the real self buried under the debris of one's ego—should be the primary goal in one's life. One needs to remove the dirt and clear the way for the self to emerge. Serving society helped me in a way to do this, but finding the real self, and thereby meaning, remained my responsibility.

I gave twenty-five years of my life to serving the society, and I feel contented about it. The remainder was meant to be spent in seeking my real self. I expect this book to reflect the efforts made by me to do precisely that. Earlier, I took decisions in a mechanical way, be it decisions about what I should study, what work to do and when should I marry and set up my family. Midway through my service, my consciousness stirred awake and slowly I started taking responsibility for my life and made decisions accordingly. There were repeated temptations to return to my former ways, but I stood firm; four times I was given the offer for 'better' postings, but I decided to go to the place I wanted to work in and did what I wanted to do. When I could no longer do that, I decided to quit rather than follow meekly the path shown by the service. If my service and work years took me to different places and exciting experiences, my favourite books and their authors took me on equally exciting journeys of my mind. My consciousness, from being a tiny dot, expanded and soared. I lived with great scholars, philosophers and mystics in my inner realm. Different dimensions of life were revealed, and I became aware of the possibilities and potentialities of my life. Today, I'm still a work in progress.

Looking at it in another way, Part I represents my physical, mechanical life consisting of career and family. The unconscious decisions took me from banks to the police service in a distant land, took on family responsibilities at an inappropriate time of life and family faced the consequences of such decisions. During this period, I came across the works of G.I. Gurdjieff and even saw and heard J. Krishnamurti personally, but the accidental inputs remained buried in my subconscious mind. This part also represents my awakening consciousness; I realized the importance of expanded awareness and acute alertness to the demands of my career and family and to say 'no' whenever needed. But the mechanical ways continued, though slightly abated. The chaos finally ended, peace descended and prosperity ensued. I became a consultant with some big corporate houses. I continued my studies, though connected purely with my career of security; an MPhil in defence studies and a PhD in aviation security. Later, I landed in San Francisco, to study MFA in art, and am continuing, as I write this, with research studies (PhD) in philosophy, cosmology and consciousness. All this while, thanks to my wife and sons who took over the responsibilities of running our day-to-day life, I stopped working and shut down the sensory inputs coming in from job, career, money and a significant part of my family life.

Part II remains the most important aspect of my life; the ideas, books and authors carefully curated, so that a clear map of the journey of my mind and consciousness emerged, or so I hope. The ideas of the Fourth Way formed the basis of my quest for self-knowledge and the context for myself in the broader canvas of the cosmology and psychology of my heredity, environment, essence and personality. While my early childhood and subsequent professional evolution, from a career in banks to one in the police service, gave me a personality, it's the essence I was eager to study, to know what exactly was me—Sampath. Religious studies contributed to understanding the religion I was born into and learning about astrology gave an insight to the kind of influences my essence is subjected to. Connected with these were cosmological and energy aspects of the yoga and chakra systems, as energy appeared to be the basis of the expansion of consciousness. With studies and practically implementing what I had learned, through diet and relaxation of the body, I experimented with my self-consciousness, which means developing a deeper awareness of my body. Rolfing contributed considerably in this context.

The important lessons from this eventful life are the spirit of enquiry, the metamorphosis of the earlier spirit of adventure and constant seeking of change into an investigation turned inwards— into unconscious decisions, their consequences and the questions that arise: Why does this happen only to me? Or Who am I? The answers came in the form of philosophies of J. Krishnamurti, G.I. Gurdjieff, Ramana Maharishi and others.

The essence of all my experiences, be it in banks, government, police, security or corporate environment—or a foreign country and its cultural differences—can be summed up in one sentence; life is accidental and random in occurring, unless your consciousness level is high enough to neutralize them. I don't know about the level of my consciousness, but all through the trials and tribulations, victories and defeats, joy and sorrows, and ups and downs, one thing which was constant in me was the feeling that I was bigger than my circumstances. This feeling is alive to date and keeps me going with cheer and gusto.

I think, this is the core of my life. This spirit is the cause of my further explorations of the very boundaries of life and consciousness. It appears that among the archetypes of truth, beauty, justice and others, knowledge and understanding have been the guiding forces in my life.

Part I

The Mechanical Life
and Awakening

The search for the truth is in one way hard and in another way easy—for it is evident that no one of us can master it fully, nor miss it wholly. Each one of us adds a little to our knowledge of nature, and from all the facts assembled arises a certain grandeur.

ARISTOTLE

1

First Encounter!

When it comes to human dignity,
we cannot make compromises.

—ANGELA MERKEL

The police patrol jeep stopped at the unmanned railway gate. I looked to my left, at the track stretching from a great distance and disappearing into the horizon to my right. As the gate bells rang, I wondered when the train would appear so that we could reach the headquarters, file the report and get back home. It was my wife Jaya's birthday. She would be waiting, fully dressed and ready to go to the temple. The noon sun was harsh and the air, humid. There was hardly any vegetation as far as the eye could see. I removed my sunglasses and wiped the sweat off my face. 'This is a godforsaken place, and the arid heat sure seems to affirm that, eh?' Sukhram Singh, my driver, grinned. 'Yes, sirji. Four days of chasing that woman across Chambal is four days too long.' He was alluding to the unfinished police action that week to track down, Phoolan Devi, then the only female dacoit, who had become the nightmare of the hundreds of villages around the valley. This time, however, I was on a different mission.

The security gunmen seated at the back were silent. Everyone was weary from the long journey that started at 4.30 that morning. I was on the trail of a murder that had been eluding the police for a long time. I suspected one of my men, a sub-inspector, of tampering with the evidence and attempting to hush up the case. I decided it was time I visited the scene of the crime, talked to people and got first-hand knowledge of the situation before coming to any conclusions. And now, I had enough evidence now to recommend the transfer of the sub-inspector.

I heard the distant whistle of the approaching train and consulted my watch; it was 3 p.m., and I was ravenous. 'About time,' I muttered. 'We should be back at the HQ soon enough now.' The train approached the gate with a roar and zipped past. I counted the carriages. There were nine. I could hear howling and laughter as the ninth carriage approached. It was full of children running about and waving at the police jeep. School children probably on a field trip, I thought, either on their way or returning.

As the ninth carriage passed, the driver started the jeep getting ready to roll. That's when I noticed it, and my jaws dropped. I rubbed my eyes and looked again as the train receded quickly. There was no mistaking the human body tightly tied in a white gauze bandage, a simple woven strip material, on the last car marked LV—Last Van. The bandage job appeared to have been the work of a professional, like they do in hospitals for victims of multiple fractures. This type of dressing is used by trained nurses. The hands were outstretched and tied to the side coupling chain of the car and the feet tied firmly to the bottom railing. I shouted, 'Stop, did you see that? What...' I was at a loss for words. 'Yes sir, a dead body,' Sukhram Singh, the driver said without a trace of emotion, 'It is the police.'

'The police?' I asked agitatedly. 'The police killed that person?' Several questions sprang to my mind—did the cops shoot the man, or whoever it was? How was the body displayed so brazenly in the open, on the back of a train car? And most importantly, how was it that my driver Sukhram knew about it and I didn't?

One of the gunmen from behind spoke for the first time, 'Sir, whenever a body, mostly unidentified, needs to be sent to the morgue, the police send it this way,' he explained. 'We have only one morgue within 100 km, and the budget leaves little room for first-class travel.' The gunmen tried—and failed—to suppress their laughs. It happened so frequently that no one was surprised or shocked. Why couldn't the police have an arrangement with the railways? After all, everything is government work, I thought. 'Chalta hai sir,' quipped Sukhram. 'It happens.' I hated that line. Whenever there was something which deserved an explanation, and no one had any, 'Chalta hai—it happens' filled the gaps. It was a perfect alibi for inaction.

The station to the right was only a few yards away and I noticed the train slowing down, preparing for a halt as it crossed the gate. I got down from the jeep and ran to the stationmaster who, almost immediately, was already preparing to wave the train off, as it was a small station and there was hardly any passengers boarding or getting off. I showed my badge and requested him to stop the train for a while. 'Do you have your first-aid team at your station?' The stationmaster answered in the affirmative and called out, 'Suresh.' Soon, the man came running from behind the stationmaster's cabin. I told him what I wanted him to do immediately. He ran back into the cabin, brought his toolbox and went to the back of the last car and started unravelling the bandages. The material appeared synthetic, and torn in many places, exposing a hard hand and the backs of both thighs. In the meantime, I spoke to the nearest hospital, which had an ambulance service readily available to send to the railway station, and then sat down waiting for the body to be brought down. The ambulance was likely to take about twenty minutes to reach. I wondered what Jaya would be thinking. It wasn't going to be a pleasant thing to tell her about the cause of the delay, though she knew it was in the line of my duty. I looked around and saw a few curious onlookers watching the proceedings from a distance. The passengers inside the train had puzzled looks on their faces at the inordinate and unusual delay the train was taking in leaving the station.

As I waited for the ambulance, I contacted the police stations located before this station to check whether it was true that the body was indeed being sent to the mortuary hundred kilometres away, and got an affirmative response from one of them. I expressed my annoyance to the station house officer of the concerned police station for resorting to this method of sending a body and asked for a written explanation in three days. In the meantime, two more men had joined Suresh. Finally, the body was brought down and placed on a bench. I signalled the stationmaster to let the train go, and it started moving as soon as he blew a whistle and waved the green flag. In seconds, the platform was empty, barring my men, the stationmaster and a stray dog. I waited until the ambulance arrived, and the body was on its way to the morgue, and then left.

On my way back the thought of that lone body heading to its final resting place in such a bizarre way kept popping up in my mind, but brushed aside the thoughts and got myself into the right frame of mind to not ruin Jaya's birthday by such reflections.

I had decided to do something about this though, and one of the first things I did on reaching the office the next day was to examine the issue of transportation of dead bodies. I dug up the budget proposal and studied it thoroughly. It was evident that the remoteness of operations and small allowances reimbursed by the government had resulted in this original but detestable idea. I issued a note raising the allocation of budget for such purposes and suggested all station house officers take up the matter with the railway authorities for a proper solution.

2

Back to the Past—Early Years

The further backward you look,
the further forward you can see.

−WINSTON CHURCHILL

Much before family planning was a thing, my parents decided to have only two children, so we were a small and compact family; I had only one brother. And it's a legacy that has passed on. I also followed in their footsteps and had two sons, though my brother, by having three girls, fulfilled the desire of the family to have daughters. During childhood, my brother stayed with my maternal uncles in north Chennai, while I went with my parents to Visakhapatnam in Andhra Pradesh, where my father got posted. He worked for the Government Coast Battery, a defence establishment, the rough equivalent of the present-day coastguard service. The only memory I have of this establishment was when my father took me for a 'firing show'. The cannons were lined up on the beach and balls were fired into the sea. The bullets went like fireballs and fell into the sea splashing water to great heights. Out of over-enthusiasm I must have wandered very near to one of the cannons when it suddenly fired. The recoil and the sound were too much for my tender ears, so much so that the ears remained shut and swollen for a week!

Visakhapatnam is a beautiful place with rocks, mountains and beaches everywhere. One day, when I was taking some Tamil magazines to my mother's friends who live a couple of streets away, I had to cross a small bridge that spanned a rivulet, which had swelled over with water due to the heavy rains that year. It had big rocks lining the banks and I was mesmerized by the running water. I went near the handrails and looking down, promptly fell over. I don't remember whether I cried for help, but I do remember seeing a man jumping in, carrying me to a cycle rickshaw, and taking me straight to my home. The shock was visible on my mother's face when she saw her son fully drenched and wearing a dazed look. Later, it transpired that the rickshaw puller was a regular to our house. He had noticed me walking alone and followed me for a while when this happened. I was scared my mother would be angry because the magazines had gone wet with the water. But she was not. She cried and hugged me tightly and thanked God for coming in the form of a rickshaw puller and saving her child.

I remember another incident when I went out with a friend of mine, Raghavendra, and wandered to the nearby railway yard. Coaches were in the shunting yard, and fascinated, we got into an empty one. I was used to trains because of our frequent trips to Chennai. I didn't remember who suggested the ride but, before we realized what happened, the train was moving and picking up speed. We didn't know what to do. The train stopped, and the inspecting staff found us huddled in a corner, frightened. Even as we had our own adventure, our mothers were running around looking for us. No one knew anything about our whereabouts, until a shunting railway man returned us both, and chided the ladies for being careless with their children. Though my mother was relieved to see me in good shape, I couldn't escape admonishment and a couple of slaps on the back. The incident was one of the earliest expressions of my tendency to venture into unchartered territories, perhaps early indication of what was to follow, when I wandered all my life!

Our house was near a mountain, which was frequented by sheep and goats that came there to graze. We would hear occasional cries of the sheep during the night, which my mother put down to the wandering tigers and wolves hunting their prey. They also sometimes strayed into the colony and took the hens. I was warned not to go near the mountain alone. Another sharp memory is of her singing 'Jaga Janani' and other songs from the movie Meera, an ardent devotee of Krishna, to make me sleep. Her mellifluous voice is etched in my memory forever. There was no electricity those days, and only a chimney lamp with a flickering light hung from the ceiling. I didn't know when my father came back from work on most of the days. My clearest memories of spending time with my dad were the bicycle rides he took me on to buy soft drinks. It's a taste that has stayed with me and led to type-II diabetes.

When I was seven, my father returned to Chennai. Until then, I didn't go to school. My mother homeschooled me, and she managed to get me admitted directly into the second standard. The teacher tested my knowledge to see whether I knew the basics of the first standard. Everything was okay except for one thing; where I was required to write the Tamil alphabet 'a' with stronger intonation, I had written the alphabet with the 'smaller' tone. When the teacher said the bigger one was required, I wrote the little one again, but this time a 'bigger' version of it. Everyone laughed, and I got admitted. Clearly, that was an indication of lateral thinking! Since I spent my early years in Andhra, I was more fluent in Telugu to start with than in my mother tongue, Tamil. When I came back to Chennai, it took me some time to pick it up and forget Telugu. My relatives were dismayed to find that I was talking only to my mother and that too in Telugu.

My brother and cousin were also studying in the same school where I got admitted. When school started, my mother gave me strict instructions to come back home along with my brothers, who were older than me. She instructed the two boys to bring me back carefully, as it was my first day at school, and first day in Chennai after our return from Vizag. After she had left, my brother showed me a place where I should wait for them after the bell. When school ended for the day, I headed to the spot, but didn't find my brothers. I didn't wait and decided to walk home alone. Our house was on the Thiruvottiyur High Road in north Chennai, and the school, Ganapathy Higher Secondary School, was in the interiors, about 3 km away. Several bends needed to be negotiated, including the crossing of the Thiruvottiyur High Road where traffic used to be heavy. I came out of the school and followed the same route that I had that morning, when I came with my mother, correctly remembering every turn we took in the morning. My mother, who was busy at work, turned around and saw me. She couldn't believe her eyes. She asked me where my brothers were, and I mentioned that they were not there at the appointed place and time. At the same time, my brothers came rushing home saying that I was missing and all hell broke loose. When they saw me standing there, their anger and relief were palpable. They pounced on me, and we were rolling on the floor. That incident became folklore of sorts as I was only seven, new to the city having arrived only a day before from Vizag, and having gone to a far-off school for the first time, successfully negotiated my way back without help and any GPS!

The rest of my school days went off without much ado. I stood first in the class most of the time, enjoyed one more double promotion, and won the admiration of my teachers.

In Chennai, our house was situated near a temple, on a street called Sanjeevarayan Koil Street. The temple used to host an annual car festival, during which time the entire neighbourhood bustled with activity for ten days. With blaring loudspeakers and crowds thronging, the Gods rode different vahanas, or vehicles, every night for ten nights. The vahanas, in various shapes like horses, elephants, the Sun and the Moon, used to take a long time to create, and appeared late in the night. Those were heady days with lots of fun and profound discussions about mythology and the afterlife. I used to wonder what we did after we died and encountered God. Would we sit on His lap or would we form a part of His furniture or tapestry? It was confusing. It never occurred that we could be accommodated somewhere in His Kingdom.

When I reached the fifth standard, I was put in another school, KCSN High School, which was farther away than the earlier one. Here too, I continued doing well at studies, maintaining my first rank. I became part of the debating team and participated in many interschool debating competitions, and won prizes.

One vivid memory was the elections for the school pupil leader, which was held every year. One student who was a known gang leader of sorts contested the elections. The school management didn't want him to be elected and thought of me as the ideal candidate to fight against him. When the voting finished, I had lost badly, and my ego was badly bruised as well. I was under the mistaken impression that I was popular, but I only got votes from those who knew me well. Another blow to my ego came from the school final exam results. Contrary to everyone's expectations, including mine, that I'd stand first in the school, I came third! It took me several days to reconcile to the fact.

There used to be a marriage hall in front of our house, and most of the days of the wedding season, that hall would be host to innumerable celebrations. Central to the celebrations were film songs blaring through the speakers every day, and I enjoyed listening to them; this, my parents thought, could have been one of the reasons for my failing to make it to the top. Even to this day, I remember many of the songs I learned during that period. That was also the period when I fell sick repeatedly, suffering from all sorts of fevers such as typhoid, chicken pox and flu. I used to borrow a radio from my uncle and keep listening to songs during such times. Otherwise there was no radio or fan at home. My mother was always at my bedside, tending to my needs when I was down.

I read a lot of novels too during that period, especially detective novels by the likes of such as Perry Mason, Agatha Christie and Ian Fleming, who created the character James Bond. I used to go to the neighbours whenever there was a cricket match to listen to the commentary. I remember the day the first table fan arrived during one of my illnesses, to give me relief from the raging fever, and a Philips radio to listen to music, which I loved. During those high school days, I had a large circle of friends, and we formed a cricket team and played matches. At other times we used to play annual games such as kite flying, stamp matching, marbles, gilli and tops. While flying kites we chased falling kites on rooftops unmindful of the danger of falling. During one such instance of kite-flying, I suddenly lost my voice, and we rushed to the family doctor, who promptly asked me whether I was chasing kites in the summer afternoon with eyes on the sky. I said yes. He smiled and gave me a tablet which cured my throat instantly. On another occasion, while playing tops, I broke my friend's head. The game goes like this; five or six people play with tops. All had a top in the hands duly rolled in ropes, and all the players have to pitch them into the centre of the circle at the same time. I did so a bit prematurely and the boy who was organizing the tops in the centre hadn't moved away. My top, with the nail edge, squarely landed on his head. The next moment he was on the ground, blood pouring from his skull. There was pandemonium, and the parents came running. His parents rushed him to the hospital, and the wound required several stitches and two days of hospitalization. When I apologized, the boy's mother said it was not my fault; probably her son was not quick enough to move away. I was appalled that a mother had more confidence in me than her son.

Somehow, I never got into organized sports events of school or college. Though I was considered a good all-rounder in cricket, I never tried to join the school or college teams.

The Hindi Language Issue in Tamil Nadu

We heard the stones falling on the roof. First, it was one or two, but soon it became a torrent. We could hear people shouting outside. The teacher stopped the lecture and asked all the students to take cover as some stones came rocketing through the windows. I gathered my books and along with others, ran towards the veranda which led to the interior classrooms. The class we were in was adjoining the road and so was more vulnerable to attack from the mob.

I was learning Hindi, and the mob outside was protesting the imposition of Hindi on Tamilians. They saw the spread of Hindi in the state as a threat to their culture, their identity and job opportunities. It all started when the government of India, through a provision in the Constitution in 1950, made Hindi the official language of the country replacing English, which was deemed to be the legacy left behind by the British. The provision also provided for a transition time of fifteen years from 1950 to 1965, by which time Hindi would completely replace English as the official language.

The southern states, particularly Tamil Nadu, hated this and saw the move as the imposition of a language spoken by people in the northern states on a non-Hindi-speaking people. The Dravidian parties of Tamil Nadu, took up the cause, albeit for political reasons, to oppose the spread of Hindi. The Dravidian parties whipped up Tamil sentiments and the agitations spread like wildfire all over the state. The government arrested leaders and police action was seen everywhere to quell the mobs. I saw hordes of men carrying buckets of tar and defacing billboards and signs appearing in Hindi, be it the railway stations, the post offices or other central government organizations throughout the state.

I was fourteen years old at that time and had a keen interest in studies. My father thought it wise to put me through as many courses as possible, including Hindi classes in the evenings at the Dakshin Bharat Hindi Prachar Sabha, the central government wing responsible for 'spreading' Hindi in the southern states.

As far as I was concerned, it was just one more subject to study. But the Hindi language classes were discontinued by the organizers, who were afraid for the safety of the students who chose to learn it. Later the Official Languages Act was amended to allow both Hindi and English to be the official languages of the country.

The local parties saw the agitations as a victory. They didn't lose time in capitalizing on this perception and made it an important issue for the 1967 assembly elections. The Dravida Munnetra Kazhagam (DMK) won and was elected to power in the state, unseating the Congress. By 1972, the DMK also split into two: the DMK and the All India Anna Dravida Munnetra Kazhagam (AIADMK) and power alternated between the two parties ever since. The Indian National Congress, the party which won freedom for the country, could never come back to power in Tamil Nadu. It signalled the birth of regionalism in the country, and other regions swiftly followed suit.

Language was only one of the issues contributing to the tensions between the south and the north. According to most of the southerners, the power was mostly in the hands of the latter; successive prime ministers and presidents were from the northern parts of India. There were leaders from the south too, such as Rajagopalachari, Kamaraj and Sarvapalli Radhakrishnan to name a few, but these numbers were far outweighed by the north. The people from the south perceived a stepmotherly treatment, which was denied by the northerners.

Around the same this time, another trend was taking shape in Tamil Nadu in the form of the anti-Brahmin movement. The protagonists of this movement supposedly saw that Brahmins, though a minority, were holding important positions in the society, be it power or worship, art or music. The agitators demanded caste-based reservations in jobs and educational institutions. Hectic lobbying combined with protests, demonstrations and violence followed. The state was again in turmoil. Ever since the country became independent, there had been no time to celebrate the freedom so dearly fought and achieved by its great leaders because the independence also brought with it the pain of Partition, which in turn, led to immense bloodshed and turmoil, at a time when leaders were struggling to make sense of what freedom meant. The leadership questions were not easy to resolve, and the country was vastly divided over religion, caste and language. Added to that were the rajas and maharajas still holding on to their thrones and demanding a piece of the cake. Enormous efforts were required to accomplish a semblance of unity; Sardar Patel was engaged in unifying the provinces, and Vinoba Bhave launched a 'bhoodhan' movement to harness excess lands from the rich to distribute among the poor for cultivation. Forming the government, administering the vast country, drafting the Constitution and the various laws and rules—it was not easy. To all these problems were added new ones such as the demands for reservation, nationalization of banks and abolition of privy purses being doled out to the kings and princes of the former provinces for joining the Indian Union.

All this happened when I was a teenager. While I was not very much concerned with what happened before and soon after Independence, as I was barely a child, what was going on in front of my eyes did affect me personally and had far-reaching consequences on my future. I was born into a Brahmin family in Tamil Nadu, the Dravidian citadel where anti-Brahmin sentiments were brewing. I am a Dravidian—by my birth and that of my ancestors for centuries—but it was politically expedient to isolate Brahmins as descendants of the Aryan race. My family, just like any other Brahmin family, worshipped Rama and Krishna in our homes. When I stepped out, I found processions and protests with placards of the same gods being burnt down and desecrated openly.

Another development was the rise of trade unionism widely supported by communists. Every organization had to contend with this development, in addition to the problems posed by reservations, regionalism and corruption. I experienced all these factors at play when I joined my first job in a bank.

It was during my bank days that I started watching Hollywood movies in a big way. One rainy day, the bank closed early due to a heavy downpour. Everyone was heading to the comfort of their home, but I chose to go to the theatre instead, guessing, quite correctly, that I would get tickets without any hassle. I went to Sapphire Hall and watched *Poseidon Adventure*, a movie about a sinking ship, which seemed rather appropriate, given that it was pouring cats and dogs outside! Meanwhile, my family became worried when I didn't return home, and contacted my friends, who said there was no work in the afternoon. When I returned home, I mumbled some excuse, had my dinner and went to bed. In the morning when I woke up, I saw three heads peering down at me. My parents and brother were mockingly furious. The reason? They were waving the torn portion of the movie ticket retrieved from my raincoat. All of us had a hearty laugh! I was a diehard fan of James Bond movies during my college days and saw *Dr. No*, *From Russia with Love* and *Thunder Ball* several times. When I became a father, I even encouraged my young sons to watch movies critically and get a feel for the visual media.

Stumbling Upon a Sage

It was a holiday, and I had just finished my college exams. Chennai was a laid-back place and enjoyable for me. I was walking along Marina Beach enjoying the blue ocean front, the sands, and the breeze. Children were playing beach volleyball, and hawkers were scurrying on the sands, chasing after people who appeared to be prospective buyers of the snacks they were carrying in tin boxes. The salty murukku, roasted peanuts and green mango liberally doused with salt and pepper were favourite items available with these vendors, who were predominantly children. The parents of these children prepared these things, packed them in tin carriers with lids and sent them through the kids for sale.

I went right ahead into Santhome High Road and then on to

Greenways Road. I liked observing people and the activity going on around me. While crossing the road, I noticed a garden with a huge compound wall with sliding gates. I had passed by this area earlier but always found the gates closed. That day it was open, and I noticed people going inside. I looked up near the entrance and saw a banner welcoming all for a talk by one JK. Curiosity overtook me, and I walked in. Once I entered, I realized it was a beautiful garden tucked neatly out of sight from the road. There was total silence except for the chirping of birds and the rustling noise of the leaves and branches in the gentle breeze. Three hundred feet into the garden, the gravel laid path led to an old-fashioned bungalow, which was invisible from the gate. As I went near the building, I noticed several people moving briskly but in silence towards the left. I too, turned in that direction and abruptly came upon a raised dais standing in the garden. About hundred people sat on the ground facing towards it. It looked as though the speaker was about to appear anytime. I found a vantage point to the right of the dais with a tree trunk serving as the backrest.

The atmosphere was electrifying but calm. The air was heavy with expectation, so palpable that you could touch the silence with your fingers. I instinctively turned around just in time to catch a glimpse of the emerging figure from the main building; J. Krishnamurti aka JK. I had not seen such a human face before. He looked like an angel descending the stairs, elegantly old with snow-white hair. He had such a frail body that when he walked, it appeared the breeze carried him to the dais.

He walked up to the dais briskly, took his seat, briefly closed his eyes for a minute and started talking in calm and measured voice. When he finished, it appeared to be too soon, but when I consulted my wristwatch, an hour had elapsed. The crowd was sitting mesmerized for the time he had been talking and probably wished for more as JK rose quickly to his feet and walked away, followed by two people, probably, from his ashram. The crowd started melting away, and soon the garden emptied out, bearing no resemblance to the crowded place it had been just moments before. I rose reluctantly and sauntered towards the gate. I looked back once and had a fleeting glimpse of the old man, with his side profile, white hair and sharp nose disappearing around the corner of the garden. I had no opportunity to see him again in my life. Several years later I read in the newspapers that JK died of cancer at the age of eighty-six.

I kept thinking about the talk I had just heard. JK had described a beautiful forest, a setting much more beautiful than the garden he was sitting in and talking. The trees and shrubs, the birds and the greenery, the wind and the sweet smell of the fresh soil; all that description of a beautiful forest lulled the audience into a hypnotic sleep. JK went on to describe a lone bullock cart winding its way through the forest path with the bell around its neck jingling in the light breeze. The audience was in a deep meditative state, experiencing the sylvan surroundings described by him. What he said next startled them out of their slumber; the bullock-drawn cart carried a coffin with the body of a dead man.

I walked away, my mind mulling what I had just heard. 'We don't know what dying means because we don't know what living means too. Death is always there everywhere, only we dread facing it and treat it like a dark, frightening monster that deserves to be kept at bay behind the closed doors. Instead of burying our heads in the sands or postpone our fears, we had one more choice, to learn from death how to live life.'

What JK said before or after vanished from memory but what lingered on for long was the powerful imagery he gave for the meaning of life. He said many things about the nature of mind, thought, conditioning, sorrow and conflicts and many other issues facing human life, which, at that point of time made little sense to me. But I knew that my life wouldn't be the same again. The talk transformed me subliminally. I wanted to understand life and death and live the right way but for a young man like me, I reckoned,

I had many things to do before sitting in contemplation of such 'grave' issues.

The Career Trail

Banks

Soon after graduation, in 1971, I opted for a freelance job with the Indian Institute of Public Opinion, which was surveying the food habits of people in Tamil Nadu. The job involved codifying details of study reports submitted by field officers all over the state and making the data fit for analysis in pre-designed formats. I also started attending classes at the Indian Statistical Institute, Nungambakkam, because someone in the family felt statistics had a great future. Given my strong anti-math sentiments, I should have known better than trying to comprehend a subject like statistics. I quit both, the course and the job.

The same year there was an advertisement from Reserve Bank of India (RBI), the central/federal bank of India, calling for assistants and I applied. There was a written test, and I stood first in the entire state. The interview was only a formality, and I got selected. A bank job in those days was a prestigious one, and my folks considered it a significant achievement to have gotten into RBI. I was posted to the annuity deposit section (ADS), which dealt with the issue of interest warrants to depositors. It was boring, but I concentrated on two things. One, I joined a distant education programme with Sri Venkateswara University, Tirupati, for a master's in English literature. Secondly, I started preparing for the Certified Associate of Indian Institute of Bankers (CAIIB) exams, which happened in two parts. Passing CAIIB was a requirement for bank employees for the promotion to the rank of officers. I cleared these two exams and even gave an entrance test for the United Commercial Bank (UCO) and got selected as a probationary officer. I enjoyed my banking stint, and continued pursuing my passion for books, music and movies.

While I was awaiting orders from the UCO bank, a life-altering encounter took place in my life, in the form of meeting a gentleman called J.P. Birdi. He was one of the officers from RBI, Mumbai, who were on a training visit to Chennai. I had opportunities to interact with the group, and one day J.P. came to me and said 'Sampath, you are wasting your time in banks. Why don't you appear for the UPSC exams? With your talent and knowledge, you would make it easily.' I asked him what UPSC was and J.P. explained to me that the Union Public Service Commission (UPSC) conducted examinations for admission to various government services, including the Indian Administrative Service (IAS), Indian Police Service (IPS), Indian Foreign Service (IFS) and other class-I services, which were far superior to banks. He also added that he had written the exam himself and was awaiting the results, saying he was ready to quit the bank if he passed. I also had a chance meeting with an old college friend, Veeraiyan, who used to be pretty good in mathematics and who had, by this time, entered the customs service. He too spoke highly about All India Services (AIS). He seemed to be particularly enamoured by the IPS and tried to impress upon me as to how it was one of the top three services in India. Thus, the idea of appearing for the UPSC took shape in my mind.

I started preparations for the examinations in 1976. Only a few were familiar with UPSC, IAS or IPS in our part of the country, so I had to study on my own. I was not aware of any coaching institution in Chennai. I started reading *Competition Review*, a magazine devoted to the UPSC examinations and began reading up on the current affairs in newspapers. I cut select articles from the papers and pasted them onto an album to maintain continuity. I took care not to choose math as a subject for the examinations! Instead, I chose European history as one of the main topics even though I was completely in the dark about the subject.

My studies for UPSC continued. I spent most of my time on

the open terrace. I would spend the entire day pouring over books for the examinations while my mother sent up food. Frequently, I took a walk to the nearby Trisulam hills and used to wave a white hanky to my mom who waved back from her kitchen window. There were fewer people and less number of houses, and hence it was possible to have an unhindered line of sight view for a few miles. In the meantime, the appointment order for UCO Bank came through, and I resigned from the RBI. I served the bank for about eight months.

The upper age limit for UPSC examinations was twenty-six at that time, which meant I had just one chance to clear the exams. I had opted for all the three services—IAS, IPS and IFS. I qualified for IPS. The next step was to take the medical examination from a government hospital. The results said I had myopia over and above the prescribed level of -4 in each eye. Luckily, the government provisions had room for review in which case vision needed to be non-pathological. So I went through a second medical examination and, to my relief, was declared as having non-pathological myopia, and the certificate sent to the ministry of home affairs which subsequently issued the appointment order.

3

The Holy Grail–
All India Services (AIS)

Disbelief in magic makes a poor soul
believe in government and business.

–TOM ROBBINS

There were three sought-after postings in the IPS—the director general of police (DGP) of a state, the commissioner of police of a metropolitan city or the head of a central (federal) police organization. Only a few privileged officers managed to achieve all three. I didn't wait to become one and quit the service as an inspector general of police. The places I worked at didn't have the police commissioner system and institution, and becoming the head of a central police organization without becoming a deputy general of police was out of the question.

There was another much sought-after category—home state. Even though Tamil Nadu was my home state, my home cadre was Uttar Pradesh (UP), maybe because my grades were lower than the cut-off marks to be considered for home state posting, and hence got assigned to another state.

Another parameter by which the success or otherwise of an

officer is determined is the number of years one spends in the 'field' job. Anyone worth his salt loved to call himself a field specialist.

Only a few thought I looked like a police officer. To others, I seemed more like a professor or a baniya, a businessman—anyone but a cop. I was thin, looked boyish and didn't have the quintessential moustache—or a pot belly. But those who worked with me eventually learned how tough I was from within, though, at first glance, my smile and soft-spoken demeanour misled my colleagues into believing otherwise. The government wanted to recruit educated youngsters to higher levels of the police hierarchy just for this purpose; to bring in fresh blood and new ways of thinking. It expected such recruits to have the primary qualities of mental toughness and physical courage together with a sharp intellect and exemplary character and integrity. The AIS policy also believed that by shuffling officers at the top administrative level, by making them work in different states than the one they were born in, would serve the purposes of national integration and function impartially without favouritism or interference. But this involved considerable sacrifice on the part of the officer concerned, like getting uprooted, with his or her family paying the price of stability.

Indian Police Service (IPS)

I joined the firefighting training at Nagpur and became a full-fledged member of the service on 13 November 1977. I was pleasantly surprised to find J.P. Birdi, who motivated me to write the UPSC examinations, in my batch, he had failed in his earlier attempt. The training at the Nagpur Fire Institute was light and comfortable, in complete contrast to what was to follow at the National Police Academy (NPA), Hyderabad. Most of the teaching was in Hindi, much of which I couldn't follow because the Hindi I learned in Chennai was no match to the 'real' Hindi spoken in these places. One outstanding feature which came up was that most of the boys from north India had excellent knowledge of the services, unlike their fewer south Indian batchmates. A considerable number of them were either sons or daughters of senior government officers or had at least one officer in their families. I had no exposure to any police officer before, and I had no relative in the AIS. I had one maternal uncle in the port services, who later retired as chairman of the Vizag Port Trust. I also noticed that many of them were planning to appear for the UPSC exams the next year to get into the IAS. Those who had the idea of writing again took the police training lightly.

Until then, UPSC was just another examination I had passed, and I was going through the motions of resigning from the previous job, getting the medical tests done, leaving and travelling far away from home and joining the services. The real import of what it meant hit me only when I landed at the NPA. It was now going to be the beginning of some real hard work. Until now, I was a young man from college going through a couple of jobs and earning a decent enough salary to indulge in entertainment and other activities and having no significant responsibilities on the home front. The activities didn't include physical labour and I had never even heard of intense physical training. I had not seen my elder brother, or my father work out. My dad thought bicycling to work was good enough.

National Police Academy

At the NPA, I was exposed to what was almost a bewildering array of physical activities, including parades, drills, sports and development of skills such as driving, swimming, rock climbing and rifle shooting among other things. All of this was overwhelming. After the early-morning rounds of parades and breakfast, my body felt tired, and I slept through the indoor classes on law enforcement. It was a severe jolt to my physical and mental homeostasis, but once I adjusted to it, I finally began to enjoy myself. But the training started in full swing and only got harder and harder, and I barely managed to keep afloat. Right from day one, however, there was no time to reflect, feel or contemplate. The body took over and laboured through the punishing routine, day in and day out. The watchword for this period of my life was hard physical work. As for my family, there used to be an inland mail once in a while occasionally, particularly from my parents enquiring about the training and the food, which I replied. Beyond that, there was hardly any sharing of information. Looking back, I feel I should have shared more then; it was possible they expected me to, but probably I was too overwhelmed by my new life.

The training of a police officer is designed to make a strong personality out of an ordinary college student. Though I was not a candidate fresh out of college like many of my batchmates were, I had spent five years in banks. But after leaving college, for all practical purposes, I was still raw. I had not done any physical training before in my life, and moreover, I had no idea what being a police officer involved. As I looked very much unlike a police officer, I did expect that the police training would also take care of building my body and improve my overall personality. To my disappointment, the training was oriented more towards making a good cop out of me rather than making me 'look good' in the real 'police sense'.

The academy was situated 20 km from Hyderabad on the Hyderabad-Mumbai highway. Ours was the second batch to undergo training there. The sprawling campus was full of boulders and rocks, devoid of any vegetation. We had a lot of shramdaan, physical work, to do to improve the school. That was an essential part of the curriculum, to dig pits, carry sand and brick from one end to the other and plant trees. When I visited the campus several years later, I felt proud and happy that the trees had grown tall and the school looked green.

Training at the academy was gruelling. The routine started at 5.30 a.m. We got up, washed, had a cup of tea and rushed to the parade ground to fall in line by 5.15. The instructors were tough but polite. They knew they were dealing with future senior officers, but at the same time, they needed to impart proper training. If someone in the squad misbehaved, the trainer would shout, 'Get out of the squad sahib!' The daily parade consisted of team drills, which was to ensure proper coordination of limbs. If you were asked to run two rounds of the ground with a rifle in hand, it was considered as punishment. Other training included shooting practice at the range where all varieties of firearms were available for target practice, physical training, horseback riding, swimming and rock climbing among others. A few of the probationers took to all of them like fish to water, but for others, some parts of the training were a nightmare. I belonged to the latter group. Horseback riding was one of them, as I had seen running horses only in movies. Added to that innate fear were the stories of probationers getting killed by falling off speeding horses. The fact that no one confirmed or denied such rumours added to the dread.

A little later, when we were undergoing training at the Moradabad Police Training College, what I feared most came true for me. We were all lined up for a cross-country horseback ride. Next to me was Satya Narayana Rao, from Andhra Pradesh. His horse was swaying and I cautioned Rao to take control of the reins. In the process of controlling, Rao must have touched the horse in some sensitive spot, his horse kicked mine, and my horse bolted, running at breakneck speed through the crowded streets. People watched in amazement. I was perched precariously on horseback or hanging sideways. I could hear shouts from behind and could sense that the trainer was following me on another horse shouting instruction in Hindi, which I hardly followed. Before I could realize, I was rolling on the muddy track with my horse bolting ahead and vanished from sight. I thought I was dead and slowly opened my eyes to find myself on the side of the road after rolling down several yards from the impact. I went straight to the hospital and received some dressing for the bruises. But my fear left me, and my resolve to master the skill of controlling the horse increased.

I did manage to do very well during my subsequent rides on the same horse which had ditched me!

During the first class of rock climbing, we were taught the 'three-point' climb. The method was to keep three points out of the four—two hands and two feet—in touch with the rock and one point in the air. Then we were asked to try it out on a rock nearby, and it worked. We were encouraged to go higher and higher and we gladly obliged. At some point, I looked down, and I was so high up that the instructors and the fellow probationers appeared like ants, far down below. I couldn't move an inch after that. My instructor shouted from below through a megaphone: 'Sampath Sahib! Don't be afraid we are here. Come down slowly.' Only then did I look down again, for a safety net below, but I couldn't locate one. I steadied myself and slowly took one step after the other backward, and after what appeared to be an eternity, placed my last step on the ground, and heaved a sigh of relief. I soon realized that most of my batchmates felt the same. One positive outcome of the experience was that we all rushed to an insurance agent in Secunderabad to insure our lives!

The director, R.D. Singh, was a tough and highly disciplined cop. He expected the probationers to imbibe all his ideas. One of his aims was to make us completely self-reliant, wherever we got posted. He made us learn to cook, polish our own shoes and stitch buttons. It's another story that most of us forgot all that by totally relying on our orderlies for everything. I realized this fact much later when I went to the US as a student and lived there a few years. I was paralyzed in the beginning when I was required to drive, get groceries, tend to the garden with my wife and cook and wash dishes in addition to scores of other chores.

The director came to the parade ground on horseback and shouted at erring probationers until froth appeared in his mouth. At least a couple of candidates fled the training because of the terror he was creating, and still many gave their forthcoming IAS exams and ran away from the service. He frequently invited distinguished speakers to the academy. To keep the routine of morning parade, forenoon indoor classes and evening games intact, he chose the hour before lunch! For the probationers, it was the most inconvenient slot as they would all be so tired after the first two spells that a lecture was least welcome, especially before lunch. What was worse were the times when the lectures ate into lunch time and extended much beyond into the badly needed break time.

One day, the invitee was Pyarelal Nayyar, personal secretary to Mahatma Gandhi during the freedom struggle. All of us arrived from the indoor classes tired. The director spoke at length about Pyarelal's contributions to public life, and finally, he rose to speak. We were famished by this point, so much so that many of us ate during the talk, then left one by one. To say that the director was angry was an understatement. The next morning we were lined up and chided for acting like juveniles, without regard for the chief guest to lunch and leave first. At the end of his long rant, the director punished the batch with a 10-mile cross-country walk. The instructors were strictly told to enforce the penalty without exception. We had regular 'shammers' among us who invented new tricks to avoid inconvenient exercises. But this time, nothing worked. Some of the probationers walked a couple of miles and complained of knee pain, chest pain and heatstroke, but the accompanying instructors were ruthless. We could hear some trainees vowing to take it out on the trainers and coaches who worked with them when they became district superintendents of police.

Another guest lecturer was the then serving director general of police (DGP) of Odisha. Thankfully this time he was a guest speaker during our indoor classes. He spoke about how difficult it was to get funds allocated for police welfare schemes, and how every time he took the file to the minister concerned he came back empty-handed. I got up and asked him, 'In that case, sir, why didn't you resign from the post to make them understand the importance of welfare?' The whole class was stunned at the audacity of such a question, and the speaker was speechless for a minute. The whole class was waiting to see his reaction. The speaker slowly turned towards me and asked my name. I told him. He said, 'Sampath, you are right, I should have resigned.' And he wound up his lecture, got up and left the class. My friends felt there was no need for such impertinence on my part, and told me I was gone for good once the director learned about this. But nothing happened. The speaker must have been a good man and must have seen the point I was trying to make and taken my comments positively.

Towards the middle of the training programme, we had overcome the fatigue of the punishing schedule and started enjoying it. It was also the time we began enjoying the 'feel' of uniform, and the prestige which goes with it

I hated disclosing my identity as a cop and believed in my strength rather than that of my uniform. A few years later when I was working at Agra, I was standing in the queue of a movie hall when a police inspector spotted me and came running, saying, 'Sahib, we would have gotten a pass. Please don't do this.' I waved him away saying I would rather do it the way I wanted. A few years later a similar episode occurred when I was riding a scooter with my wife seated behind me near the Taj Mahal. We had grown tired of being driven around by a police driver and followed by a couple of gunners, and decided to enjoy a little bit of freedom by riding the scooter. I may have gone a little over a mile when I heard a motorbike following me and stopped to the left. The motorbike also stopped behind me, and my deputy came running. 'Sahib, you shouldn't be doing this,' he said. 'How did you know I was sneaking out?' He smiled, 'It's known all over the district sahib, as the street patrol is reporting it over the mic!"

But a more serious incident occurred when I was returning with family from Chennai after a brief holiday. Kaushik, my son, was about a year old. When the train reached Gwalior station, I got down to get some water from the tap on the platform with the child in my hands. I filled water when my turn came, and by the time the bottle was full, the train started moving. I rushed back to the compartment, and to my dismay found the doorway blocked by passengers and the travelling ticket examiner. I understood it was the crowd having no tickets and the examiner was making hay when the train moved. I pushed the crowd hard with one hand and got a foothold even as the train gained speed. I was enraged. What if I slipped with the child in my hand? I went up to the ticket examiner and grabbed his collar. 'What were you doing at the doorway with so many illegal passengers inside the train?' I asked him angrily. He asked me to mind my business and stop manhandling a government servant. My rage went to my head. I gave the child to my wife, grabbed the puny man, lifted him and advanced towards the door. I was going to throw him out of the speeding train! There was pandemonium with passengers dividing their loyalties between the two of us, with one set of people pulling me back. Jaya, my wife, was pulling me hard. Better sense prevailed, and I set the man down. He adjusted his uniform and threatened me with dire consequences at the next station, where all of us were to disembark. 'I will call the police and have you arrested for manhandling and threatening to kill a government servant!' he yelled. I smiled to myself. He was going to have to call *me* for that!

Soon, the next station, Jhansi, arrived. The TTE looked like a wounded tiger ready to avenge his enemy. The platform was swarming with police officers. The TTE must have been bewildered as he was yet to call the police. Soon, he understood what was happening; the police posse came to our compartment, saluted and helped us get down from the train. I looked around for the TTE. To my amusement, he was trying to get out silently through the other door. My inspector got hold of him and brought him to me. Realizing the possibility of getting arrested for selling tickets in the black, he apologized profusely. I let him go with a stern warning. He looked grateful. While being escorted away, he asked me one last question: 'Why didn't you reveal who you were?'

One more enjoyable item on the training agenda was Bharat Darshan, a tour of India. The idea was to give an 'all India' feel to the trainees. We divided the batch into several groups, with each group visiting 7-8 states. I was part of the team which went to Maharashtra, Rajasthan, Punjab, Haryana, Delhi, Himachal Pradesh and Kashmir. The academy hired exclusive trains for each group to carry us from place to place. The programme typically consisted of visits to local police officers such as the DGP of the state, the commissioner of police and other senior officers, police control rooms and police stations to observe and learn how the cops work in different states under different circumstances. We also had the opportunity of visiting famous places and tourist spots wherever we went such as Mt Abu, Pahalgam and Vaishno Devi among others. The tour lasted for about twenty days, and the itinerary was so crowded that after a few days we started moving around like zombies. The food was another problem, especially for vegetarians like me. In Kashmir, I found no vegetarian food, except apples. Perforce I tried to eat an omelette one day, but failed to swallow the first morsel. For me, it was the beginning and the end of eating 'non-vegetarian'.

The Wedding

Five days after my wedding, I left my new wife behind, promising to take her to Hyderabad as early as possible. Once I got back to the NPA, my first concern was to find accommodation for a month, since we were not allowed to keep family inside the campus. I had to find a place that was close by given my rigorous training schedule. I stood outside the academy gate and looked around. As luck would have it, I saw a farmhouse right across the road, and decided to check it out. I entered the gate which bore the name Roy Cottage. It was a big farmhouse, inhabited by a joint family consisting of at least a dozen people. I approached Mr Roy, the owner, and explained my need for accommodation for a month to live with my wife. He told me sternly that he didn't like the probationers who'd made his life hell on a previous occasion. I walked back disappointed when he took pity on me and agreed, provided I didn't exceed the one-month limit. It was not a great deal, but good enough for my purpose as it was right across NPA. I thanked him profusely, and called my wife, Jaya. So, it was that we started our married life in that small room, which functioned as a bedroom, living room and kitchen. We needed to clean up the place and share the restroom with the owners in the main building. This stay lasted for a month and soon after the passing out parade (POP), I sent her back to Chennai, promising to pick her up on my way to UP, while I headed to Arunachal Pradesh, for the army-attachment leg of our training.

Army Attachment

Like Bharat Darshan, army-attachment was another important aspect. We were attached to the Fifth Mountain Division, Seven Guards Battalion of the Indian army, which was stationed at Arunachal Pradesh. The idea was to get first-hand experience of how the army works and under what conditions. It was, indeed, an eye-opener for all of us. We reached Calcutta (now Kolkata), and took a flight, my first, to Arunachal Pradesh. The army authorities received us and took us to their base camp. The streets were clean, lined by trees and greenery. We could even spot a few elephants loitering in the fields.

After some rest, we started out and reached Seven Guards after an eight-hour mountain drive. It was pitch dark, with the only light coming from the camp. It was cold, and chilly winds pierced my skin. I was not used to cold weather. Being from Chennai, I had only experienced three seasons—hot, hotter and the most humid. The place was about 10,000 ft above sea level. We climbed down from the army trucks and went into the mess, had some food, and hit the sack. In the morning we found the place to be a valley, surrounded by mountains and forests. We stayed there for a few days and studied the army working in difficult terrains. The military personnel were in strikingly high spirits.

We embarked on our next drive to a place, which was about 15,000 ft above sea level. We learned that our stay at the valley was part of the acclimatization process for the greater heights we were about to scale, equipped with suitable winter wear. It was late November and was likely to get worse in December and January. But it was cold enough as far as I was concerned. We stopped over at the highest point and explored the area. A storm was looming, and we all took shelter in tents. The tents were covered with dripping ice, forming frozen cones above our heads. One soldier made tea for us. He was cheerful and seeing him we felt better and tried to chase our gloom away. The storm had subsided but covered the mountains with snow. The sight was splendid and eerie at the same time. The next morning we continued our journey further up. After miles of driving, we came to the place where the road curved. As we took the bend, we saw a lone soldier standing on duty in the snow, waving at us. Tears lined our eyes as we drove past him. The road climbed down on the other side of the mountain, towards the Chinese border. The army explained to us that the route we were taking was where one of the earliest incursions by the Chinese military in 1962, took place. We climbed down to about 9,000 ft above sea level and stopped at a place called Tawang. Lunch was arranged at a Tibetan monastery. From here, the Indo-China border was about 20 miles. The place was serene. The cold was less oppressive and the sun was shining. Monks were around in total silence. We were shown around the monastery, and after spending some time there, we retraced our steps through the same route to our base camp at Seven Guards. The remaining attachment period went without an incident, and we were seen off at the airport. We reached Kolkata and went to our respective home towns, where our state-level training would continue for another three months. At that point, we hadn't realized that we might not be meeting our batchmates for years as our destinies were chalked out in different directions.

Typically, probationers come to know their cadres before the end of training signalled by the POP. In our case, the announcement didn't come in time as the political scene was chaotic to say the least. The then prime minister Indira Gandhi had imposed a state of emergency putting opposition leaders in jail and announcing a slew of sweeping 'reforms', including population control, nationalization of banks and abolition of privy purses to the former princely states. The atmosphere in the country was rife with barely suppressed anger and resentment towards the government, but the prime minister misread the mood and decided to lift the Emergency after two years and hold elections. She expected to win, but was resoundingly defeated. The Janata Party came to power for the first time. The political atmosphere was fully charged, with high expectations from the new government but there was much chaos and confusion on the ground. The cadre allotments, which must have been at the bottom of the priority list, were announced but never came. The rumours said I was going first to Maharashtra and then to Karnataka, but finally, I ended up in UP.

The states register their requirement of AIS officers with the government well in advance. The batch strength is decided based on these vacancy positions and once training is completed, the states are allotted the number of cadres as per their requirement. For the probationers, the general preference was his home state, for obvious reasons—less adjustment to a new place, its culture and language.

The downside of such a scenario where everyone went to their home states was the chances of favouritism. In fact, the concept of AIS was to make it a pan-Indian service. The slogan of 'unity in diversity' rested to some extent, on the shoulders of these officers, who were down the merit list, if not as much as it did on other factors. To decide who went where the government considered the ranking of the officers. For instance, if Tamil Nadu had two vacancies and had four candidates, the first two ranks went there, and the rest were allotted other states. I often wondered why a higher-ranking officer was not sent out to other cadres, as they were supposed to be 'better equipped', by their ranking, to cope with challenges. The roster system decided who went where against a list of states with vacancy positions. The officer who had to go out had to learn the local language and adjust to the local culture, all the while performing the tough job of policing. It was through these officers and their families, who upheld the traditions of the service and ensured impartiality in work, by making personal sacrifices. What the world saw was, of course, the 'privileges' enjoyed by them. It is hard to say which one outweighed the other. In my case, the difficulties far outweighed the advantages.

There was yet another category within the out-of-home-state officers—those who got into better places than their home states. For instance, an officer who comes to Andhra Pradesh or Tamil Nadu from UP or Bihar stands to gain in the long run because he got to work in a better environment than what supposedly prevailed in his home state. Such officers were the most fortunate since they got a better standard of living and better opportunities. I didn't comprehend what it meant for my family and me until I arrived in UP. Jaya and her family too, would not have even dreamt that she would have to go to live in UP.

4

Uttar Pradesh—The Armageddon

Change leads to insight far more
often than insight leads to change.

—MILTON ERICKSON

State Training

We packed our bags for our next adventure to UP, where I was supposed to go to Moradabad, where the Police Training College was situated. Before going there though, we went to Delhi, where I left Jaya at our relatives' house and proceeded to Moradabad, to find out what lay ahead, and, if possible, to find accommodation for both of us. The train to Moradabad was bursting at the seams, with people attached to every part of the train, quite literally, spilling over from the compartments, or even hanging on for dear life on top of it.

The train finally reached Moradabad, a sleepy overgrown village at that time, and I got off and hailed a rickshaw. The driver immediately understood when I said PTC, short for Police Training College, and everyone seemed familiar with it, as it was one of the premier institutions located there. He asked for ded rupiah—one-and-a-half rupees, but I bargained and agreed to give only dhai rupiah, two-and-a-half rupees. He agreed promptly to my price and said, smilingly 'Baitho sahib, ho jayega.' It was only later that I realized the reason for his enthusiastic agreement to my haggling—I had, essence, upped the asking rate; he wanted 150 paise, and in an attempt at bargaining, I offered two rupees and fifty paise. It was all because of the confusion in the language I had, but I quickly realized my folly and made up by paying what I promised, trying to explain away my ignorance by saying that I was offering one rupee more for the extra services given by him for carrying the luggage into my room. He smiled and left. I could see that I couldn't convince him. In hindsight, I should have probably just copped to my ignorance.

The first to welcome me at the PTC was Mullah, the mess in-charge. He asked, 'Sarkar, where are you from?' That was the first time I heard the word 'sarkar'. My friends later explained the different meanings the word had, the most obvious being 'government'. But the word could also be used to address officers, as they were the representatives of the government. In my time there, I quickly realized that Mullah extracted an appropriate 'price' for his niceties, in the form of tips, but he was a kind soul and helped me in locating a house for rent, not very far from the PTC. Having found a place, I went to Delhi to bring Jaya.

At the PTC, the training started in full swing. It was not very different from what we underwent in NPA, but with emphasis on local conditions and laws and regulations about UP. The downside for me though, was that all training was in chaste Hindi, and I could understand only a little of what was spoken. I needed to undergo specialized training in Hindi and appear for exams at Allahabad. But even there, the classes didn't have anything to do with the practical Hindi which was required to deal with real-life situations. My wife bore the brunt of being in a new land, far away from home, with no proper communication facilities—and an unknown language. But she was a friendly person by nature and within a few days made friends with neighbours and the house owner's family.

My mother joined her a little later. We used to go to the crowded and narrow marketplace to pick up provisions and vegetables, as we had no help because I was still undergoing training. I used to get up early in the morning, wear the uniform and disappear into the thick fog, as my wife and mother watched from the balcony.

I received posting orders to Ballia, a rural district in the eastern UP for six months of practical training. Ballia was crime- and poverty-ridden where even basic English wouldn't work. I brought this up to the director of the training college, who, in turn, spoke to those concerned, to change the practical training to Agra, a district in the western part which was comparatively better developed and had a cosmopolitan atmosphere, primarily because it housed one of the seven wonders of the world—the Taj Mahal. The added attraction was that it was on the Grand Trunk route, with direct trains to Chennai, which meant a big deal at that time. Before I proceeded to Agra, I had yet another training to complete at the Mussoorie Academy, which I had missed at the beginning.

When we boarded the train to Dehradun so that I could finish the training schedule I had missed, Jaya was pregnant. We had not made any reservations for the journey, but decided to take a chance. When we reached the station, we learned that the train was running several hours behind schedule. The platform was swelling with multitudes of people by the minute, and when the train arrived well past midnight, the crowd literally jumped as one into the train, sitting wherever there was place. I had to muscle my way into the compartment with Jaya and baggage in tow. We finally reached Dehradun and caught a bus to Mussoorie, which was an hour-and-a-half uphill. The winding roads and the rickety bus took us into chilly Mussoorie late in the evening. We found our way to our room, put down our luggage, had a hot shower and lovely dinner before hitting the sack.

For me, most of the next day was spent in registration and other formalities, during which time Jaya wandered and found some friends. One of them was the family of a faculty member,

Ramakrishnan, who had had adorable twins. Jaya had a great time with the kids, while I busied myself with the training. Within a week, Jaya developed breathing trouble, and we went to the academy doctor. After examining her, the doctor advised that given her pregnancy, it would be advisable to go down to the plains. I decided to drop her off all the way home, to Chennai, until I completed my training, which was for four months. I rushed to the director and explained the situation. He was concerned but said I had just come for the training and no leave was possible but reluctantly agreed to give me five days. It would take two days to go and two days to get back with one day in Chennai. We rushed to the bus terminus and boarded the Delhi bus just in time. The next morning, we reached New Delhi Railway Station, and the GT Express was ready to leave for Chennai. The station superintendent was an understanding man and gave me two berths. After thirty-six hours we reached home, had a good meal and a sound sleep and then the same day, I embarked on the return journey to Mussoorie.

By this time, the strain caught up with me, and I was running high temperature while travelling. I reached the academy. It was the time of the festival of Holi and the whole Academy was celebrating it with coloured powders and water cannons. It was festivity all over. I was so tired and unwell that I went straight to my room. Just at that moment, a huge mob rushed into my room, all of them my friends, with bucket loads of coloured water and powders, and poured all of it on my head and all over the bed! My pleadings for mercy fell on deaf ears. I had to bathe in cold water to wash off the colours.

Anti-dacoity Operations and Encounters

When I reached Agra, there was a jeep waiting for me at the station. Jaya and our four-month-old son, Kaushik joined me a little later. We were given accommodation in the transit hostel on Circuit House road. From there the Taj Mahal was within walking distance. B.P. Singh was the senior superintendent of police (SSP) at the time, and Vikram Singh was the additional superintendent of police. I joined as assistant superintendent of police (ASP) under training. Harbhajan Singh was the ASP. S.K. Dutta was the range director inspector general. All of them were very considerate and helpful. Dussehra is a huge event in UP where the Ramlila is celebrated with great pomp and show. Every district in the state has a Ramlila ground to host the annual festival, including the effigy burning of Ravana when thousands gathered to watch the show. As I had gained considerable expertise in handling a horse, I decided to be on horseback during crowd control duties. As the event passed off peacefully, I thought I had come a long way since the horseback-riding debacle at Moradabad.

The SSP came home occasionally to take us for dinner at his residence or to Kinari Bazaar, a place known for chaat items in Agra. Whenever it was possible, he took me along with him for raids and inspections. During one such ride, I saw a dead body of a woman lying on the roadside. It was shocking to see the headless body with flies all over. I expected SSP to stop the car and have a look. He didn't stop. He passed some orders into the wireless mike and continued with our conversation. I was shocked by his nonchalance. He said it keeps happening, and while the police officer should take appropriate action, he couldn't afford to panic. It was the first lesson I learned from him, to face death boldly and impersonally, if not indifferently.

B.P. Singh tirelessly pursued dacoits and criminals with the help of his extensive informant network. The raids were held mostly at dawn, preparations for which commenced the previous night. We used to lay siege at remote villages and strike at dawn. The logic of such a strategy was that we would be moving in when it was still dark and still able to shoot with the aid of the lack of light. These were villages without electricity, and the nights were pitch dark. Vikram Singh used to be a very enthusiastic police officer, had a great sense of humour and an able aide to the SSP. Both used to devise anti-dacoit plans and execute them with precision.

Introduction to Third-degree Methods

As part of the training, I was to stay in a police station for about a month to learn to police at the station level. I trained with the Bah police station in the Agra district, which was about 100 km from the district headquarters. The police station was in a dacoit-infested area, near the infamous Chambal Valley, where from all legendary dacoits, including Phoolan Devi, operated. The room where I stayed was just behind the police station. Being a rural station, it had no electricity supply and mosquitoes made after-dark hours an impossible nightmare. The food consisted of the customary—dal, roti, sabzi and a little rice.

During the day, I spent time in the front office observing the staff working and the complainants coming in to lodge first information reports (FIRs). I would read the reports and compared them to what the applicant had to say in the first place. After lunch, I would retire to my room. Usually, at about 11 p.m., the inspector would come and say, 'Chaliye sahib', which meant he and a few others were going for a raid. On one such occasion, we marched into the bihad, the arid dunes, with rifles in hand. It was a long walk, at least 3 kms into the dunes. It was pitch dark, and torchlights were not allowed, lest the party we were going to raid get alerted. The inspector said we should develop the ability to find our way in the dark only by looking at individual stars. One of the accompanying constables lit the torch briefly to avoid a slithering snake, but the inspector was unhappy about it. It must have been well past 2 a.m. when the party stopped at a small hut. The inspector went inside, and we followed. There was a fireplace in one corner, and an old man was lying on a rope cot near the fire. The inspector woke him up and asked where the arms and ammunition were. The old man shook his head saying he didn't have any. The next thing before anyone could anticipate, the inspector took out an iron grip from the roof of the hut, put it inside the old man's nose and pulled hard! Blood came out from his nose, and

I was frozen! I said, 'What are you doing? You are not supposed to resort to third degree, especially in my presence!' The inspector nodded but said nothing. By this time the old man led us to the backyard and showed a place on the ground. They dug the ground, and lo and behold—we found several firearms hidden there. The inspector later explained to me that these were the weapons held for the use of the dacoits to kill and loot people. 'Tell me, sahib, should we or should we not?' asked the inspector. I had no answer, though the episode gave me an uneasy feeling.

We reached the station around 4.30 a.m. with the old man in tow, but my mind was back in that hut, replaying the incident. Once we interrogated the man, we would come to know the details; who he was, how he came in possession of the illegal arms and ammunition in such a large quantity and who was behind it. But what bothered me most was how to solve the problem of third degree and violence especially when it appears that there is no better way to deal with the situation.

How It All Works

After completing my practical training, I was posted to Jhansi, my first regular posting in the police service. It was March 1980; we had been training continuously since November 1977.

Typically, a district had a superintendent of police (SP) as its executive head for policing. It is subdivided into circles or sub-divisions, and each circle had a deputy superintendent of police (DySP) as its in-charge. Each subdivision had a few police stations headed by an inspector or sub-inspector, depending upon the size and jurisdiction. The inspector had a few sub-inspectors, constables and head constables under him. A junior cop would be there for registering the cases and other duties such as maintenance of records. Most records were in chaste Urdu and Hindi. Disputes over jurisdiction arose from time to time, as in the case of a murder in one police area and the body getting recovered from the neighbouring area. The main reason behind such disputes was that no police station liked taking responsibility of solving the crimes of another. It is another matter that sometimes the police wanted to show lesser crimes happening in their area, which is called 'burking', and sometimes cases were downgraded to show a less significant crime in place of a grave one. A good police administration discouraged these tendencies.

There were other positions such as the deputy inspector general of police (DIG) in charge of a range, which consisted of a few districts. The DIG coordinated activities among the areas under his jurisdiction and inspected various district offices and police stations to ensure proper functioning. There was an inspector general of police (IGP), over and above the DIG, with a few ranges under his belt. Then there were administrative and operational heads at the headquarters. The DIG was the chief executive of the state, who would be directing all operations. He would be reporting to the chief minister of the state. The department also had other wings apart from the executive arm. Some of them were the intelligence wing, the crime branch, special branch, police welfare, radio and wireless, to name a few. Crimes, which had state-level ramifications, or which required lengthy and impartial investigations, were referred to the crime branch. The intelligence wing and special branch took care of intelligence collection and security. Armed battalions were available for crowd control and law-and-order problems.

The IAS looked after overall district administration. The collector or the district magistrate was the head of the district administration, with sub-collectors and subdivisional magistrates and tehsildars their immediate juniors. The 'dawali', the functionary who always accompanied the collector wherever he went, was the symbol of authority for the collector. He and the superintendent were expected to function in close cooperation at the district level to maintain law and order. The collector functioned under the commissioner of the division, overseeing developmental activities. The administrative head of the secretariat was the chief secretary, who reported to the chief minister. Essentially, the British put the structure of police and administration in place. The Police Act of 1861 drafted by Lord Macaulay remained unchanged in several states.

Any officer who joined a district was expected to 'call on' the senior officers, first alone in the office, and then with the officer's wife at his residence. It was an unwritten rule, but necessary to develop a rapport and ensure smooth functioning. Any violation would have grave consequences, though indirectly. Something to this effect happened with me right in the beginning at Jhansi. When I arrived, the first thing I thought of was this unspoken rule, and I went to SP's office only to learn that he was on tour and would be back only after two days. Why not call on the DIG, I thought. In the Jhansi Range, Jhansi was the biggest district compared to others such as Lalitpur, Etawah and Banda. Hence, the DIG had his headquarters at Jhansi. I reached his office, and he promptly received me and offered a cup of tea. We exchanged pleasantries for a while before I left. The next day the superintendent arrived, and I called on him. He had on a very grim expression. I didn't know what went wrong. But he was good enough to ask me whether I called on the DIG, to which I replied in the affirmative. 'I am your boss. You should have called me first,' he told me. I was silent. Then he went on to say that we were both IPS officers whereas the DIG was from the state police and had 'conferred' IPS status and that I should have shown more respect to him rather than to the DIG. He told me I shouldn't meet the DIG without his permission. I didn't understand why he was so angry, but I wisely stayed quiet. I had so many unresolved personal issues that I thought this was a petty one, but the superintendent didn't think so.

One of the biggest problems, as I discovered later, was to get living quarters allotted. The public works department, which was responsible for allotments, came under the district magistrate; you had to call on him and make a request for a house. Invariably, the number of officers in an area would far exceed the quarters available, which would result in wrangling. Until the time you succeeded in getting quarters allotted, you lived in guest houses or some other arrangements, as I did. There was an old building in the police lines, which had an oddly shaped hall and a lawn in the front. We had a partition erected in the living room to create a makeshift bedroom and kitchen, which was good enough for a few months. By now we had become quite adept in spoken Hindi.

Catch Me If You Can

It happened during my tenure as the ASP. I was sitting in the station getting ready for the weekly 'durbar'—when members of the public could meet me in person to air their grievances or give petitions. It was 11 a.m. on a Friday when my wireless mike crackled. It was a call for help from the inspector of Babina, a police station, about 25 km from the headquarters. A robbery had taken place in a bank, which was 16 km on the Jhansi–Babina Road. The gang had looted the bank after shutting off the staff in a locker room. There was no time to even think. I told the SP briefly about the call, got into the jeep with three men and sped along the road. As the city receded, the stretch of road for about 5 km was scenic, after which the industrial belt began with the sprawling Bharat Heavy Electrical Ltd complex (BHEL) being the prominent one. I had stayed in their beautiful guest house with Jaya and Kaushik a few times, whenever I was there on duty. After BHEL, there was a stretch of about 7–8 km where the civilian population lived before the cantonment started, which extended up to Babina. The cantonment was full of army men and their vehicles busily going about their daily routine. It was in this stretch that the bank was situated. Though not thickly populated, the area was still bustling with people; it was a daring daylight robbery that occurred there in the morning.

We reached the bank, which occupied the ground floor of a three-story building. Located on the main road, the bank's entrance had a sliding iron grill door which remained open during business hours. It had a small signboard in the front and smaller signs at the entrance showing hours of operation and holidays. There was no guard outside, which was common at the time, because bank robberies were a very rare occurrence. Much later, when banks got robbed routinely, and people got killed, bank authorities decided to post security guards with licensed guns to bank premises and subsequently, ATM centres.

The business area had papers and cash littered all over. The staff huddled inside the locker room with the collapsible gate closed and locked from inside. We found them in a state of utter shock. I had the doors opened and asked my men to get them some water to drink and we waited while they got their bearing before we questioned them for information. From what I gathered, the robbers just had about half an hour's headway. I had no time to waste if I wanted to apprehend them. I came out and looked at the scene. Five roads branched off from near the bank; one heading towards Jhansi, from where I had come; another to Shivpuri; a third to Datia, and a fourth to Gwalior—all in Madhya Pradesh in various directions—and the last one was towards Babina proper. I had one minute to decide which way to go; my instincts said Gwalior. I had no time to think and rationalize my decision. We raced towards Gwalior, stopping at several places along the way to question people milling about at tea shops or on the streets, and check if they had seen a car speed past. No one knew anything. It had rained heavily in the last two days, and waterlogging was a problem. The causeways were full, and water was flowing to the brim. At places, we had to get out of the jeep and push the car as the water had entered the hood of the car and damaged the self-starters.

We reached Gwalior and drove straight to the superintendent's office. He was holding an internal meeting with his office and had to wait a few minutes before he waved all of them away. I explained the crisis to him. He thought for a while and called his crime assistant to bring some files. After examining them carefully, he handed three of them to me. I looked at them carefully. The first file was that of a habitual petty offender. Next was a photograph of three individuals who were suspects in an attempted bank robbery. The third one showed a gang of six, and I looked at the faces closely. Two of the faces resembled the descriptions given by the bank staff. I thought it could be the gang. The superintendent also concurred, but said they didn't operate in the area anymore and moved north towards Delhi—even more reason to go further on, to the Gwalior–Delhi road and look for more clues. I thanked him and took off for Delhi.

As before, we stopped at different points and asked about a speeding car. We had the photographs to show this time. We reached a narrow bridge that allowed only one car at a time. Rainwater was flowing over the bridge. As my men were pushing the car slowly, I noticed a forest guard in a small bunker near the edge of the bridge. I went over and asked him whether he saw a white Ambassador speeding that way. I showed the photographs. His face lit up in recognition. He said their vehicle had stopped at the bridge, and two people got down from the car and pushed, and he identified one as one of the people in the photograph. That was enough for me. We raced towards Agra, and as we were near the Circuit House, the state guest house, I spotted the car abandoned on the road. It was evident that they had switched cars and fled, probably towards Delhi, which was four hours away. We decided to stay at the guest house for the night; I had to strategize our next move.

Next, we planned for the car to be seized and headed towards Delhi. Kiran Bedi was the deputy commissioner of north Delhi. My officers met her and explained the case to her. We discussed the details with her and the inspector in charge of crime; she suspected some criminals in the Saraswathi Nagar area. My party, together with local police raided a house and apprehended the criminals along with the stolen cash.

I had two jobs on hand—get the criminals identified and take them to Jhansi. I contacted the bank manager and requested him and his staff to come to Delhi immediately. We had to wait overnight for him to arrive and identify the criminals. Only then did I remember my home and realized how my wife must be feeling without any knowledge of my whereabouts. Those were the days of no cell phones, and even subscriber trunk dialing (STD) was rarely available. Mostly we had to book a trunk call, and the costliest and the quickest was called 'lightning call', which took anywhere between five minutes and half an hour, sometimes more. I booked a lightning call and waited. My wife came on the line and burst into uncontrollable sobbing. She was alone with our infant son, not knowing where her husband was for three days, and there were no friends around. She had asked the superintendent, who told her that I went chasing the robbers, but he too was not aware of my whereabouts. I realized what a big mistake I had made by not informing anyone about what I had been doing. I consoled her that I would be back the next day.

The bank manager arrived next morning and was taken straight to the police station. He looked at the robbers, and they gave him a hard, intimidating look—the 'you identify us, and you are gone' kind of glare. The manager appeared threatened, and did the most unexpected thing; he swooned! We splashed some water on his face and helped him stand, but he sagged. After all the efforts we had taken to trace the criminals and recover the money, this was the least we wanted. Somehow, we managed to convince the Delhi police and brought the criminals to Jhansi, and had them identified by one of the staff from the bank and proceeded to charge them.

His Highness and the Humble Cop!

As ASP I was also in charge of a subdivision called Samthar, which was about 75 km from Jhansi, and the headquarters of the yesteryears Province of Samthar, before it was annexed to the state. The descendants of the maharaja still lived there in the fort, and the set-up was feudal. People still respected the current raja, Ranjit Singh Judeo. He was a respected member of the province and a new officer made it a point to call on him on joining the precinct. Ignorant about this unwritten rule, I just stayed in the guest house on my first visit to the sub-division.

My wife and I had arrived late in the evening on the previous day. At around 9 p.m., before we could reach the guest house, a small group of weeping villages stopped our jeep. I asked what the matter was. The villagers said dacoits had entered their village and they were looting and killing people. I passed on the message over the mike to the police station and ordered reinforcements. I asked the driver to take the jeep to the guest house, which was around the corner, to drop off my wife before I proceeded to the spot. As we approached, a loud voice shouted, '*Thuum, kaun aatha hai*,' which meant, 'Stop, who's coming?' My wife thought dacoits had come there to attack us. We went inside, and I sprinkled water on her face to bring her around. I then gently explained to her that it was merely the police guard at the gate and the shout was part of the procedure to confirm the identity of the approaching vehicle. If you were found to be an enemy, then he would be justified in shooting you down! It was a routine procedure, but sounded odd in the jungle-like atmosphere, with an ongoing dacoit situation that had taken place just a few hundred metres away.

I rushed to the spot, and the inspector also arrived with reinforcements. Two bodies of the villagers were on the ground. We went searching for the dacoits in the dark in and around the village. Shots were fired at us and we returned the fire. We got two of the dacoits killed but the remaining fled away. The villagers told us there were six of them. The scene was grim with no lights and people running here and there. It was well past midnight when I was done wrapping up my job and leaving the scene of the shootout; sending the bodies for post mortem, clearing up things, registering cases, and arranging for security in the village. I returned to the guest house where my wife was waiting, with fear in her eyes. I assured her that everything was okay, and we slept fitfully that night.

The next day I was at the guest house preparing for an enquiry against a person suspected of involvement in a crime. At that time a few rowdy-looking men arrived at the door. They politely bowed and said, 'Raja Sahib ne aapko yaad kiya.' As polite as that statement was, that the Raja of Samthar was remembering me, I knew the underlying command sent by the prince, that I was to go and meet him. I was weary from the last night's episode. I suppressed my irritation and said I would be available for the next half an hour and the raja was welcome to come to the guest house and meet me. The goons were incredulous. No one had ever responded so 'disrespectfully' to your boss's 'invitation'. They went away, filled with disbelief and hostility. I continued with my work. After about twenty minutes, I saw a crowd of about twenty-five people approaching the guest house. Leading this posse was a short-statured, smart-looking man, holding a pack of Alsatians by the leash. It didn't take much to understand that it was the Raja of Samthar. I stood up, welcomed him and took him inside. I asked for a cup of tea and some biscuits. He asked some routine questions to know where I was from and said, 'Oh, you are from Madras? A perfect place. Hard-working and honest people. We like dosas. Come home sometime.' Saying this, he put his cup down, signalled his men, and went away. I detected a trace of anger in his voice.

I also left for the enquiry. The person we were in search of was sitting in his shop in the bazaar street, a crowded place. The interrogation was of sensitive nature, and I wanted to do it myself. So, I went up to him and started asking questions. He was arrogant and gave vague replies. I came to know later that he was one of the raja's men. I attempted to slap him, right in front of the crowd. After a short while, after the enquiry, we returned to the guest house and on to Jhansi. What I didn't know was that the man went to raja and complained. The already miffed Raja saw an opportunity to take it out on me. Before long, the Samthar sub-division observed a total bandh and a busload of people went to the headquarters to give a representation to the superintendent and deputy inspector general, with copies faxed to the deputy general of police at the Lucknow headquarters, the chief minister and Prime Minister Indira Gandhi. When I reached there, all pandemonium had broken out, and the SP asked me what happened. I explained and categorically admitted having beaten up the shopkeeper. He said the chief minister was concerned as there was an enquiry from the prime minister's office (PMO). I handed my resignation letter to the superintendent and told him I would like to go back home. I heard nothing about the incident afterwards, but I suspect the SP handled the situation; he had contacts and more importantly, he was a good friend of the raja's, something which I learned only later.

Several years later when I had returned to UP, I was posted at the Lucknow crime branch. We were living in an apartment in the police lines. One evening, we heard a commotion outside the compound, and I looked down to see what was happening. There was a motorcade with revolving red lights entering the compound. Someone was asking for directions, and the man was pointing towards our block. I left the balcony and came inside, as this was a familiar sight there. Some VIP must be passing. Exactly five minutes later, the doorbell rang. I opened the door. To my astonishment, it was the home minister of UP, in charge of the police department, and it was none other than our raja of Samthar. I was secretly resigned to the fact that my career had prematurely ended, considering our very recent history. On the contrary, he hugged me and spoke highly of my integrity and courage. He invited both, my wife and I, to his house for dinner and proudly introduced me to his family members. He took me aside and said, 'Sampath, I know you have gone through a lot of ordeals in UP. I am the home minister, now tell me where you would like to go, and I will post you there.' I thanked him for his gesture and said I would let him know when I needed help. I thought of jokingly asking him whether he could post me to Chennai, but I didn't say it aloud. I was all the while admiring the man, who had come to my home, despite our ill-fated first encounter. He could have summoned me if he wanted, but maybe, his previous experience reminded him that I might not turn up! It spoke volumes about his magnanimity. I consider this the highest tribute I ever received for my service, equivalent to the police medal I received years later from the president of India.

Qawwali Singers From Mumbai

Jhansi had its share of festivals and fairs. The district had areas predominantly populated by Muslims, and there were mazaars, tombs, fakirs, samadhi and sadhus who dotted the cultural landscape of the region. One of the tombs here was that of a fakir, who had a group of followers claiming that the fakir's original tomb was in Babina, not Jhansi. Hence, the annual Urs festival, a religious commemoration in his tribute, was performed at both the venues, causing considerable tension in the district, for the people as well as the administration. That year, the pressure was rather high. The Jhansi group had invited a famous qawwali troupe from Mumbai to perform during the Urs. This group enjoyed the support of the administration, and was permitted to have the event at the district headquarters, which was convenient to monitor from a law-and-order point of view. And so the Babina group was declared unlawful. In the meantime, the Babina party came to know about the Mumbai music troupe arriving at Jhansi; the train from the city had to pass through Babina before reaching Jhansi.

The day of the Urs came, and all arrangements had been made to ensure the event went off without a hitch. In the meantime, I received information that the Babina party was planning to stop the train, hijack the music troupe and compel them to sing at the parallel function organized by them at Babina. I tried to contact Vikram Singh, sub-collector in charge of Babina but he was not immediately available. So, I decided to go over to Babina and see the situation for myself. When I reached the police station there,

I found a large gathering outside. I took the inspector from the station along with me to the railway station. It was time for the train from Mumbai to arrive, with protesters and travellers crowding the platform. We were about a dozen policemen with lathis only, as I had asked everyone not to carry arms. The train arrived, and despite the commotion which followed, we successfully managed to get the Mumbai troupe out. There wasn't much of a problem doing that, as the protesters also wanted the same. They were intrigued and so was inspector, Babina. I took the party to the Babina police station in my jeep, with the lead singer in between the driver and me in the front seat. When we reached, we found the crowd had swelled to hundreds, blocking the road leading to Jhansi, with tractors and bullock carts. Some of them were reported to be carrying arms and knives. Later Vikram Singh told me that he could not reach Babina because of the blockade. The wireless couldn't reach Jhansi, and there were no other means of communication. Everyone was waiting to see what I was going to do.

I asked the party to get down from the jeep and get inside the station. They were given a cup of tea to refresh themselves and wait for my signal. The crowd became a little weary after about an hour, as nothing was happening. My jeep was parked in the porch, away from the gaze of the crowd. A few people were trying to peep in and see. I thought that was the right time to make a move and I asked the troupe to get into the jeep quickly, and we reached the road where it forked, with one road leading to the left and the other to the right. To the left was Jhansi and as far as the eye could see, the road was completely blocked by people, bullock carts, cars and even boulders and rocks. I thought there was no point in battling it out as we had an insufficient force and a showdown was the last thing the district administration would want. The crowd also was curious about our next move. I told the driver in a whisper to go up to the main road slowly and take a sudden right turn instead of left. As we negotiated the right turn and sped fast exactly in the opposite direction, the crowd was stunned.

A few people realized they had been fooled and tried to follow us on their motorcycles, but Sukhram, my driver proved too swift for them. We were racing at about 100 km an hour, and soon they were shaken off our trail. I told Sukhram to go 20 km and take a right, which would lead us into a thick forest area. After about 50 km, the road opened up on the other side on a highway near Raxa Police Station, and from there it was just a 10-km drive to the venue of the function at Jhansi.

My driver smiled when he realized what the plan was and did as told. In effect, we would be covering 80 km instead of mere 25 km had we taken the direct road. I thought the detour was worth the trouble as we would only be slightly delayed for the programme, but the troupe would escape unscathed. But that was not to be. One of the musicians, who was down with fever, was feeling very ill as his condition worsened after the train journey. All the tension at Babina proved too much for him as he was throwing up frequently. We had to halt now and then for him to vomit before proceeding. We reached the avenue as planned, albeit an hour late. The crowd and the administration were waiting to see how I was going to bring in the performers. I offloaded the troupe near the dais and went straight to my home, which was only about 100 yards from the venue to wash and dress up and bring my wife to the function. I also arranged for an ambulance to take the sick man to the hospital. When I entered the pandal, the celebrations had already started; the main singer was singing a beautiful qawwali. When he saw me he stopped singing, stood up and did a bow announcing in the mic, 'Here comes the hero who saved our lives.' The crowd erupted in applause.

During dinner that night, the superintendent of police, the deputy inspector general, collector and Commissioner Mr Punia all had a word of praise for the way I handled the situation single-handedly and averted a major law-and-order problem for the administration. Even twenty years later, when Punia was helping me get relieved from police service, he didn't fail to recall the incident with admiration. It was a pleasant evening for me, though only briefly because by midnight, we received the news from the hospital that the ill member of the troupe had passed away.

Murder Most Foul

It was about two warring families in a village. Every few years there would be a murder in the family, and someone from the opposite camp would go to jail. But nothing would deter them from taking vengeance; it was a tradition that stretched back generations. A young boy from one of the families who was inclined towards academia had grown fed up of this cycle of vengeance and had left the village to join a college in the town. During the holidays though, he went home and didn't come back. The university authorities thought he was at home, but the family never saw him. It was evident that the boy was kidnapped on the way home and was either kept somewhere or killed. I also came to know that the local police were involved and sided with one of the families. The father of the missing boy came to me and complained. He told me about the entire background and the involvement of the inspector. I contacted some of my police informers, who confirmed that unfortunately, the boy had been killed and body thrown into a well.

Early the next morning, I picked up the informer and the inspector of an adjoining police station, without the knowledge of the inspector of the jurisdiction, and proceeded to the spot. The informer showed the well from a distance. I got some chains from the village and lowered them into the well. What greeted us was horrific; the young boy's body had been cut up, and the body parts came out one by one. The police arrested the suspects. The news made sensational headlines the next day.

What followed was even more bizarre. After a couple of days, at around seven in the morning while I was reading a newspaper and sipping a cup of coffee, the doorbell rang. There was no one around. I got up and opened the door only to see the father of the young boy who had died so tragically, standing and holding a bundle in his hands. What happened next was horrifying; packets of hundred-rupee notes fell at my feet. He was sobbing and thanking me for recovering the body and arresting the culprits. He requested they should be hanged and asked me to accept the money as a token of his gratitude! I felt heat behind my ears as the blood rushed to my face. It was a bribe, and I didn't know what to do. I stepped back, closed the door, and shouted at him to take the money and go away immediately. He persisted, and I told him firmly that if he didn't leave, I would arrest him. I heard footsteps fading away. I carefully opened the door to ensure that he was gone and no currency was left at my doorsteps, and heaved a sigh of relief. More than the scene, it was the thought of what would have happened if someone had witnessed this and reached the wrong conclusion that had me worried.

One of the outcomes of such crime-chasing activities was that my wife started getting anonymous calls threatening the life of our child. The call would come every day at 4 p.m., when I was either at the police station or out on rounds. The caller would say, 'We know you are from the south. Ask your husband to be careful. He is unnecessarily harassing us. If he doesn't stop, your child will die.' We tried to trace the call, but we only had a small telephone cross-bar exchange those days and that was hardly capable of such functions. But our efforts to locate him scared the caller and the calls stopped. He must have been a criminal whom we were after.

On another occasion, we received information that dacoits were going to raid a village that night. We had planned an encounter, and around 10 p.m., we reached a spot a few miles away from the actual village to not alert the dacoits, lest they abort their plan. We had with us one company of about a hundred men of the Provincial Armed Constabulary (PAC), the armed wing of UP police. We walked through the jungle and reached the vicinity of the village. As we were nearing the village I asked for the division of the force into three parts to approach the village from three sides, the fourth one being a small rivulet running behind the village. I was about to tell my men to get down to the ground and start crawling when a bullet whizzed past my left ear. We all dropped to the ground as more bullets flew past. One of our sub-inspectors got hit in the shoulder. It was evident that the dacoits had sentries posted on rooftops of the houses, and seeing movement in the dark, had started shooting blindly. We too returned fire, while simultaneously advancing slowly on our bellies. By the time we reached, the dacoits had sensed that we were police and fled. Inter-rivalry among gangs was not uncommon. In our frustration, we opened the doors of every house and searched. I was the one to enter the hutment first with a revolver in hand, kicking open the flimsy doors, but alas, we returned empty-handed.

At that time, I was working as superintendent of police, CID, Crime Branch, which was situated on the Raj Bhawan Road in Lucknow, UP, once rated among the top three crime-ridden states in India. The crime branch was such a department, where difficult cases that could not be solved by the local police got referred for detailed and professional investigation. I oversaw the region of Bareilly, which spread across the western and northern parts of the state and bordered Delhi. On taking charge, I found many pending cases, while some case files were untraceable; a few of the cases were closed. To my shock, I found those missing files in the attic, where they were gathering dust. I had those files brought down, dusted them off and started reading them and making notes. I called the investigating officers (IO), discussed the case and the reasons for the delay in solving them and how I could help in further investigation.

Nearly one-third of the pending cases were related to dowry deaths. An ancient and obnoxious system of taking money from a girl's family as a condition for marriage, dowry was a malaise that was prevalent across the country, and in UP as well. The criminal cases involved bride burning, where the girl's in-laws burnt her to death for not bringing enough dowry. Investigating these cases involved visits to remote villages where such cases occurred frequently. Most of the stories went typically like this: the woman walks towards the backyard with a kerosene lamp at 4.30 a.m., accidentally trips on the haystack, which catches fire from the lamp and gets burned to death. Though it looked evident that the woman was murdered in cold blood, proving the same during investigations was next to impossible; there was no evidence, save that of the offenders themselves. The scene got murkier with politics, corruption, allegations and counter-allegations. During my investigations, I also found that in some cases, women made false allegations of dowry harassment against their husbands and in-laws, to wreak vengeance or to extract money. It was a daunting task to differentiate the real from the false and then again prove the murders in the court of law.

Discovering the Life of Mind—Gurdjieff

On a cold evening in November, I got out of my office to stretch my limbs. The winter was just setting in. As I walked out and glanced in the direction of the crime branch library, located in a corner of the building. Ever since I had taken up this post in the crime branch, I had wanted to spend some time in the library, but couldn't find the time to do so. That evening proved to be just the right time to do something about my long-suppressed wish, and I entered the library. It was more of an oversized living room with dusty carpets and a few chairs. There were about half a dozen book racks at the most. There was no librarian entirely dedicated to the task but an administrative assistant who shared the work, and it showed in the way books were maintained. There were no catalogues and one needed to go book by book to see the subject, author or contents.

I started with the first rack and picked a book which interested me. As expected, most of them were law related, but I had the persistence and time to examine the books one by one. In the third rack, as I was looking at the three huge volumes of Criminal Procedure Code, I noticed a small hardbound book wedged in between them. I picked it up and checked the title, *Gurdjieff* by Dr Kenneth Walker. The cover image was that of a bald man with a big moustache and penetrating eyes. I was intrigued. What was the meaning of the title, who was this man on the cover and what doctor had anything to do with writing this book?

I picked up the book, made an entry in the borrowing register and came back to my desk. It was 7.30 p.m. by the time I returned and got ready to shut shop for the day. I got into the car with excitement and immediately started reading. After dinner, I shut myself in the study. When I finished the 165 pages, it was well past midnight, but I couldn't sleep. As I was reading the book, I could feel the neurons in my brain firing incessantly with powerful ideas.

The author spoke at length about Western philosopher and thinker G.I. Gurdjieff (G) and his ideas about life. How one is born with a body, psychology and cosmology. How one takes birth with essence and later develops personality. How society and the family play a role in the development of personality and how one becomes habit-bound when one grows and lives a mechanical life, a life driven by external circumstances rather than one's inner promptings. He went on to describe the nature of knowledge and understanding, and how one can't *do* anything, and everything happens until one starts observing oneself and cultivates self-remembering and working on oneself to raise one's level of consciousness, resulting in a change of being to attract better things in life.

The author quoted G as saying that one's level of being attracts the kind of life one lives and to change a life one needs to change that level. Reading the book had brought up old memories, of accidentally stumbling upon a lecture by J. Krishnamurti in Chennai. The ideas I just read made miraculous connections with those buried deep in my subconscious. After all the tumultuous events in my life in the past ten years, I knew for certain that life happened randomly and many of the events made no sense. What G had said about life in general and personality development interested me. A baby is born with pure essence and no personality. The essence is the core seed, and all its reactions come from it. It is curious, happy and all smiles and laughter, making life a heavenly experience. Slowly, the personality starts forming; like the kernel in the fruit. The exposure to the environment, the family and the society all help in this formation. This character development takes place at the expense of the essence, which in many cases remains dormant all the while. Only after the child grows into an adolescent and then into an adult is it ready to face life on its own. Therefore, it is necessary for the child to grow a vibrant all-round personality to live a healthy life.

Babri Masjid Demolition

9 a.m. on 6 December 1992. Along with several of my colleagues, I was in the anteroom of the chamber of Mr Tripathi, the director general of police, at the time. With horror in our eyes, we were watching the live coverage from Ayodhya unfolding on TV. Scores of people swarmed all over the Babri Masjid dome with axes and other weapons and tools, hammering away at the structure, which slowly crumbled. Simultaneously, there was a tussle going on the ground between the security forces and the mob. There was a flurry of phone calls from Delhi, from the chief minister's office and from ground zero for information or instructions. We ran in and out of Tripathi's office conveying the messages to him and in turn getting directions and pass them on to the forces on the ground at Ayodhya. Mayhem and confusion prevailed. As we trained our eyes on the TV set, we watched as the Babri Masjid dome came crumbling down, and with it, the dread of communal tension that was to grip the nation. The aftershocks of the destruction resonated throughout the country, most impossibly, several thousand kilometres away in Mumbai, with the city in the throes of horrific riots that killed hundreds. And as though the tragedy of the riots weren't enough,

a series of bomb blasts in Mumbai which followed in March 1993, killed scores of innocent people.

The reverberations never truly died down, even after a decade. In 2002, a train carrying kar sevaks who were returning by train to Gujarat from Ayodhya, commemorating the tenth anniversary of the event, was allegedly set on fire at Godhra, and 59 people were burnt alive. What followed was grim; hundreds of Muslims all over the state of Gujarat were allegedly hunted down and killed. The then state chief minister of the BJP government, Narendra Modi, who went on to become the prime minister of India in 2014, and his state government were accused of conniving to hunt down the Muslims. The Congress government at the centre set up an enquiry committee to probe the allegations, which went on for years. Earlier there were demands for reconstructing a Ram temple in Ayodhya, the birthplace of Lord Ram. That in fact, had been the reason given for the demolition in the first place, that the Babri Masjid stood on the site of a Ram mandir which had been brought down to construct the mosque.

The Agony and the Ecstasy

First Promotion as Superintendent of Police (SP)

The days of my posting at Jhansi were coming to an end. I was beginning to enjoy my life. The AIS officers received nothing short of adulation. The set-up was predominantly feudal and the state lagged in some aspects such as technology, but there was no dearth of hospitality and respect for IAS, IPS officers. Later when I returned to the south, I noticed a stark difference—the police forces there were shabby compared to UP, where the police force had more area and population to cover and other problems of the predominantly rural economy, accessibility and a high crime rate, to name a few. But the general opinion is a complete contrast to the ground reality, and it is one that has remained with the state. Personally, I gained a lot in experience, my perspective widened and my capacity to deal with complex problems increased.

While south Indians had a perception that UP and Bihar were backward postings compared to theirs, my observations told me that there were only a few differences. Smaller states did have an advantage in the sense that they were much more manageable, and promotions came quicker.

In UP, transfers were always in the making, and people were always on tenterhooks. If officers got together, the talk would revolve around who would be going where, and in our case, the lists were finally out. There were many transfers, and at the end of each list, there was a newly promoted officer from our batch. UP had the biggest contingent of officers in our batch, with about fifteen of us, and it was always a problem when it came to promotions. It was difficult for even a big state like UP to find so many posts at the same time for the entire batch.

I watched all my batchmates getting promoted except me; it was hard to know what was happening in Lucknow. I was frustrated. I didn't know whether I had a poor record due to which my promotion was withheld or something else. For two long months, the ordeal continued before the orders finally came. They said that the list containing my name was 'stopped' by another officer, through a writ in the court, seeking justice for himself. Hence the delay in getting the writ cleared, making a fresh list and getting the government order (GO) issued all over again. They said it was quite acceptable as it didn't affect my seniority, but no one cared how that would have adversely affected a young officer who had a good record and deserved a timely promotion. I was posted to Nainital, as the superintendent of regional intelligence, for the Kumaon region comprising Nainital, Almora and Pithoragarh districts of the Himalayan region. I was disappointed because of several reasons—one, I thought it was unfair to post a young performing officer to intelligence so early in his career. They should have posted me to a district as additional superintendent, where there was scope for learning, and more of community policing. Second, the posts of regional intelligence were a new concept, and there was no infrastructure available. Third, it was farther away from home. I also felt that the attitude of the department was one of indifference to the individual needs of the officers concerned and it paid no attention to performance. The size of the batch was also partly responsible for this problem.

I sent my family back to Chennai and went to Lucknow, first to the headquarters to get a briefing and exposure to intelligence work and then proceeded to Haldwani, in district Nainital to start work. In UP, once you got transferred, the public works department would issue notice for the vacation of the house after some time and withdraw the help staff. I didn't know the situation in other states, but in UP, all those problems were taken as necessary evils and tolerated because of the high value placed on the services. I didn't share that view though. The public impression was based purely on the high standards the services boasted in olden days, especially before and immediately after Independence when the IAS was known as Indian Civil Service (ICS), and the IPS, as Indian Police (IP).

There were briefings and other formalities before I went to Haldwani to take charge of the new posting. I found the atmosphere in Lucknow to be slack and the staff, less disciplined than in the district of Nainital. I had a friend in the IAS who came by the officers' mess one day. We had dinner together, and he left around 9 p.m. We went out of the mess, and our cars were ready to take us back to our respective places. It was a little late, and from the way the driver banged the rear door of the car shut, I sensed that he was not happy about the late hour. After my friend had left, I got into my car and asked him as to why he behaved rudely in front of another officer and what impression would that officer carry about the department. The driver stopped the car in the middle of the road and started walking away. I could think of no other way except to get down, drag him back to the car and order him to drive me back. We finally reached home. Next day, there was a cold reception in the office. I could guess that the driver must have complained. I expected the Director General of Intelligence (DGI) to call me and talk to me about the incident. But he never did. No one was interested in knowing my version. They only told me that my briefing was over, and I should proceed to Nainital on the new posting.

I proceeded to Nainital. The train reached Haldwani, which was the last but one station before the Nainital hills started. The mountain air was fresh and chilly. At the station, the local police inspector received me and escorted me to the guest house. From then on, I was on my own. It took a few days for the car to arrive from Lucknow, and until then I moved around pillion of the old motorcycle belonging to the lone plainclothes head constable. I had to find a building on rent for the intelligence office and appoint personnel. I had a lot of things to do, and everything required follow-up action. I was allotted old house as my residence and once again, I called my wife and son. My health bothered me on and off, and finally, I became bedridden. What started off as a sore throat turned into a fever that never climbed down for over fifteen days. There was no proper medical care available in the town, or so I thought, until I came across Dr Sharma, who was a godsend for me. He looked at my throat, which he said had turned almost black due to infection, cursed the one who was treating me so far and gave me an antibiotic together with half an anti-allergy tablet. I was up and running in two days!

After setting up the office, I started moving about on the hills of Ranikhet and Almora. I visited these places infrequently initially, as there was little happening there from the intelligence point of view. In fact, the whole of Kumaon had different kind of life; placid and laid-back. The political front didn't have much activity, and the region remained economically backward. An outfit called Parvatiya Sankritik Utthan Manch was slowly coming into its own, holding rallies and highlighting demands for better developmental activities. The people of the region felt neglected, which later culminated in the formation of a separate state, Uttarakhand, carved out of UP. On the western side lay the town of Kashipur, which had a sizeable Punjabi population. At the time of Khalistan agitations in Punjab, this area was said to have witnessed some tension, but by the time I arrived in 1980-81, there were hardly any situations worthy of acting upon or reporting.

Jaya and I moved around the Kumaon hills freely. Nainital Lake was a wonder, and we had a government guest house overlooking the lake. There were more lakes such as Bhimtal, which were less frequented and therefore retained their pristine beauty. From Ranikhet one could have a clear view of the snow-capped peaks of Trisuli mountains. Rishikesh, Dehradun and Mussoorie were other places we managed to visit and enjoy. A ten-mile trek in the ice-capped mountains of Kullu is particularly unforgettable. My only regret was we could not make it to Badrinath during my stay at Haldwani.

On the work front, things were frustrating, with practically little work, no proper infrastructure and no life for us. The work was hardly contributing to my growth. I was in no mood to enjoy the pleasures of living near Nainital Lake, as there were so many fundamental problems plaguing us. I resolved to get out of UP and return to Chennai at the earliest, with or without a job. I resolved that from then on, I would dictate the course of my career and life, and not the service. I came to know that Intelligence Bureau (IB) was recruiting officers on deputation and insider news was that even a Chennai posting was possible after serving a few years at the headquarters at Delhi. I applied for a position in the IB, and the posting order came swiftly.

I moved to Delhi and was temporarily put up in a transit accommodation provided to us at Lodhi Colony. Jaya joined me with five-year-old Kaushik and one-year-old Dhananjay. We spent one year in Delhi, and meanwhile, I was keeping tabs on vacancies in my home city, so that I could get back to Chennai, which was the sole aim of my life then. To my dismay, I came to know that it was possible to get posted elsewhere before getting posted to Chennai, for which there was already a big queue. I went to M.K. Narayanan, who was the then additional director of IB, and requested for a home posting as I was given to understand that in one year I would be able to go to Chennai on an internal posting. He said it was not possible immediately. I wrote a representation requesting for a posting to Chennai, failing which I requested a repatriation to UP, my home cadre. The home ministry considered my application and agreed to the latter. I was back to square one.

Again, the usual routine was tiring; that of finding an accommodation and settling down for another round of work. Jaya's brother came to Delhi from Chennai to escort her and kids back to Chennai, until I settled down in UP. I had left my luggage at batchmate and friend, Ashok Maheepathi's place in Delhi. We had neatly stacked it up in the balcony of his house. After settling down, I went to Delhi to bring the personal effects back. To my horror, I found the entire lot soaked in water. Delhi gets one of those storms and rains, which probably took the cover off and the rain drenched the luggage consisting of furniture, clothing, utensils and books, among other things. I brought back whatever remained of it to Lucknow. Five years later, the same fate was to await my household goods, which were sent by truck from Chennai to Lucknow at the end of my first deputation to Chennai airport. It was summer, and it rained heavily, quite unexpectedly in Madhya Pradesh, and the protection cover proved insufficient. Our wedding photo album stands testimony to this event even today.

Considering the IB debacle, it was likely that they might not consider me for another deputation for at least three years. So, I resigned to my fate and settled down as I had no more energy left to fight an impersonal machinery called the government. Life was a little better in Lucknow compared to Haldwani. I had to tour extensively, throughout western UP, which also gave me an opportunity to go to Delhi to find out about possible vacancies in Chennai. During one such visits, I found a slot at the Chennai airport, and requested V.K. Jain, who was then the special secretary, home, also from UP cadre. My application was accepted, and I was posted to the Bureau of Civil Aviation Security, Chennai, as the regional deputy commissioner.

5

The Homecoming and Adieu, IPS!

Not all those who wander are lost.

−J.R.R. TOLKIEN

Bureau of Civil Aviation Security (BCAS)—Chennai

As we approached Chennai Central Railway Station, I could see the joy in my wife's eyes. There was a vehicle at the station and a representative from the Bureau of Civil Aviation Security (BCAS) to receive us. I was to join the next day, 1 April 1987. The office was situated at the old international airport terminal. It was on the first floor, which contained the airport director's office. The corridor ran from right to left from the staircase. To the right where the corridor ended, there was a small room to the left, and my predecessor, Upadhyaya from the Tamil Nadu cadre rose to welcome me. The smallness of the office space struck me at once. The entire room must have measured about 200 sq ft, partitioned into four. The deputy commissioner occupied one cubicle, while the two assistant commissioners who were on deputation from the Railway Protection Force (RPF) were assigned two cubicles. The remaining staff of four packed into the last cubicle. What little room was available was occupied by some fax machines and copiers. I surveyed my kingdom for the next five years, and my heart sank. The first resolution I took was to do something about the office.

My predecessor quickly left, even vacating the living quarters at the earliest, making way for me to move in. The flat was situated right across the airport. I could walk to my office, which was a good thing, since there was no earmarked vehicle for BCAS. If someone needed a vehicle for operational reasons, he needed to requisition for it the previous day and get it detailed for a fixed time, which was a major drawback as no senior officer from the police would like to be without a regular transportation. What followed was an indicator of things to follow. I had, by this time, understood my surroundings and took out a file and tried reading it. While I was at it, a visitor, who introduced himself as Raghavan, the vigilance officer from Indian Airlines (IA), walked into the office. He appeared confused to find a stranger in the seat, till I explained that I was the new deputy commissioner. He thought for a minute and said, 'What about the ID card for Mr Rajagopal? Did Mr Upadhyaya say anything about it?'

Rajagopal was the DIG of the Chennai office of the Central Bureau of Investigation (CBI) and needed an airport entry pass, which was, in those days, a symbol of prestige and power. Raghavan had a close working relationship with CBI, and my guess was that he had promised the deputy inspector general to get him an airport ID, even though the officer didn't need a permanent one issued to him. I said I didn't know anything about it; in fact, I was not even aware of the procedure. Raghavan felt disappointed and slightly annoyed. 'The DIG has already arrived and is sitting in my office,' he said. He probably expected me to find the ID card or have it issued in a hurry and hand it over to him. I did nothing of that sort. I politely said it was not my fault, and the DIG would have to come again when the pass was ready, which would take at least a couple of days as I needed time to study the procedures. The officer left in a huff, and must have made his way directly to the CBI officer to recount what had transpired, but I didn't hear anything about it again until I ran into Rajagopal in the terminal after a few days. He was there to catch a flight to Colombo. I introduced myself. He said, 'Ah, Mr Sampath, pleased to meet you. I learned about you from Raghavan.' I could guess what Raghavan would have told him! But what he said next was unexpected. 'Sampath, why don't you come to CBI? I need upright and bold officers like you. Think it over and let me know. I will be back from Colombo in five days, and if you are willing, I will speak to the home minister and get your deputation orders issued.'

I thanked him for his offer and left. I could see that he had taken the ID card issue in the right spirit and appreciated my point of view. I didn't, of course, express my willingness for CBI, as I had just taken over civil aviation, and I wanted to do justice to my new role, the lack of facilities notwithstanding. Having said that though, the offer to join the CBI was a big honour, for two reasons. It was a well-established department unlike the civil aviation office, and then there was the prestige of working for the CBI, of course, which was the Indian equivalent to the FBI. Still, I decided to stick around and start from the scratch in BCAS.

My next encounter with 'airport culture' came on the heels of this one. I was sitting in my office one evening when the news came that the Indian Airline staff had gone on a flash strike and the flights were inordinately delayed. The pilots were demanding action against a security man for his 'high-handed behaviour' with airline staff. At the time, the evening flight to Delhi on which the union home secretary was travelling, was on the bay. I rushed to the terminal to find out as to what was happening. During those days it was the state police which was entrusted with the security of the airport before the responsibility was handed over to the Central Industrial Security Force (CISF). The BCAS issued the policy guidelines and supervised the functions, but the police did the actual policing on the ground. On enquiring, I found out that when an IA car carrying the flight crew entered the gate and was stopped by security personnel, the driver got down and slapped the security guard, saying, 'Don't you see the airline emblem on the car or the pilots inside?' The policeman hit him back and said the emblem was not enough and they had to have a pass and show it as and when the security demanded for identification.

By this time, I received a call from the deputy general of police for Tamil Nadu, and I told him what had happened. He asked me to suspend the constable pending enquiry and ask the pilots to withdraw the strike so that the flight could take off. After all, the suspension was not punishment. I told him politely that it might cause loss of face for the security force, as the incident was triggered first by the IA driver's manhandling of a police officer, and refused his recommendation for suspension.

We assured the IA staff of enquiry, and the flights took off after a delay, but with our pride intact. Later, I called a meeting of the security personnel and explained to them what to do under such circumstances. While they were justified in retaliating if someone used violence against them, it wasn't a simple question of who was right, but who had the might. And IA was mighty those days, or at least, that's what they felt. I explained to the security personnel how to deal with such arrogance effectively and without inviting criticism. Instead of reacting immediately, they were told to record the incident and file a first information report with the police, which was very much in their hands. The best way would be to complete the investigation and file a charge sheet quickly. The erring individual would come to know when the court summons reached him, and by then, it would too late to take any preventive measures. The logic worked. The IA employee who slapped the policeman was charge-sheeted for obstructing a government servant from discharging his duties. The individual, who thought he had gotten away with his behaviour was in my office, begging for mercy. I politely told him I could do nothing as the matter was already in court, but we would render all assistance in getting the damage minimized. We later softened our stand and finally withdrew the report. The whole episode had a salutary effect on the general attitude towards police and security. People looked at security with new respect. There was yet another incident involving security and customs department. This customs official wanted ingress into the high-security area through a locked gate, which the policeman refused, and asked him to come through the other gate which was open. The officer glared at him and went away. He did return sometime later, this time through the open gate, and addressed the police officer with an expletive. In this instance, the policeman promptly reported the matter to his seniors who, in turn, registered a case against the customs official for abusing a government servant on duty. The customs officer learned about the case only after he received a court summons and when he came to me with an apology, I asked him to apologize to the constable who he had abused, and dropped the matter.

The question could arise as to why we had to compromise in the above two instances. We could have, as well, gone ahead and prosecuted them, but the situation was not that simple. Had we done that the entire airport would have been hostile to us, and it would have been difficult to function on a day-to-day basis since security would lose the cooperation from other agencies. Very few people went by what was right or wrong; they went mostly by their emotions. Under such circumstances, a veiled threat paid more dividends than actual prosecution. Those incidents set the trend among the constituents of the airport, and the climate became condusive for the smooth functioning of security.

I still had the infrastructure of the office to take care of. The office space was dismally cramped, the furniture was old and rickety, and no proper office equipment was available. The two assistant commissioners, who must have had decent facilities in their parent departments, were also marking time. At BCAS, they were provided with house rent allowance (HRA), which was a pittance compared to the then current housing situation. I felt sad when I found these officers riding an official motorcycle for official duties. The other staff such as the personal secretary, attendant and others were mostly on deputation from the airworthiness office, or the office of the director general of civil aviation, who were also on the lookout for repatriation to their parent departments.

The ministry of civil aviation was the apex authority for all civil aviation-related activities. A cabinet minister presided over the ministry, assisted by a minister of state and had several departments under its jurisdiction—the director general of civil aviation (DGCA), the airworthiness inspection directorate, the BCAS, and the government-owned Air India and IA, International Airports Authority (IAAI) and the National Airports Authority (NAA) are some of them. The ministry also dealt with all other matters about foreign air carriers, international organizations, such as international civil aviation organization (ICAO). While the IAAI looked after the international airports, the NAA was responsible for domestic airports. Later, there were frequent changes in the structure of these two organizations and were finally merged to be called Airports Authority of India (AAI). Similarly, the IA and Air India, which were operating domestic and international services joined to become Air India.

I met M.A. Khan, the director of Chennai airport and explained the poor condition of my office. He was surprised and said no one brought this to his notice. I remembered my staff mentioning that nobody bothered about the working conditions of the security department. I could see how problem-solving depended on proper representation of facts to the right person. Khan came with me for inspection of our small office and agreed that it was indeed poor. He took me to the second floor of the old terminal as airport operations had just moved to the newly built terminals a couple of kilometres away. On the first floor, the customs department, had shifted into the new terminal as well, and their back office on the second floor was empty. It had independent cabins for all of us and sufficient space for office and visitor areas.

We moved into the new office immediately. After a little follow-up and persuasion, we received a new car and some more vehicles and office equipment from our headquarters. We were set to concentrate on our work. In due course of time the two assistant commissioners were repatriated to their home departments and replaced by two assistant commissioners from IB. They were with BCAS long after I left in 1992. We also inducted army ordnance corps officers for the newly set up Bomb Detection and Disposal Squads (BDDS) at the four metros of Delhi, Mumbai, Kolkata and Chennai. An officer of the rank of an army major headed these units and procured the paraphernalia for bomb handling and sniffer dogs from the Border Security Force (BSF) Academy at Tekanpur, Madhya Pradesh. Since they needed to be available at the airport round the clock, the jawans had to be allotted living quarters near the airport and the dogs had to be provided with air-conditioned accommodation in the airport vicinity. We also got enough funds for the construction of the BCAS office building near the new terminals—it was a two-story building with plenty of space for office, training and recreation.

On the operational side, the BCAS drafted the first National Civil Aviation Security Policy, for which we all made our contribution. Inspections were carried out to ensure compliance. The BCAS carried out 'dummy checks' at the airports wherever their officers went, which meant hiding a weapon in handbags and observing whether the security screening personnel were able to detect them on the X-ray machine. The downside of such a procedure was that wherever we went, the security personnel were informed of our programme well in advance, and therefore the security personnel became overly alert and checked and rechecked all baggage to the annoyance of fellow passengers.

During one such visit to the airport at Visakhapatnam, Andhra Pradesh, I found the scenario to be quite different. The airport terminal had a bank and a post office counter, purportedly for the use of the passengers. The airport handled only one or two flights a day, but the terminal was still teeming with people; I soon discovered the reason for this; the hall was full of visitors who had come to see off the passenger, and there were also a large number of people from the neighbourhood who had come there for banking and postal transactions—inside the terminal. As a result, the passengers didn't have space even to stand. I ordered everyone except the passengers to get out of the building. I instructed the police to put barricade and restricted the entry for passengers only, much to their relief. After the flight to Delhi had left, I returned to my office to find a man waiting for me, who introduced himself as the personal assistant to the then chairman of the Vizag Steel Plant, an IAS officer. He said he was there to convey the appreciation of the chairman, who had been a passenger on the Delhi flight, for having dealt with the problem of overcrowding at the airport. The gentleman did not stop there; he even extended an invite, on behalf of the chairman, to the use of the company's newly built hilltop guest house. I stayed there along with the family during my subsequent visit. The guest house was exquisitely done up and was close to the scenic Gangavaram Beach. We have seen many such beaches afterward, but nothing quite compares to this visit—and the memories it fostered.

One insistent and annoying problem I faced during my tenure was that of hoax bomb-threat calls. People knew about the setting up of the bomb disposal and detection squads, and also knew that the aircraft would get delayed for the check. Those who had grievances against the airport authority or even passengers who were delayed getting to the airport, gave a bomb threat to hold the aircraft until they arrived. We could not afford to ignore such alerts, for obvious reasons, and had to run through the entire drill each time—take the plane to the isolation bay, disembark the passengers and check the aircraft thoroughly only to find it clean. Whenever we found suspicious or unclaimed baggage in the terminals, we took it to the 'bomb pit', dug up at a safe distance from the runways and the terminals, but within the airport perimeter. We even bought a robot for remote handling of suspicious objects. Though we had bomb blankets and other safety equipment the robot was convenient for handling explosives. The technicians could remain at a safe distance and operate the robot remotely to lift and open the baggage to check for explosives. Unfortunately, the robot went out of order, and for lack of spares, the imported robot went to the attic.

I was nominated by the ministry of civil aviation for a training programme with the Federal Aviation Administration (FAA), the apex authority for civil aviation operations in the US, located in Oklahoma. Mr Suradkar from the Mumbai airport was my companion. The training was interesting and informative, along with the fact that it was my first ever visit abroad. From there I went to Montreal, Canada, to visit the International Civil Aviation Organization (ICAO), a body of the UN, which dealt with global civil aviation issues. Most of the countries in the world were members of this organization, which met at regular intervals to discuss major issues facing the world civil aviation community. Through its rule book called Annexe-17, the security regulations were circulated to all member countries to follow. That was how we see uniform security procedures all over the world.

The first ever meeting of ICAO countries took place in Chicago in the year 1945, and the deliberations formed the primary document, called the 'Chicago Convention'. Annexes to this paper dealt with various aspects of civil aviation operations; Annexe-17 dealt with Security. We drafted the National Civil Aviation Security Programme based on these documents. I was also nominated to represent India on the ICAO Panel of Security Experts, for their exchange programme through which assistance was provided to organize aviation security in countries which needed help, particularly in developing countries, though no opportunity came my way to render such services.

Assassination of Rajiv Gandhi

Rajiv Gandhi landed at Chennai airport around 8 p.m. on 21 May 1991, from Andhra Pradesh, on a whirlwind election tour. We were at the airport to receive him, with snacks and tea at the VIP lounge. After tea and some small talk with officials and party workers, Rajiv Gandhi, the ex-PM set out for Sriperumbudur to address an election meeting. In about an hour's time, a suicide bomber identified as belonging to the Liberation Tigers of Tamil Eelam (LTTE) of Sri Lanka, assassinated him.

Rajiv Gandhi had succeeded his mother Indira to the prime minister's office after she was gruesomely assassinated by her security guard in 1984. Those were the days when the Khalistan secessionists were very active, and their demand was to have a separate state, Khalistan, to be carved out of Punjab. Tipped by intelligence agencies that Khalistanis were hiding inside the famous Golden Temple with a huge cache of arms and ammunition, Prime Minister Indira Gandhi ordered a raid on the holy temple of the Sikhs and flushed them out. After the raid, because of the ill feeling fostered by the separatist movement and in an uncertain, conflicted environment, Indira Gandhi's personal, and trusted security guard, Beant Singh fired from his service rifle, when she stepped out onto the lawns of her sprawling bungalow after breakfast, on her way to meet the people outside. Tragically, the fate that befell her also claimed the life of her second son, Rajiv, this time, at the hands of a suicide bomber with affiliations to the dreaded Sri Lankan militant outfit, LTTE.

In the early days of the civil war in Sri Lanka, India played a big brother role to the island nation as it was unable to contain the violence. The war was between minority Lankan Tamils and the Sinhalese majority over freedom. Many organizations sprang up to represent the Tamils, including the LTTE. What followed was an internecine struggle between the groups resulting in the killing of many leaders. On the other hand, the government forces were also fighting to establish supremacy. Rajiv decided to send the Indian Peace Keeping Force (IPKF) to Sri Lanka to help. There were again allegations of misconduct against the IPKF and the resentment of the Tamil population rose against it. So much so that when Rajiv was on a state visit to Sri Lanka as a prime minister, a Sinhalese soldier tried to hit the visiting prime minister with the butt of a service rifle, even as the prime minister was inspecting the guard of honour. Rajiv escaped the attack by ducking just in time, but was not so fortunate the second time, when he was on an election tour of Chennai. The elections were just a month or two away, and it looked like a sure win for him for his second term as prime minister, when the tragedy struck.

Along with me, a host of other officials saw him off from the airport to Sriperumbudur, small temple town 50 miles west of Chennai, where he was scheduled to address an election rally. There was a minor issue at the airport, and I proceeded to the main terminal. Hardly in about 45 minutes, the wireless set crackled, and a message came about a bomb explosion at Sriperumbudur in which several people had died. As airport security, we were kept abreast but there was unfortunately nothing we could have done. Then, we got a call from Delhi saying a human bomb had assassinated Rajiv Gandhi. All hell broke loose for next several days. I later learned from intelligence reports that Dhanu, a Sri Lankan Tamil girl, was responsible for the killing. Purported to be a recruit of LTTE, she was one among the crowd gathered at Sriperumbudur with a garland in hand to greet Rajiv. When he came near her, she stooped down in a gesture of touching his feet, pushed a switch to fire the explosives tied all over her body, killing several people including her intended target and herself.

While we were waiting at the terminal, there was news that Sonia, Rajiv's Italian wife, boarded a special aircraft to escort her husband's remains back to Delhi. Their two young children Rahul and Priyanka waited to see their father returning home lifeless. Thirteen years and a few elections later, Sonia became the president of the Congress Party, which remained in power unhindered for ten years. Rahul, who, at that time, was in his early forties, led the party, along with his mother, in the general elections of 2014 in which the Congress lost badly. It is ironic that, for the last several years, even though his party was willing to offer Congress leadership on a plate, he was hesitant to accept it.

Aviation Disasters

Two incidents were memorable during my tenure. One was a hijack attempt by a Sri Lankan youth who tried to seize an IA flight from Chennai to Bengaluru. He had a round object covered by his handkerchief which he brandished as a 'bomb' on board the aircraft, and threatened that if the flight were not taken to Jaffna in Sri Lanka, which was known for being an LTTE stronghold, he would blow up the aircraft. But the crew did not take him seriously, because he was clearly an amateur and was shaking terribly. They talked him out of the 'hijack' drama and landed safely at Bengaluru airport. The boy was found to be carrying a cricket ball covered with a handkerchief. He was handed over to the police. Nevertheless, the authorities banned all 'round' objects from being carried on board for some time after the incident. Some overzealous security personnel banned apples from being carried in hand baggage. There was massive protest at the Kolkata airport when the security roundly rejected rasgullas from carry-on luggage. Due to public protest, the authorities lifted the ban later.

The second incident was tragic. IA had acquired new-generation Airbus A320 aircraft for passenger flight operations, one of which was plying from Chennai to Bengaluru and back. When the plane took off from Bengaluru on its return journey, it failed to climb to a sufficient height and crashed on the ground near the airport, killing all the occupants. Either the aircraft had defects, or the pilots were not trained to handle the new-generation aircraft.

Another memorable incident didn't take place during my tenure but just before it, so I did have the opportunity to follow up the investigations. The incident had far-reaching consequences on the security measures at the Chennai airport. On 2 August 1984, a powerful bomb exploded inside the airport terminal killing at least thirty people and injuring an equal number. It made the authorities sit up and think about the procedures regarding baggage identification systems. During investigations, it transpired that a Sri Lankan militant group was responsible for the blast. The bomb was initially meant for an Air Lanka flight to Colombo, but the baggage wrongly found its way to a London flight and was detained because there was no passenger to claim the luggage. The militants had purchased a ticket and managed to put the baggage inside with connivance from some airport employees, but no passenger appeared. In fact, they were watching the movement of the baggage from within the airport and were alarmed when the baggage got detained. They probably went a little away from the airport, for fear of apprehension, and alerted the police about the bomb. The customs inspector who held the baggage refused to budge, and the time set for the blast was approaching. The Colombo flight had left in the meanwhile. Ultimately, the customs relented and allowed the baggage to be moved, but it was too late by then. The explosion occurred.

When I took over in early 1987, the impact of the incident was still felt in the airport. Procedures were drawn up afresh to ensure that the passenger accompanied the baggage and baggage identification became mandatory.

Return to UP

On completion of the deputation with BCAS, I faced the prospect of going back to UP. Our boys had grown up and were studying in good schools. I postponed the dilemma by taking leave for about six months. Finally, I landed alone at Lucknow in November 1992, leaving the family back in Chennai for the sake of the children's education. I was posted as assistant inspector general (AIG) at police headquarters. My primary job was crisis management and mobilization of forces either from within the state or federal/central paramilitary forces. The posting offered an instant connection with all the districts and officers all over the state. I was concerned about my absence from the state for five long years, and the posting at police headquarters came as a golden opportunity to re-establish contact. But within weeks the demolition of the mosque shattered the peace for all concerned including me.

I went on leave for about six months and returned to UP as senior commandant of 15th Battalion of PAC, at Agra, which was my second posting to the city. By this time, our batch was due for promotion to the next level of DIG. As it happened before, during the elevation process to the superintendent level, the government could not accommodate all of us as DIGs. Added to that was the problem of state cadre officers winning a court case and joining our batch! As a result, we were all retained in whatever capacity we were in, at the pay scale of DIG! For instance, I continued as senior commandant/DIG of the battalion until an apparent vacancy arose. I didn't have the patience to wait nor was there any motivation. The charm of promotion was gone, once again.

Soon after, I requested for a study leave to pursue my master's in philosophy from Madras University. All India Service officers are entitled to a two-year study leave once during their service, which comes as paid leave. I landed in Chennai and after completing my MPhil studies, extended my leave, until I got my second Government of India deputation to Chennai, this time with Central Industrial Security Force (CISF) as its deputy inspector general, south zone. I had, earlier enrolled for a PhD programme at Dr Ambedkar University in Agra, and completed the same after three years in 1998.

Central Industrial Security Force (CISF)

The region had about fifty government undertakings all over the four states of Kerala, Karnataka, Andhra Pradesh and Tamil Nadu. Establishments such as airports, seaports, mints and currency presses, coal mines, space organizations and oil refineries came under CISF for security. This elite force had elaborate training arrangements for manning sensitive establishments, VIP security wings and safety audit arrangements. I had to travel extensively all through the region for inspecting the units, taking care of the welfare of a vast workforce in the area and investigating incidents involving security. I had the responsibility of carrying out security surveys and audits, determine the size of the security force and investment required.

The Naxalite Problem

The bomb exploded precisely when the bus was crossing the road, killing about ten jawans and injuring another twenty-five. The two busloads of CISF personnel were slowly winding their way to Hyderabad after completing the first phase of elections in Andhra Pradesh in 1999. The sixty-odd jawans were weary after the gruelling election process in the Singareni–Ramagundam belt, which suffered heat upwards of 45°C in summers. The road was winding through a zigzag mountain road. That was when the blast occurred.

I was in my office in Chennai closely monitoring the movement of the battalions all over Andhra on election duty. On getting information about this incident, I rushed to the airport, where fortunately, there was a flight to Hyderabad leaving in about an hour's time. While waiting at the departure gate, I was constantly in touch with my people on the ground and coordinating the situation in Hyderabad. I also asked for a vehicle to be kept ready at the airport. By the time I reached, the injured had been moved to Osmania Medical College hospital, where I went directly on landing. It was a heart-rending scene. Many people had died by the time they reached the hospital and many more had lost their limbs and sustained other grievous injuries. I had a busy time coordinating with the hospital authorities for removal of dead bodies to the mortuary, informing the relatives of the jawans and passing on the status report to the headquarters and higher-ups. I stayed on for a few more days before returning to Chennai. Once there, I had more work to do to ensure timely payment of compensation to the families of the dead and prepare the citations for gallantry awards for those martyred officers. What was intriguing being the fact that Naxals chose to bomb the CISF bus when they usually made the local police their target. I asked one of my informers to find out the reason behind this change of strategy, and found that they were indeed aiming for the police but mistakenly bombed CISF bus.

Whenever I visited Ramagundam in the past, I used to move incognito—in plain clothes and private cars with no escorts or shooters—to avoid unnecessary confrontation with the Naxalites. On one such occasion, as per an informer, one Naxal leader knew about my movement.

The Naxal movement originated in a place called Naxalbari in West Bengal, and hence the name, as a militant armed organization specializing in guerrilla warfare against the state. The states most affected by the activities of this outfit were West Bengal, Andhra Pradesh, Odisha and Chhattisgarh, though at one time, their activities were noticed in several other states such as Bihar, Jharkhand and Karnataka. Their main demands related to redistribution of lands and release of their cadre from the prisons, arrested in previous attacks and killings.

The CISF is one among about half-a-dozen such paramilitary forces. The Central Reserve Police Force (CRPF) helped the central and state governments to maintain law and order. The BSF, as the name suggests, helped the army in securing the borders. The Indo-Tibetan Border Security Police (ITBP), and the National Security Guard (NSG) for VIP security, especially the Z category of VIPs. The CBI, though not a paramilitary organization, was for primarily for criminal investigations including anti-corruption operations. It was during this tenure with CISF that I was decorated with a medal and citation for meritorious services by the president of India.

During my tenure with CISF, we had a director general, the head of the force, who had the habit of coming to Chennai every weekend. At first, we were enthusiastic and implemented the full protocol in welcoming him, including a ceremonial parade. He inspected a unit en route and proceeded to the Aurobindo ashram in Puducherry for a two days' stay, and left for Delhi on Sunday evening. The next weekend he came again and followed the same routine. I cut the parade and went to the airport to receive him in full uniform. He showed his dislike for abandoning protocol for a director general visit. The next Friday, I went to the airport in civilian clothes to receive him. My plan was to stop doing even that the next time. He got down from the aircraft, looked at me and said, 'How can you be in private clothes to receive your DG?' I replied, suppressing my smile, 'The DG is on a private visit, sir!' Obviously, he didn't like my response and the lack of protocol, and remained hostile for the rest of his term, but such random visits continued. Then, I decided to take a different course of action; I wrote a petition complaining about these visits, and how they disrupted my functioning at the regional level, and sent it to the central vigilance commissioner (CVC), asking him why there was no control over a senior officer's movements at Delhi. I gave a copy to a friend who had direct contacts with the home department. The DG's visits stopped abruptly. I got a call from the CVC's office saying that it was the first time they received a complaint from a serving officer against his boss, complete with his signature! People generally didn't complain, and even if they did, it was through anonymous applications. Later, my friend told me he faxed my complaint to the home minister, who then called and chided the director general!

Adieu, IPS!

After twenty-five years in the service, I decided to call it quits in 2002. The last promotion was the elevation to the rank of inspector general, which came at the end of my tenure with CISF. A proposal for promotion, the creation of this post for the southern region and my retention at Chennai in that post was drawn up by CISF and sent to ministry of home affairs (MHA) for approval. Since my tenure had ended before the approval came, the ministry extended it by three months, but even then, the proposal couldn't come through. I decided to go back to UP, claim my promotion and resign from the service. I submitted my resignation to the deputy general of police, CISF, who promptly forwarded it to UP. I gave time for it to reach UP and then decided to go to there for follow-up.

This was my last trip to the northern state and I went alone, leaving my family behind for the last time. I landed in Lucknow and deposited my luggage in the guest house. The staff confirmed receipt of my resignation and informed me that it might take time to relieve me. It was required to pass through the chief minister's office, then on to the home ministry's office in Delhi and finally sent to the president of India for his final approval.

I walked out scanning the offices on both sides of the corridor. The rooms were occupied by senior officers of the state government. Red and green lights were blinking alternately on the wall, indicating the availability or otherwise of the official concerned. An attendant was invariably found sitting on a stool in front of each room, ready to respond to a call bell from inside. I came across one office and stopped. The name appeared familiar. The red light was on. Beneath the name of the officer, it said, 'Secretary to the Chief Minister'. I finally remembered the name as that of an IAS officer who had served as the commissioner of the Jhansi division, where years ago, I served as the assistant superintendent, my first posting in UP after training. I decided to meet the officer and greet him. I sent word through the attendant. In less than a minute, Punia appeared at the doorstep, gave me a hug and took me inside, where we reminisced about the days gone by over coffee. When I told him about my intent to resign, he couldn't believe his ears. He listened carefully to my story and while empathizing with me about the difficulties I had faced, reassured me that he could get me a posting of my choice. It was the fifth time in my career I got an offer of help to get a good posting!

I smiled and thanked Punia for his support, but told him my decision to quit was final, and it would be of immense help if he assisted in getting the resignation accepted and let me go as early as possible as my family was waiting in Chennai. Punia understood my situation. He picked up the intercom and gave instructions to the person at the other end. In less than fifteen minutes my file was placed on his table. Punia took the papers, asked me to wait and entered the adjacent room. Only then did I note that this was the office of the chief minister. In exactly three minutes, Punia was back with the file, which he placed on the table in front of me. I looked up in bewilderment. He stated, 'You stand relieved Sampath!' I was speechless. 'But Mr Punia...'

'Yes, I know what you are going to say—that it needs to go to the MHA in Delhi and then on to the president of India? Don't worry, that will all be taken care of. You can head back to Chennai,' he reassured me. I couldn't believe my ears. It was an irony that in my entire service, one thing which happened swiftly in UP in my favour was the relieving order! I couldn't thank Punia enough and left. In the next three days, all formalities such as my promotion orders as inspector general, pension papers and arrear cheques were cleared and I was free.

Among other reasons for quitting, I always felt it was a waste of time and energy to devote one's entire work life to one profession. The police department demanded your time and energy 24x7 for over thirty-five years if you wanted to reach the ultimate position of director general of police. It was not always exciting or rewarding. Much of muck came along with years spent in unimportant postings before you tasted a posting or two of your liking. Officers got identified with one party or the other and got shunted out to insignificant assignments or off to godforsaken places when the 'other' party came to power. The rewards were dismally low, as were the salaries too. The only reward was the high perception which the public had about the services and the satisfaction that one served one's country, which is certainly not insignificant. I figured that all the above conditions suited the purposes of society, which extolled the services and members of the armed forces, but from the individual's point of view, it would be better for his evolution to serve for some time and move on. In fact, no one, I thought, should be preoccupied only with what one knows. I thought this quality that exists in most of us is a big obstacle in our path towards personal evolution. You may be a great actor, singer or a politician but instead of clinging to it until you are driven out, you should know when to retire gracefully, during a flourishing career, to make way for others and also to sharpen some other faculty. This quality of clinging has been the cause of many evils in our society. Of course, it takes courage to do that, and not many could claim to possess it.

After some time, I joined Reliance Industries as their security consultant and director of Security.

6

The Corporate Jungle

You must take a chance,
make a choice and change your life.

–ANONYMOUS

Reliance Industries

When it was time for repatriation from Chennai to UP, and the promotion and extension of service with CISF was not coming through, I considered other options. I did not even consider returning to UP as a viable alternative because my second son had reached an important point in his education and uprooting him wouldn't have been right. Moreover, I was away from my cadre for so long that I was not sure about rebooting my career there from scratch. The only other option was to quit the service as I was eligible to apply for voluntary retirement, which carried a pension after twenty years of service. The next question was my next move after retirement. One needed to plan for such an eventuality well in advance, identify potential employers and have some assurance for a job suitable to one's seniority. I was tech savvy, even in those days when mobile phones and digital cameras had just started appearing on the market. Only a privileged few had cell phones, and the government issued them only to very senior officers. The internet used to be slow, and making one's webpage was almost unheard of. I created my page and had uploaded my complete details on the page. The scion of one of the biggest private corporates at Mumbai, Mukesh Ambani, was also a visitor to the webpage and was impressed with my profile. He spoke to his brother-in-law Shyam Kothari, who oversaw the company's southern operations, and based in Chennai. I met him and had a chat, and it was decided to hire my services as a director of security operations for the company, an avenue that I had had no experience in when I was in the services.

But with the assurance of this job, I went ahead and applied for voluntary retirement. However, I decided to tread carefully. My government 'sensibilities' told me not to accept a direct position in the existing hierarchy of the company. I found becoming a consultant to be the solution as it would provide the necessary distance and functional freedom. So, after I was relieved from government employment, I started a consultancy firm with a handful of staff, and the corporate house became my client. I also negotiated a settlement that allowed me to work from Chennai. But before I plunged into my private sector stint, I took a brief holiday to visit my older son Kaushik, who was studying in Chicago. When I came back and was all set to go to Mumbai to formally meet Dhirubhai Ambani, the chairman of the Reliance conglomerate, I got the news that he had taken ill and had been admitted to the hospital. Within a week he died, and within a few weeks of his death, trouble started brewing between the brothers.

Reliance Industries, one of India's top private sector companies, was valued at $14 billion in 2002, went on to become a $110 billion company in 2017, and suffered a partition between the two brothers of the family in 2005. I was one of the most affected in this division. Within a week of my joining and before my role could even be defined, Dhirubhai Ambani, the chairman and founder of the company, passed away. He was ailing and admitted to the hospital for some time, but no one had expected him to die so soon, at least not me; he was just seventy. His two sons, Mukesh and Anil, fought a succession war, which came out in the open in 2005 and they parted ways, albeit temporarily. They did make peace of sorts, but the chasm remained. The brothers divided between themselves, the many properties all over the country, and not many knew the formula based on which such a division took place. The Mumbai headquarters was the worst affected. Though I had earlier negotiated with Mukesh, the elder son, for a consulting position in security and had served the government with a notice two month before voluntary retirement, as was mandatory, it was anybody's guess that he would not have made that decision without his father's approval. Dhirubhai was a man who had great respect for the government and his death was a setback for my career in the company right in the beginning.

To start with, I found that the company already had a security set-up which was operating on a basic model of a few security officers and a set of standard operating procedures (SOP). I felt the need for a good security manual for the entire group of companies. As a first step, I prepared a presentation for Kothari and followed it up with a draft manual in the next three months. I travelled extensively to visit various facilities all over the country to do security surveys to assess the current systems, the risk factors and any additional requirements. Kothari was so impressed with the presentation and the draft manual that he spoke to Mukesh Ambani immediately over the phone and fixed an appointment for me to go over to Mumbai to give a presentation to Mukesh. I was glad I had got an opportunity to meet him with my first effort. But, I was too happy too soon, which was something I realized only after reaching Mumbai. The problem came in the shape of the head of the human resources department, V.V. Bhat, who also had the security department under his thumb. He had recruited a junior officer from one of the central police organizations and was running the security office through him. It was hard for me to say if Bhat saw a threat to his fiefdom in my entry into the organization.

Many of the private companies in India were family-owned, which metamorphosed into corporate houses with the advent of economic liberalization and subsequent import of western management styles, particularly from the US. Still, the interests of the family remained the core aim of the company, though in a hidden way. One member of the corporate family rightly quipped, that they were 'modern-day princely rulers'.

In those days, when an entrepreneur started a business, he surrounded himself with a handful of individuals with or without some expertise in chosen areas. Even if one was not an expert in a subject, his services were valued as he was a friend. In the pre-1991 era, India had trade restrictions and a whole lot of other licences and permits were required to start a business. During those times, India was a democratic country following socialist principles. If the 'Licence Raj' was in place, the babus or government clerks ruled the roost, and private businesses had to innovate to circumvent cumbersome procedures; even corruption was not ruled out in such manoeuvres on their part. It is hard to decide who to blame: the government procedures and red tape or the entrepreneurs? The country's system was not progress-oriented for the economy and the nation suffered low growth rates and balance of payment deficits. As a result, currency reserves plummeted, forcing the country to pledge its gold reserves to the UK. In the early 1990s, the government decided to throw away the yoke of socialism and permit a liberal and globalized economy. Corporate houses got the much-needed shot in the arm for doing business in a free atmosphere. The Indian economy recovered rapidly.

Reliance Industries Limited, under Dhirubhai was rumoured to have earned a reputation for 'fixing' all such problems in obtaining licences for many business activities and progressing rapidly. It was not altogether acceptable to some sections of the people, especially among government officers, who saw the company's success as an outgrowth of graft and corruption. Reliance took shape during those earlier pre-liberalization times, and V.V. Bhat was one of the close associates of Dhirubhai. He belonged to the 'extended' Reliance family, next only to the core members, who were rewarded richly for their loyalty; including undisclosed amounts as salary and other perks such as first-class travel and stay in luxury hotels and foreign trips. They headed essential and vital functions and carefully watched the performance and activities of 'outsiders', meaning those professionals who were hired to perform the tasks of the business. Such outsiders could enter the rarefied circle by showing their loyalty over the long term. Once they reached these levels, they never got sacked and were looked after well long after their retirement, which eventually came only when they were physically incapable of working.

Under the circumstances, therefore, my entry was probably seen by Bhat as unwelcome. However, since I had the recommendations of a family member, the brother-in-law of the boss, he couldn't help but take me into the fold, but it was clear he was wary of my presence. I first became aware of this when I reached the headquarters in Mumbai for the presentation and with a draft copy of the security manual. It was Bhat, and not the chairman, who saw the powerpoint presentation. I presumed he must have been busy and had assigned Bhat to see it on his behalf. Once I returned to Chennai, I told Kothari about what had transpired. He was surprised and said he had forwarded a copy of the draft directly to the chairman, who had marked the same to Bhat with the directions that the measures suggested by me be implemented with 'immediate effect'. Despite that, I didn't hear anything for a long time, but noticeable changes in security procedures were ordered by Bhat, without acknowledging my authorship. I was nevertheless happy that I had made my contribution and the company had benefitted from my expertise and skills.

I continued to do my work in the southern region with headquarters at Chennai. The company had launched its new branch for the telecom arm of the business and was planning to enter the mobile phone market with low-cost handsets and low tariffs. The company sold cell phones for as low as Rs 500 (about $10). Mobile towers, intermediary stations, and other installations had to be put in place all over the country. I travelled over 10,000 miles by road to ensure proper security for all such facilities. Finally, I began to experience immense satisfaction in my work. Reliance had some sound business principles worth emulating by other firms. It believed in flooding a new project with resources to enable the project to be established. You could probably ask for a chopper, with proper justification, and you would get it. Once the establishment was up, and production started, then you couldn't get even a pencil sanctioned! Such was the control over the resources. I saw this happening during those early days of Reliance Communications and contrasted it with the battles I had to wage for getting barest minimum resources from my headquarters in the government. The second principle of its founder was the creation of wealth for the entire staff and shareholders of the company. I also saw this principle working in my case, reflected in the generous salaries and perks. The stocks of the company were ruling the market and whoever invested in the company immensely benefitted. But never once was I asked to do anything illegal nor did I have any reason to suspect any wrongdoing anywhere.

In all that time, trouble was brewing between the brothers, and in about two years, the internecine war broke out. I was in danger once again. One day, I received a call from Bhat, conveying the decision of the management to make me the country head of security for Reliance Communications. I understood the implications, which were that Reliance Communications was going to the younger son Anil and that I had been shunted to his camp by Bhat. I also learned that Mr Kothari, who had been my well-wisher, decided to stay away from the goings-on. That left me all alone. My efforts to contact Mukesh were futile, as a lot was going on between the brothers and he must hardly have had time to sort out others' issues. I didn't know Anil or his associates, as they were rarely involved in the affairs of the company, since Anil headed Reliance Power at that time. And all things considered, I had come on board as Mukesh's recruit. When I joined, no one had brought up meeting Anil. I too, was hesitant to go on my own and meet him, and that had its roots in bitter experience. I hadn't forgotten the episode early on in my career as a cop, when, as a fresh recruit, I called on the director inspector general of the range before I met the immediate boss of the district because he was out of town.

Reliance Communications

During the first couple of years, I was with the group I never came across Anil in any meeting or social gathering. No one I interacted with in the company discussed him. Everything about him was only hearsay. And then I was being sent to Anil's camp without my consent. However, after much thought, I agreed to take on the challenge as a professional advisor and consultant. My job, after all, was to advise on security irrespective of the company. I had witnessed a mass exodus of property and personnel to Mukesh's camp, so much so that, only a lady security executive remained with Anil.

But what followed was bizarre. The Anil camp was silent, and no move was made to issue required emails asking me to take over the new charge. I suspected there was no proper agreement of division and partition on many issues, and security was one of them. I even thought of the possibility that while the Anil camp thought I was a deliberate plant from Mukesh's side, Mukesh must have thought I deserted him. Such was the talent of Bhat, who played his cards so deftly against me.

Finally, the decks cleared for me to take over the reins of security at Reliance Communications, thanks to Kumar, who was the human resources head at that time. I moved from Chennai to Mumbai and stayed at Dhirubhai Ambani Knowledge City (DAKC), Navi Mumbai. I built the security department literally from scratch—putting the security manual and standard operating procedures in place, recruiting security executives and agencies for manning the installations and streamlining the operations. In two years the security department was functioning smoothly. All this while Anil Ambani never met me even once nor did he attend security briefings.

Even though I quit government service, I never lost touch with my friends and called them occasionally. R.K. Raghavan, who retired as the director of CBI, was heading the security division for Tata, another corporate giant and I made it a point to keep in touch with him, as also M.R. Reddy, who retired as the chief of National Security Guards (NSG), and was heading the security for another corporate group called GMR Group of industries, headquartered at Bengaluru. During a conversation with the latter, where he mentioned that his company was bidding for construction of two airports, one at Hyderabad and another at Delhi, Mr Reddy asked me whether I would be interested in joining them, as I had enough aviation experience. That made sense and got me thinking.

I quit the job, having served the entire Reliance Company for five years. Much later, I came to know that both Kothari and Bhat were no more.

GMR and Adani Groups of Industries

My consultancies with GMR and Adani groups lasted for brief periods. With GMR, I was designated as the executive director, Security, and collaborated with the security wings of the Delhi and Hyderabad airports, both of which GMR acquired after the government privatized them. In my tenure, we also surveyed the Turkey airport for acquisition and development by the company and purchased two Falcon business jet aircraft for company use from the France-based Dassault Corporation. I had opportunities to visit Dubai, Istanbul and Paris, all of which were memorable. After leaving GMR, I briefly worked for Adani Group, Ahmedabad, before leaving for the US.

Working for the government, corporate and joint sectors added great value to my evolution. I saw different types of people, and their thinking, values, and even their intrigues were fascinating to watch. In government, people were honest and straightforward, albeit a little too proud of power, however big or small their position might be. In the corporate sector, even among top executives, fear ruled, probably because they lacked the constitutional protection available to government officers. Free interactions among the officials were rare, or so it was with me, as I was an outsider and a former cop! Another guiding principle that I found was predominant among corporate executives was the profit motive—just as government officers having an urge to cling to power at all costs.

Thinking about the outsider syndrome, it was not new to me; I was an outsider in my state in the IPS, an outsider in my cadre, UP and an outsider to the corporate culture. I was going to be an outsider in the US too. It could be that my spirit is unfettered by considerations of being an insider for anything! Except, of course, to my family! Which is why I accepted the proposition of moving to the US, where my sons had settled. By this time my younger son also went to the US for his PhD studies and both were in the Bay Area, California.

7

Family and Relationships

It is not what we have but
who we have in our lives that matters.

–J.M. LAURENCE

My father, Ramanujan, was a government servant and mother, a homemaker. My dad was an ardent nationalist and followed political developments carefully, though he didn't join active politics. He admired C. Rajagopalachari, aka Rajaji and his Swatantra Party. Subsequently, he became an admirer of Indira Gandhi and the Congress party. His respect for Gandhiji remained constant throughout his life. On the personal front, he had less to worry as his two sons were hard-working and his wife took care of home. He made his first home in 1969, making a shift from north Chennai to Nanganallur, a southern suburb of the city near the airport. I remember how we listened to the live broadcast covering the *Apollo-11* landing on the Moon, sitting in our new home. Later, he built a house for me near it. All the while I was away at UP and all I did was to send money to him, and he took care of the rest. This home came in handy and useful when I availed of study leave later on in the service, providing a roof over our heads.

My father died in 1995. I don't remember him as having had any health problems. One day, I was told by my brother that he has admitted him to a local hospital due to some respiratory issues. After two days, we shifted him to a city hospital where he died the same night. My mother was with him as we had just returned home from the hospital to have a shower, have some food and get some sleep. He was seventy-two at the time of death and was quite hale and healthy until the end. He was a vegetarian, had no bad habits, ate and slept regularly and used a bicycle to move around. He had come to stay with me in UP along with my mother several times, at Jhansi, Nainital, Agra and Lucknow. He spoke broken Hindi but had a flair for learning languages. He was fluent in Telugu through his posting in Vizag and understood Malayalam. Two instances that occurred during his visit to UP stand out in my memory. Once he went to the mochi, a cobbler, at a street corner in Lucknow and got his slippers repaired. The charge was fifty paise, but he didn't have change. The shoemaker sensed his problem with the language; he waved his hand and said something to the effect that my father could pay later. He came home and sent the money across but kept wondering how generous he was to say that to a stranger like him! On another occasion, when we were at Nainital, I took him to the Jim Corbett National Park near Kashipur. It was late in the afternoon by the time we reached. As we drove inside, it was becoming dark, and my father was getting increasingly uncomfortable. We were lucky, according to me—probably not according to him—that we spotted two tigers at close range drinking water from a pond. While everyone else wanted to stay if possible and take some pictures, he insisted on leaving as he was feeling uncomfortable being at a close range of wild animals. We reluctantly turned back, and as we were nearing the gate, a wild elephant was on the road, blocking the passage; he appeared to be in no hurry to leave. We waited at a safe distance for about half an hour, but he didn't move. Finally, my driver picked up a stick, rolled a waste cloth over at one end, dipped it in the gas tank of the jeep and lit it. He asked me to hold the burning torch just outside the window facing the side where the elephant was, so we could slowly move towards the beast. As we approached, the animal ambled away, and we drove away heaving a sigh of relief. By then, my father's face was ashen with fear.

My mother, Kamala, was one of several brothers and sisters, but she was especially close to her eldest brother, who later went on to become the chairman of the Visakhapatnam Port Trust. We visited our uncle during our summer holidays almost every year. He had three sons, and the five of us had plenty of fun playing together. My mother was a gentle soul, soft-spoken and not given to extreme emotions. I have never seen her get angry or speak harsh words. The only form of protest she showed was not to talk for days on end, and whoever was responsible for her anger apologized and begged her to speak. If she was angry with my father, she used to communicate with either my brother or me. She cooked well and was proficient in Carnatic music.

Years later, when I was working in Mumbai, I got a call from my brother that my mother had a malignant tumour in the abdomen. I immediately left for Chennai. We had the tests repeated. The cancer had spread to several vital organs. The doctors felt that at such an advanced age (seventy-eight), she should not go through the rigours of chemotherapy and we should try alternative medicine. We did as suggested, and the ayurvedic doctor we consulted assured us of her recovery. He managed to bring about marginal improvement, and my mother also felt she would recover. The treatment continued. My brother Narasimhan and his wife Srimathi took excellent care of her, as I was moving around from Chennai to Mumbai to Bengaluru.

I changed jobs and shifted from Mumbai to Bengaluru to work with GMR Group. I visited my mother at Chennai every other weekend. Once, Jaya and I visited her on a Saturday and told her we would be leaving the next day as I had a couple of things to round up before going to Bengaluru. Though she said nothing, I could see the disappointment in her eyes. I assured her we would be back next week. She held my hands briefly. The next day we picked up our luggage from the hotel where we were staying in the city and drove towards the highway. The road went through a junction from where my mother's home was only a couple of miles away, and I had a sudden urge to meet her once again before hitting the highway.

We took the turn and drove towards home. My mother was happy to see me again. She was entirely in control and had full consciousness, but she looked pale and tired. Her body had considerably thinned out. She even spoke a few words about her brother and sister visiting her earlier. Once in few days, she had glucose drips for strength and energy. My brother told me she had glucose only the previous day. As we watched, her face contorted in pain and she went breathless; her gaze slid slightly upwards and, within a second, it froze. I shook her, but the body was motionless. I could hear my brother and my wife rushing out to bring the doctor. I looked again at her eyes. There was no movement. She was gone.

I always knew that my brother Narasimhan, who is older to me by about three years, cared for me deeply. He worked for a private company in Chennai. Even at an early age he showed responsibility and helped my parents in many ways. As a child, when I went away to Visakhapatnam with our parents, he stayed back in Chennai with the joint family of grandparents, uncles, and aunts, and he learned early to bond with the family. He and his wife, Srimathi have three daughters; while one of my nieces went on to become a doctor, the other two became computer engineers. All of them are married and have families with children.

From my parents' point of view, they raised a good family, and both their sons had done reasonably well in their lives.

Jaya, my wife, came into my life when I was twenty-seven and she, barely twenty-two. The youngest of six siblings, she was born in Tiruchirappalli, a temple town about 300 km south of Chennai. Her father V.K. Srinivasan was a pious man and initiated Jaya into religion. He had a good sense of humour and appreciated excellence. Her mother, Komalavalli, was an energetic person, who was never tired of taking care of her children and grandchildren. She trained Jaya in cooking and housekeeping, which stands her in good stead even today.

The family settled in the temple town of Mylapore, staying within a stone's throw near a Srivaishnavite temple, where she spent a lot of her time as a child. Endowed with a sharp brain and phenomenal memory, she earned a degree in commerce from Delhi University and a job with the IA, but she didn't join it due to our wedding and moved with me to UP. Years later when we returned to Chennai, she worked for a short while with Saudi Airlines at Chennai, but domestic responsibilities again ended it prematurely. She qualified to be an interior designer and worked with a partner on a few construction projects, and designed the apartment we made in the city later. She is a Maria Montessori qualified teacher and on and off works with schools.

Just as I didn't, she too knew hardly anything about the service when she married me. She must have had the jolt when I showed her the garage/dump house that passed off as our first home after the wedding. But being an excellent housekeeper, she turned that into a comfortable place in no time and even managed to cook and entertain guests. My uncle, who came along to see how we were doing, was pleasantly surprised to see Jaya making the best of the situation. Later, when the boys grew up, and my job took me from place to place, she settled down to become the bedrock of the family, enabling all of us to follow our passions, even today in the US. As she was exquisite with her hands, be it fixing things around the house or knitting and sewing or gardening, she excels in whatever she undertakes. The hallmark of her work is speed, sometimes at the cost of safety. Her hands and body sometimes found it difficult to match her thoughts and resulted in small cuts and burns while cooking or cutting vegetables. She is extremely friendly and goes out of her way to help. When our sons were old enough to take care of themselves, she had time to pursue one of her passions—painting and portraiture. She wanted to learn the art of Tanjore painting and even found a teacher to help her learn. Both would be at it for hours together and at the end of two years, produced over a dozen paintings and hung them all over the house in beautiful frames. While I excelled in theory and rationalizing, she is above par in execution. In short, she is my extended arm; we complement each other that well.

Our elder son, Kaushik went to the US at the turn of the millennium to pursue his MS in electrical and computer engineering at the University of Illinois in Urbana-Champaign. Soon after completing his graduate studies he joined a start-up in Silicon Valley, where he worked for six years. By this time, he was married to Preeti, an architect, and a civil engineer. Kaushik was always passionate about films and soon started taking filmmaking classes at a local community college to take his mind off the gruelling hours of his start-up. Kaushik quit his start-up and decided to pursue his passion full time. He applied to film schools and got into the prestigious USC School of Cinematic Arts, from where he recently graduated with an MFA degree in Film Directing. His graduate thesis film, *GROOMING*, premiered at the Cannes International Film Festival and was nominated for a BAFTA US Student Film Award. He is now working hard to get his first feature film off the ground. They have two sons Avyukt and Mithran.

Our second son, Dhananjay followed his brother to the US to do his PhD in computer engineering, with a scholarship. Even when he was ten years old, he showed extraordinary interest in computers, which were, then just beginning to proliferate across the world, capturing people's imaginations in a big way. On completing his education, he had no problem in finding a job in the Bay Area. He held another position with a research organization before quitting that too to begin a start-up with two other friends. A little later, he utilized the experiences to start his own cybersecurity company. He has a great passion for cinematography, and his dream is to join his brother to make movies one day. His wife Medha works for a software company in the Bay Area. The couple has one son, Vedant.

When they left for the US, we felt a vacuum in our lives, especially Jaya, since I had at least work to do. I had taken up security consultancy with corporate houses after retirement and that too involved trips away from home. All these changes had taken their toll on Jaya. She was expecting to settle down permanently at Chennai and follow her passions and dive deeper into spiritual life, something she had grown up enjoying. I've always believed that our childhood never indeed leaves us and knowing how much Jaya wanted to resume her involvement in temple worship and festivities only proved that belief. She sorely missed her temples when I was posted in UP; both of us would go in search of south Indian temples and made it a point to visit the ones we discovered. When we came back to Chennai, luckily for her, the living accommodation allotted by the government was near a temple. And when we bought our own home, it was a three-bedroom flat just opposite the same temple. She enjoyed the proximity for about three years. Even in the US, she is actively engaged in teaching slokas to children, in addition to managing the household.

After all the years in UP and Delhi, my job as a corporate security consultant took us to Mumbai, Bengaluru and Ahmedabad. All these movements and scratchy living here and there were frustrating for Jaya. Added to the agony was the absence of the kids. At this point, I decided to put an end to this situation. The solution appeared to lay in both Jaya and me joining the sons in the US. While the idea of moving to the US seemed exciting to Jaya, I was not sure, as I had a job on hand. I brainstormed with Dhananjay and hit upon the idea of pursuing a degree in creative writing in the US! I wrote the required tests and applied for a master's degree in fine arts (MFA) in creative writing and consciousness and got admission to a school in San Francisco. Jaya and I secured our visas, closed shop in Chennai and embarked on yet another adventure.

8

San Francisco Beckons

The arts are not a way of making a living; they are a very human way of making life more bearable.

–KURT VONNEGUT

Art and Life in California

The California Institute of Integral Studies (CIIS), which I chose for my master's programme in fine arts, was a private institution of higher education founded in 1968 and based in San Francisco. CIIS consisted of three schools, and I studied at the School of Consciousness and Transformation. The other two were the School of Professional Psychology & Health and the School of Undergraduate Studies. Many of its courses combined mainstream academic curriculum with a spiritual orientation, especially from the teachings of Sri Aurobindo of Puducherry, India. It was my spiritual interests and familiarity with the teachings of Aurobindo and Mother among other spiritual traditions of JK, G, Ramana Maharishi and Paramahansa Yogananda, which motivated me to choose the institution. The California College of the Arts (CCA), which I joined earlier, was a school devoted to arts and writing, was also an excellent school, but the emphasis on consciousness development in CIIS was what attracted me. After completing two semesters with CCA, some of the credits got transferred to the new school. Both schools are only a few miles apart in San Francisco.

The school opened for the fall session, and after the registration formalities and a briefing from the international student coordinator, I went and sat in the class. It was a new experience for me. The classroom atmosphere was very informal. Students were mostly American, and I was the only Indian. Later, I came to know that two batches earlier, there was a student from India who graduated and went back. Some of the students were eating and drinking during classes. Students called the lecturer by first name and exercises were read out aloud by each one by turn, followed by discussions. I could barely understand what was being spoken because the accents were different and the contexts, alien and it was hard to halt them or request them to go slow now and then. I reckoned the atmosphere here was possibly different from any engineering college in the US, where you would be inclined to find hordes of Indian students and the subject being science and formulae, the language probably didn't matter much. In my case, it was art and philosophy with an American twist suited to an American audience. I decided to keep listening and hoped to improve my understanding by and by, which I did. The first semester was tough and taxing as I was returning to college after a long time. I managed much better at CIIS and handled my subjects in such a way that my credits over the duration of the course were evenly spread. I was required to take forty-eight credits in two years or four semesters. I carefully spread the number of credits over a period of two years. An international student couldn't take less than nine credits per semester, couldn't stay away from school for more than five months at a stretch, and couldn't leave the country without 'travel authorization' from the school, among other such conditions. If anyone broke the rules, he was liable for termination of his course. There were also provisions for taking lesser credits on medical grounds, and I utilized such rules to the fullest, as studying was, after all, my post-retirement initiative! I managed to extend the course by a year, for which there were provisions in the rules, and I ensured that I didn't lose the status of a student by violating them. There was plenty of reading and writing to be done for the course. Thankfully, the public library had an excellent collection of books and came in handy for my textbook requirements. The fees were hefty, and for an international art student, I had little scope for scholarships. Grants were available for American citizens only, and foreign students paid fees in full. I did get a small merit scholarship, which helped in paying a portion of the cost. Still, the tuition fees and the cost of health insurance were prohibitive.

One major difference I found between the societies in India and the US is that in India, we still keep thinking about macro issues such as poverty, lack of infrastructure, corruption, gender issues, the caste systems, among other malaises. Meanwhile, first-world problems have narrowed down to the individual at the micro level. Not that they have met all outer wants, but the emphasis has shifted to the individual. Since society has provided sufficient infrastructure for basic living, the person is free to devote time for oneself. One is not eternally doomed to the prospect of working for others. Individual freedom is equally important as the freedom of the society as a whole, and I found evidence of such an expression in the art.

Art was something I didn't experience in my busy police and security career back home. I used to find the concept of art confusing. How could art contribute to the transformation of the society? But in San Francisco, I found ample evidence of art's transformative effect in street art and art galleries. The artwork gets presented in art museums, literature and magazines devoted to various forms of art, clubs and galleries. In Santa Cruz, as you walked on the pavement, you would come across people playing their guitars, singing songs, dancing in groups, displaying their paintings on the sidewalks, painting the walls with beautiful colours and many other activities. Cafés provided spaces for open-mike programmes, dancing space for people to assemble and shake a leg. I came across people who gave up good jobs and prestigious positions in the pursuit of art. I also read articles about how homeless people didn't care much for the money but wanted to voice their opinions and only needed people to hear their point of view. On the one hand, it is a materialistic society based on consumer economy and on the other, the individuals express and live art.

The subjects I had for the master's degree were fascinating. The course title said 'Writing, Consciousness & Creative Inquiry'. The programmes included writing workshops, project work, creative enquiry for artists, a comparative study of Krishna, Buddha and Christ, the art of fiction and non-fiction writing, the artists in the world, editing and publishing the in-house magazine, the structure of stories, cultural identity, unlocking the writer's voice, spirituality and moral action, the philosophy of Rudolf Steiner, to name a few. Each topic had at least six sessions lasting four hours each and carried two or three credits depending upon the subject. The comparative study of religions, the glimpses into the western philosophy of Rudolf Steiner and comparative study of Krishna, Buddha and Christ, all taught by Robert McDermott, were enthralling. Robert headed the philosophy department and was also the president of the institution in the 1990s. He had a unique approach to teaching; instead of cramming the details down your throat, he asked questions and went about noting the points on the blackboard. Before the session ended, the whole picture emerged to the delight of all the students, who also had a sense of participation in learning. Among others, I had read books by Jacob Needleman on G's ideas back in India and couldn't believe my eyes when he came to teach several sessions, for which I considered myself fortunate. Carolyn Cooke, the programme chair for writing, consciousness and creative enquiry, was a pleasant personality. The author of several books, she had a firm grip over her subject. Her enthusiasm was infectious. Christian Frock appeared to be a very strict personality to start with; she didn't allow her students to eat or drink in the class. ('It leaves an odour of food for a long time, you know!') She also insisted on punctuality and maintaining discipline, reminding me of an Indian classroom. Her subject was to teach about how an art student could survive in the world, the importance of web presence, a good business card, a narrative biodata, an elevator pitch and such other practical aspects of the life of an artist. She curated art, wrote for art magazines and enjoyed extensive contacts in the art world of San Francisco. Jody O'Connor, who was the international students' coordinator, was forthcoming with any help, be it in offering competitive healthcare insurance or fixing internships, accommodation and other vital issues faced by international students. The classes were interactive in nature. The idea was to provide the right atmosphere for creativity and encouragement to write or draw, paint or whatever it is that you wanted to do. I marvelled at the environment for learning and vividly remembered how in one of the discussions my 'cop-self' came to the fore and how I failed to invoke the artistic point of view. The discussions were about a piece of writing by James Baldwin, a celebrated African-American, who subsequently moved out of America by choice. The story belonged to the era of slavery, when once there was an execution of a slave in public for some crime committed by him. He was hung upside down over a fire, and his private parts were cut off, much to the 'amusement' of the crowd and left to burn alive. While most of the students saw that as a well-written piece of literature and examined the structure, as Baldwin was known for his style and structure, I said the piece deserved to be banned. Even if this was written by an African-American about a horrific reality that had occurred a century ago, it brings such gruesome details of a torture of a fellow human being to the reading public. What appalled me was that the execution was in the style of a picnic and families and children watched the gruesome murder and applauded. The class went silent because no one had thought on those lines. I felt that content was more important than structure and beyond a point, the structure didn't hold against content. I was able to protest because of my administrative experience and knowledge of the potential consequences such inflammatory writing could cause to racial and communal amity in the society.

In addition to the regular classes there were many symposia, seminars, evening get-togethers, celebrations and readings, held in the auditorium, Namaste Hall. There were readings and workshops outside of the school, in similar institutions and clubs and invitations keep coming for you to attend. I was mildly handicapped to participate in all such events, as I stayed 50 miles away, but still, I made it a point to make it to some of them. All such events promoted group discussions, familiarity with the art scene in the city and an opportunity to get to know others with similar interests. I also taught meditation and some basic ideas of Hinduism to interested listeners at the community level.

Given my previous job, I had an interest in observing policing in America. In general, what I realized was that the police here operate more on the principle of deterrence than prevention. There are signs everywhere warning about the repercussions of violating traffic rules, including Himalayan fines ranging anywhere from $269 to $343! There are carpool lanes on the highways to encourage carpooling, and the fines for misusing the lane are very high. Similarly, there are measures to tackle over speeding, jaywalking, illegal parking, the list is long. I also read about crimes, especially school shootings by psychopaths and defensive killings by police officers. One gunman appeared in a packed movie theatre and started firing indiscriminately at the people, killing several of them. Jilted lovers shot down their girlfriends and family members. In almost all the cases, the murderer would end up killing himself. In some cases, they were shot down after a showdown with the police. Hardly any accused in such cases went on trial. I tended to agree that the prevailing gun culture could be one of the reasons for such shooting incidents, in addition to individual psychological problems prevalent in the US society.

But what caused much uproar were cops shooting citizens, which were purportedly done in self-defence. Three cases attracted much ire from the public, particularly from the African-American community, which all three victims belonged to. I followed the shooting of Michael Brown in Missouri and Eric Garner in New York. In the former, the police alleged that he attacked the officer, who killed him in self-defence. In the latter case, Garner was supposedly selling loose cigarettes, which is a crime. The video shot by a bystander was telling—a heavyset man who, incidentally, was also suffering from asthma, attracted the attention of a couple of officers, one of who pounced from behind and held him in a chokehold. Even as the cop was wrestling with Garner, he was joined by several more officers; the chilling video reminded me of hyenas circling a wounded animal. The victim uttered 'can't breathe' before dying. In the tragic third case, eighteen-year-old John Crawford III was examining an air rifle in a Walmart store in Ohio and was shot dead by a police officer responding to a call from someone in the shop who said that a boy was wielding a gun. Later, the store camera showed the victim only had an air rifle in his hand, and the children and their mothers standing nearby were not the least bit afraid. For me, it was baffling as to how a police officer saw in it a life-threatening situation. Then there was the person who had made that call.

After studying the cases in detail, as reported by the press, and numerous other cases over the past years, I realized that the problem arose largely because the police were as suspicious of members of the African-American community as they were of the police. A catch-22 situation. After the killing of Eric Garner, two officers were shot dead by a black assailant, who, of course killed himself. Because of this fear, the police expect the victim to obey when ordered by them. They don't tolerate anyone resisting or talking back. I also felt that some of the the African-Americans who were stopped or questioned couldn't help talking and arguing too much. I thought talking less or saying nothing could have helped saving some lives.

The second reason, as quoted by the press, is the militarization of the police and the Pentagon equipping the civil police with sophisticated weaponry meant only for army operations. I had seen police officers gathering in large numbers with weapons to tackle a situation. Some blamed the predictive and preventive 'broken window' policing methods adopted by the police. As per these methods, the police had software to analyse data and identify 'hot spots', where crimes occur frequently and concentrate their efforts in such places to prevent unlawful activities. Unfortunately for innocent people, the methods mentioned above included the use of 'stop, question, frisk' ways, which, according to the public, frequently resulted in unnecessary harassment. Eric Garner, moments before his arrest and death, was complaining about these methods of harassment he faced in the hands of the police. The mother of all reasons is, of course, the gun culture, which has been proving elusive to deal with for successive governments in America.

I couldn't help but think about the situation in India. Back in 1980s the 'encounter' culture was said to be prevalent in states like UP, where criminals identified as lawbreakers were gunned down by the police. I remember being grateful for the fact that guns were not so easily accessible in India. I also recalled how I, as a serving police officer, surrendered my service revolver after observing how police officers became trigger-happy over a period. But what influenced my decision was a shocking incident of a police officer getting killed by the service revolver of another during a drunken brawl. Another officer and batchmate of mine murdered his wife suspecting her of infidelity. However, when the need arose, such as an organized raid, I did carry a weapon, only to return it promptly to the armoury once the duty was over.

Though I had visited the US several times in the past ten years, it was different living there as a resident. As a visitor, I used to go for a maximum of three weeks, visit a few places with family and return to India. Now, things were different. The first challenge we had to overcome was around the house, and doing a lot of things on our own. Jaya used to do a lot of work back home too, but now I had to pitch in, and that was quite considerable. The second challenge was transportation. When I was visiting, I depended on my sons or friends to move about during weekends.

So, we needed a car, and before that, a licence, to solve the problem of transportation. If you could drive, it was a lot easier to move about on your own. But getting the licence was not easy. The department of motor vehicles required us to take a written test for which you needed to study the rules and regulations carefully. Once you passed the test, you need to schedule a practical driving test in which a transportation official would accompany you in the car and give directions. If your driving was satisfactory, then the licence gets approved and arrive a few weeks later by post. Both of us managed to get our licences after a couple of attempts at written and practical tests.

I found the Bay Area to have good infrastructure with excellent roads, transportation systems, drainage and water supply systems, uninterrupted power supply, well-maintained parks, national parks of gigantic proportions and amusement parks of every hue. The houses were old constructions, but with systems in place for a comfortable living. The houses were constructed in the 1960s and 1970s when the economy was booming. The rentals saw a low during the economic slump in the latter half of the 2000s but skyrocketed after the large influx of immigrants from other countries. Single family homes started costing a fortune. Flipping over properties within short periods was not uncommon, as the houses were bought at lower prices, upgraded and resold in the market. Upgrades as a standard included wooden flooring, air conditioning, heating, tiles in the bathrooms and other accessories.

After the Hispanic and Latin American people, the Chinese and Filipinos, Indian Americans, or Asian Indians, as they are called to distinguish them from the Native Americans in the US, are the fourth largest ethnic group in America, with a population of over three million. The community is well represented in technical fields, especially computer software, and prefers living in cities like New York, Chicago, Seattle, San Francisco, particularly the Bay Area where companies like Google, Apple, Facebook and scores of others are situated. Earlier generations of Indians found prosperity in the silicon-chip-based industry in this area, which gave it the name Silicon Valley. Mainly comprising the southern part of northern California and the southern portion of San Francisco, which is the Bay Area, the Silicon Valley has come to represent the high technology industry of the US, where one-third of all venture capital investments take place.

At first impression, fitness awareness appeared better among the general population in the US as compared to India. The gym-going habits, availability of equipment, computer apps, magazines entirely devoted to physical fitness and numerous TV shows, ongoing research and availability of plenty of supplements for good health, mostly monitored by a regulating authority—all of this gave the impression that it was indeed a country having higher awareness levels of physical health. But you come across considerable obese and overweight population too. Vegetarianism and preference for vegan food is also on the rise and restaurants catering vegetarian food had started appearing all over. But the healthcare cost is prohibitive with huge insurance policy premium and additional co-pay requirements. The Barack Obama-led government had introduced a health insurance scheme called Obama Care, which was not cheap, and which needed more people to join the project to make the costs more affordable. This is the scheme the Trump administration wants to scrap in lieu of another scheme. You did come across some drugs sold over the counter which were not approved by the Food and Drug Administration (FDA). The food and consumable items come with labels indicating the contents and ingredients very clearly.

In addition to this, the state of California also has one of the highest tax rates in the country, probably due to the warmer climate it offered. When we moved to the state, in 2011, California was reeling under a three-year drought, which made the water supply scarce as the drought worsened. I found the costs of education, taxes, healthcare and real estate to be very costly compared to India. The most significant system was the personal identification (social security, driver's licence) to which all transactions including financial, were connected. Bank loans and credit systems relied heavily on 'credit score' systems which determined whether an individual was worthy of credit. Any misdemeanour anywhere promptly appeared on the identity and therefore, reflected on the credit rating.

There were two things about Americans that I observed were a general phenomenon. One, there would hardly be any household without any pet, usually a cat or dog, or both. I had a classmate who had a pendant on her chain with a photo of her pet cat— the photo was updated every time she came to the class! People brought their dogs and cats inside the class. Our neighbour Bill had a black cat which often walked on our fence. I once happened to mention to him that we may consider getting a dog. Bill discouraged us saying how expensive it was to maintain a cat and narrated how his cat had had a toothache and he had to take her multiple times for extraction of the tooth and other sundry expenses for medicines and special food, and that the final tally of the bill drained his savings to a considerable extent. So that put an end to the premature thought of getting a pet. The other thing I noticed was that people had a reading habit. In buses, trains, beaches and other public places you could see people sitting quietly in a corner and reading a book. While there were bookstores, online shopping was slowly edging them out, reducing footfalls of browsers to bookstores. Still, I preferred the feel and smell of a new book in my hands. I regretted the closure of Borders, the chain that filed for bankruptcy. If some corporate house wanted, it could have saved Borders. Instead, America watched it die, I ruefully thought.

The Perils of Cyber Space

One afternoon, I was sitting in the San Francisco State Library reading up on some research material for my project. A heaven-sent for book lovers, libraries in California provide the latest books and what's more, many libraries across all counties are connected by a service called Link+, which, gives you access to books that are unavailable in your local library and may be on the shelf in one of the others. It is my habit to spend some time chatting with the library staff, and on this particular afternoon, they told me how, a few days ago, a young man, who appeared to be a college student, was working on his laptop when the cops appeared and arrested him. Later, I learned that Ross William Ulbricht was indeed a notorious cybercriminal, who was running an illegal internet market called Silk Road, which sold drugs and other illegal merchandise over the dark net. After two years from his arrest in 2013, he was sentenced to twenty years' imprisonment and a hefty fine. His criminal organization was reported to have had a turnover of over $2 billion during his career.

I became part of former US president, Barack Obama's cyber initiative, which he inaugurated at Stanford University in 2015, thanks to the introduction given by the head of South Asian department, whom I had a chance to interact with during a conference. It was a good experience to be part of this task group headed by Herb Lin, research fellow of Hoover Institution. In addition to me, the group consisted of industry leaders such as Gary Belvin from Google; Sameer Bhalotra, adviser to the president on cyber security; Whitfield Diffie of the Center for International Security and Cooperation, Stanford; and Enrique Oti from the US Air Force, among other senior research scholars and fellows among others. The group brainstormed about how to effectively counter the cyber threat, which has been assuming alarming proportions in the past five years or so. I was more of a learner, but with my experience in policing and law and order, and a background of physical and corporate security, it was not difficult to get an understanding of the situation.

Global strategist, author and consultant who focuses on the impact of technology on security and businesses, Marc Goodman, in his book, *Future Crimes*, says the following about how technology came in handy for the perpetrators of the 2008 Mumbai attack of 2008: 'At every point during the siege, the LeT extremists exploited the available technology to gain situational awareness and maintain a tactical advantage over police and the government. The leaking data was captured by terrorists to identify those who stayed at Taj Hotels (the writer means The Taj Mahal Palace Hotel) Mumbai. Attackers carried GPS handsets, PDF files of hotel floor plans and used Google Earth to explore 3-D models of target venues, satellite phones and Blackberry GSM phones, and Skype to coordinate with the Pakistan-based command centre, the internet and social media to provide real-time tactical directions. A bystander's tweet regarding police force landing on the roof of Jewish Community Building was intercepted by the attackers and helped them ambush the cops. A Filipino hacking cell affiliated to the Al-Qaeda funded the LeT for the attack. The attackers proved fully capable of collecting open-source intelligence mid-attack. The hostages were photographed and shared with the remote command centre to identify them over the internet and social media. In short, it was an instance of how modern warfare is going to be in future.'

I was always interested in technology. Ours was a generation which made the transition to the computer, the internet, mobile phone era. I eagerly learned all I could about gadgets from the earliest stages of this development—the very first generations of devices like the colour television, digital cameras, desktops and laptops, mobile and smartphones and using the email, chats and other social media, were adopted immediately. Even though I had heard about hacking and stealing of identity, I didn't think it was all that serious until I became part of the cyber initiative at Stanford university. It made me realize that I was not the only one who was hooked on to the internet and allied technologies; the entire world was doing it unmindful of the dangers lurking behind it. Every government, private companies and individuals found their corner in that vast cyberspace and entrusted it with critical information, including private information, identification, photographs and the happenings in their life via social media. Data on the defence systems of a country, critical infrastructures such as the power grid, transportation and banking became increasingly dependent on the Net. The latest trend is Internet of Things (IoT), through which the internet is harnessed to interconnect devices such as computers, smartphones, cars, refrigerators and home security systems among scores of others.

It is evident that digital technology is growing exponentially compared to the non-digital technologies, which increased linearly for a long time. The problem with cybercrime is that it has not entered the consciousness of the public at large and those affected, such as banks and ATMs, underplay such events for fear of adverse publicity and loss of public confidence, which would be detrimental to their future business. We download millions of apps to help us, whether it is banking or even cooking. We are constantly connected to the internet via our computers, laptops, phones, iPads, cable boxes, PS3s, HDTVs, to name a few. Rapid medical advances have resulted in increasing human life span, reducing infant mortality, tripling per capita income around the world and increasing access to higher education and trillions of dollars' worth business through mobile technology. The downside is that the power grids, air-traffic-control networks, fire departments, water supply and even elevators in offices have been plugged into the net, resulting in increased threat of disruption. We plug more and more into the global grid.

These are times of 'cyber anxiety', and the cyber realm is the single greatest emerging threat. As of 2013, there are thirty trillion individual web pages, 8.7 billion devices connected to the internet—which is estimated to rise to forty billion by 2020 due to IoT. There are estimates that 97 per cent of Fortune 500 companies have already been hacked. Others might have been hacked too, but are ignorant of the fact. Black markets are thriving; a 24-hour denial of service is listed in the black market for $80, and $200 for larger projects.

Cybercrimes

So, what's the motivation for the cybercrimes? The answer, in one word, is data. Data is the new oil, and everything around us continuously generates data. Today, human beings have turned into human sensors. In 2014, on an average, every minute 20,41,66,667 emails were sent, Google search recorded two million queries, 6,84,000 pieces of content were shared on Facebook, 1,00,000 tweets were made, 47,000 apps were downloaded from the Apple app store, 48 hours of new videos uploaded on YouTube, 36,000 new photos posted on Instagram and 34 million messages were exchanged on WhatsApp. Every ten minutes we created as much information as humanity did in the first 10,000 generations. All the while, the cost of storing dropped exponentially as well.

Goodman says that in a matter of just a few years from using Google only for searches, we now rely on it for directions, calendars, address books, photos, videos, entertainment, voice mails and phone calls. Over one billion users have posted personal, intimate details on Facebook. Between 1998–2016, Google grew into a juggernaut. It doesn't forget, and it doesn't delete. Google started with a search engine, and it knew what you wanted. It created Gmail to know what you wrote and to whom. It created Google Voice to track whom you're calling. Voicemail deciphered the messages using voice recognition and voice transcription software. Through the Android platform, it can track your movements through your smartphones. In 2012, Google announced the merger of data from all its more than seventy products, which means easy tracking of all data in one place; it processes 24 petabytes of data every day, which, if printed and stacked, would go halfway to the Moon. Despite several lawsuits and class-action suits for privacy violations, security breaches, mishandling user data, theft of intellectual property, tax evasions and contraventions of antitrust laws, Google marches on and we are proud of Sundar Pichai, the CEO of Google, because he is from India!

Social media networks are the new public records. The data you share is scrapped, sorted, warehoused and sold to advertisers, government and data brokers, all of them eagerly waiting to consume the collective digital trail we leave behind. Facebook has the largest unpaid workforce—you and me. We are the product and not customers. It has a market cap of over $180 billion. More than 350 million photos are uploaded daily, and the 'like' button used 6 billion times. It chronicles every event in your life. In ten years, it grew from a membership of zero to 1.3 billion, each valued at $80.95, friends 0.62 cents, profile pages $1,800 and the business web page is valued at $3.1 million. On the other hand, Facebook is credited with the Arab Spring of 2010 and political upheavals in Tunisia, Iran and Libya.

We leak data through cookies planted into our systems when we visit a website or use an app. All digital devices have unique fingerprints, such as an IP address for the network used, media access control number (MAC) from the Wi-Fi network card and the IMEI or IMSI numbers from your mobile phone. These, combined with likes, pokes and tweets are enough to paint an accurate picture of you. Friends and families are leaking data about you too. 'Free' is a great business model. We pay dearly for all free services. Data is the currency here. Goodman humorously says that the sucking sound you hear is our privacy, data, and all other details that make up our unique identity being inhaled by the internet. The detail you don't even share with your friends and relatives are being filtered into a big computer algorithm in the sky, aggregated into petabytes and sold for billions. That's why Google doesn't send a bill to you and has a valuation of over $400 billion, and all that you have are free services.

Mobiles and smartphones are like electronic tags on remanded prisoners. They track your every move. Globally making calls ranks fifth in priority, after web browsing, social networking, playing games and listening to music. In the US, mobile phones generate 600 billion unique data events every day. That's why Google created Android to get all this data and has even filed a patent for 'advertising based on environmental conditions'. Facebook uses your phone's mic to detect ambient sounds, takes pictures and videos with your camera without confirmation, read your messages and gives phone-syncing option to upload photos. They can do all this because we have already signed the terms and conditions, agreed to whatever is written in small print for reams of pages without reading and clicked the 'I Agree' button.

Apps do the same. Appropriation of personal information occurs every time you download an app. Every app asks for permission to access your data like photos, contacts, etc. Google Play Store also provides all your data to app developers. McAfee discovered that about 82 per cent Android apps track online activities and 80 per cent collect locational data. An advertiser has three key questions to ask—who will buy the product, what will they buy and where are the buyers. Google owns the 'what' question through the search data, Facebook owns 'who' but no one yet owns the domain of 'where', with fierce competition on for locational data. Location data is determined by GPS, triangulating mobile location and distance between towers and Wi-Fi network used. Location Based Services (LBS) work by incorporating location into everything you do and everywhere you go. An app in Russia called 'Girls around me' showed details of all girls in the vicinity. The mobile advertising ecosystem is set in motion when a woman goes to a gynaecologist's clinic, and goes to 'Babies R Us' three weeks later, revealing the woman's pregnancy. We, in fact, live in a surveillance economy.

Governments across the word also monitor social media for threats. A survey by the International Association of Chiefs of Police of more than 500 law enforcement agencies revealed that more than 86 per cent police departments include social media in their investigations. Data brokers such as Acxiom, Epsilon, Datalogix, Tap Leaf, Reed Elsevier, BlueKai, Spokeo and Flurry, together are worth $165 billion. They get data from ISPs, credit card companies, mobile phone companies, banks, credit bureaus, pharmacies, DMVs (Department of Motor Vehicles, US), grocery stores and our online activities. Acxiom has 23,000 servers that are collecting, collating and analyzing 50 trillion individual data transactions every year covering over 96 per cent American households and 700 million consumer profiles the world over. The idea is to 'behaviour target' people to extract premium proprietary behavioural insights on you and your life. Mailing lists are rented out with details such as seniors with dementia, HIV patients, victims of domestic violence, pregnant teenagers, etc., which aggregate customers' entire purchase history with demographic statistics obtained from data brokers.

No proper regulations exist, as social media is a public place. With so much 'dataveillance' going on, with so much profit promised, who can blame the hackers if they too want a piece of the cake?

Who's doing all the hacking and committing all the cybercrimes? There are three types of criminals on the internet; the state players, criminal groups, or a lone wolf, just as our 'friend' in the library. The state player is a rogue nation, which employs cybercriminals to attack the cyberspace of its enemy to dislocate the critical services. A lone wolf is the one who, sitting in front of the computer in his apartment, hacks away for profit.

Risk assessments are about predicting likely hazards, but in cyberspace, risks remain undiscovered until an attack takes place. Three primary factors are involved in assessing risks; the feasibility of the adversary knowing and exploiting the vulnerabilities, the consequences of such exploits and the likelihood of such attacks being carried out. Always assuming the worst-case scenario will lead to threat-inflation. The fact remains that assessing the capability of the adversary is hard because of the non-physical nature of the weapons and the enemy's actions and intent.

Availability Attacks prevent access to the network, either by overwhelming it with visits, a denial of service, or even taking it even offline. Scale and impact are critical to this kind of attacks. Confidentiality Attacks monitor activities, extract information on systems and user data. Such attacks on intellectual property become strategic matters, such as the US-China cyber conflicts. The third type is Integrity Attacks, which necessarily mean entering the systems to change or alter it rather than extract information. This is particularly insidious because we use the same systems to diagnose the attacks. The last two types of attacks use vulnerabilities to enter the system.

Botnets are zombie computers attacked and converted into veritable receptacles of malware to spread among other computers. For instance, the Conficker worm virus infected seven million computers worldwide within a few months. Botnets have no geographical limits; the owner has no idea his computer has been compromised or whether it's a hostile activity by a hacker. Even if we succeed in identifying it, we can only identify the computer but not the culprit. Think of a stolen car being used in a getaway situation. There is an attribution dilemma about the scale of operations; more people are involved, which means the greater the chances of detection. But evidence beyond a reasonable doubt is difficult to come by.

The McAfee Malware Zoo, which is a collection of malware has over 110 million different species of malware. In 2010 it detected a new malware every fifteen minutes, in 2013, it was discovering one every second. In another study, as of 2010, there were 49 million strains of computer malware. A 2011 study by McAfee reported two million strains of new pieces every month. In 2013, Kaspersky Lab reported two lakh every single day. By 2012, $2.3 billion were spent on malware eradication and $20 billion on security measures, which was likely to exceed $95 billion by the end of 2017. The market for cybersecurity is about $65 billion growing at a rate of 6–9 per cent annually, to $165 billion in ten years. A 2013 study revealed that over 50 per cent of Android devices had 'unpatched' vulnerabilities due, perhaps, to the fact that there are too many players involved and even if a vulnerability is detected, it's not clear as to who's responsible for informing the consumers and issue a patch. It's found that the certification done by Trust, an agency meant for certification, is done so mechanically that even sites unworthy get certified for a fee. Consumers seldom deviate from the default settings, thereby making it easier for phishing attacks.

Anti-virus software looks for previously known malware and blocks them. Israel Institute of Technology conducted a test to see the usefulness of anti-virus software produced by forty tech giants including Microsoft, Symantec, McAfee and Kaspersky Lab. It was discovered that 95 per cent of malware remained undetected. The time taken to detect malware is also increasing. For instance, the malware Flame took five years to detect. Even big businesses and corporations are not better off than individuals. One study found that in 62 per cent cases it took at least two months to detect intrusion. According to another, the average time from breach to detection was 210 days. When they came to know, it was mostly through law enforcement or customer calls and not their internal security. It is found that in 75 per cent cases, successful penetration takes only minutes. Only in 15 per cent cases does it take more than a few hours.

According to research conducted by Ponemon Institute, the costs are likely to surpass $100 billion by 2017. To calculate this, the institute took into account, in addition to the theft amount, the costs of detecting the breach, containing the attack, investigations, identifying perpetrators, repairing and recovering the network, sales decline, credit card replacement fee, consumer credit-monitoring services, rising cyber insurance premium, stock market punishments, class-action suits from customers, shareholders and regulators. All told, cost per record was stolen, is around $188.00, and millions are being taken routinely.

The Internet

The internet has a dynamic, distributed system. The entire system is based on trust, as it functions without top-down coordination, and hence depends on the behaviour of users. The main issue of internet governance, according to experts, is one of interoperability and communication rather than the classic problem of distribution of resources, which consumed political thinkers of the past, who believed that digital resources were not scarce. So, the main themes revolve around the technical standards for interoperability, the distribution of IP numbers and the management of the internet's naming system. The Internet Engineering Task Force (IETF) develops new standards and protocols and modifies the existing ones for better performance. The Internet Engineering Steering Group (IESG) reviews all rules from a security point of view, with the Internet Architecture Board (IAB) providing oversight. The Internet Society (ISOC) is an international group that oversees most of the technical standards process.

The internet is the global brain. Complexity is added to obvious advantages of cost, efficiency and capability. For instance, let's take the Lines of Computer Code (LOC). In 1969, *Apollo-11*, which landed on the Moon, had 145,000 LOC. The 1980 space shuttles required 4,00,000. Now Microsoft Office Suite has 45 million, as does the US healthcare systems. Physical things are becoming computers and information technologies. Cars are computers we ride in, and planes are industrial control systems. Growing complexity has a direct correlation to safety and security. As all the codes grow in complexity, errors also multiply. Typically, you can find 20–30 errors per 1,000 LOC. In a code of 50 million lines, the errors amount to 1.5 million, which easily pave the way for attacks to happen.

When the difference between the expected and actual

behaviours of a computer is caused by an adversary, as opposed to a simple error or accident, then the malfunction is a security problem. A cyber problem becomes a cybersecurity issue if an enemy wants to obtain something from the activity, whether to get private information, undermine the system or prevent its legitimate use. A skilled hacker can do three things to a computer; steal its data to reveal strategic plans; misuse credentials giving the ability to change or destroy data; or hijack resources to prevent reaching out to customers. In this respect, even building a complex system can create new openings and hidden vulnerabilities to exploit.

Defending a computer means verifying and scanning all files against a library of known malware, but the problem here is that some malware can change their appearance. Heuristic detections are intended to identify suspicious computer code behaviour based on rules and logic analysis. Static analysis is carried out by virtual machines to dynamically simulate code operations to test the incoming malware and make them explode before they enter actual systems, which is like the removal of suspicious baggage in airports to bomb pits by bomb squads. One way this malware get into our systems is called social engineering, also known as phishing, which happens by just asking the victim to click on a link. This method exploits an unchanged default login or password, misconfigured applications or software vulnerabilities in the system. The other threat is what's commonly known as 'zero-day' exploits, which only means previously unknown vulnerabilities. Drive-by attacks result from visiting wrong websites. Over 90 per cent of malware spreads from previously hacked websites which are innocently visited. Botnets involve zombie computers, sending spam, selling illegal products or launching DDoS (Distributed Denial of Service) attacks, which primarily target the subsystems that handle connections in the computer and overwhelm the connection link. The most controversial of all threat vectors is what's known as 'advanced persistent threats' or just APT. A team works behind an APT with a particular target in mind, also known as 'operation shady rat'.

The tools may include a keystroke logging software to a control programme that can direct the malicious code. The actions may target individuals, corporations, government, and shift from an act of crime or espionage to an act of war. If not cleaned properly, even copiers, printers and thermostats can be used for exfiltration of information.

The simplest form of network defence is a firewall, which essentially refers to filters that only permit valid activity on the network. The next layer of protection is a set of sensors that look for invalid behaviour. Intrusion detection systems exist at the computer level or on the network. They detect attack signatures and similar behaviour, alert the administrator to potential attacks and keep logs for detailed forensic analysis. Patch management is done for zero day, or for other vulnerabilities. Wrong patches, even if they are official, may sometimes wreck the system if not properly done. Encryption helps when you can't defend the system against infiltration, but can minimize loss by limiting their ability to understand data. Air gap is another method by which a physical separation is created between the network and critical systems, which, of course, compromising operational efficiency and effectiveness. The question is how to navigate through these attacks. Simply by accepting that bad guys are out to exploit these vulnerabilities, and then by developing the best possible responses that allow us to keep benefitting from the good parts of the cyber age, short of pulling the plug. There is nothing called absolute security.

Apart from a host of measures mentioned above, we should design our systems in such a way that the system has resilience, which means that the system is operable even under attack or should be recoverable as quickly as possible. In fact, the different threats to a system's confidentiality, availability of the Internet, integrity and resiliency require different responses. While discussing cyber incidents or fears of potential incidents, it's important to separate the idea of vulnerability from the threat. For example, an unlocked door is a vulnerability but doesn't become a threat if no one wants to enter.

Cyberspace

It is defined as much by the cognitive realm as by the physical or digital. It may be global, but it's not stateless. Cyberspace was once just a realm of communication, then became a hub of e-commerce, and now, also includes critical infrastructure such as power, agriculture and food, water supply, defence and banking. The vital connector of all these areas of operation to cyberspace is a tiny device called Supervisory Control and Data Acquisition (SCADA). These are critical devices highly vulnerable to cyberattacks. In the US, 90 per cent of all critical infrastructure is controlled by the private sector and not the government, which only means that the risks are higher.

The Stuxnet worm is the best illustration of cyber war in modern times. It demonstrated to the world how physical damage could be caused through the digital space. An Iranian nuclear facility was presumably attacked remotely by Israeli and American forces to destroy the centrifuges of their nuclear facility, tearing them apart and causing extensive damage. It used four zero-day exploits, the Windows platform, and stolen private keys of popular software and digital signatures to carry out the operation. It's said that by suitably modifying the worm, it can be a weapon against SCADAs.

Earlier, in 2007, the 'most wired' state of Estonia in the Balkans faced massive DDoS attacks, presumed to have been engineered by Russia, over shifting the site of a Russian war memorial. The best part of this offence was how the radar screens were duped to show everything was okay when warplanes entered and left the state air space. After the first and the second world wars, followed by the Cold War, the world has entered the new era of cyber wars. Cyberspace is the fifth domain of battle after land, air, sea and space. The previous world wars were fought straightforwardly. The Cold War was fought more by proxy then, and the nuclear war was more of a war of deterrence. Compared to these, cyber warfare is unique in the sense that there are no geographical boundaries and the enemy is unknown. It is almost impossible to defend oneself in this wilderness and offence appears to be a more practical solution, in the sense that you get trained hackers to breach the enemy's cyberspace, which precisely is the reason why countries like the US, China and North Korea have armies of trained cyber offenders and the situation seems to be escalating.

Asking whether repealing the internet is possible is like asking whether we can put the toothpaste back into the tube. Building a smaller and 'secure' model net was also considered as an option but didn't take off. Moreover, the bigger the Net, the riskier but less is ineffective. The air-gapping option, as mentioned, reduced effectiveness. Building 'resilience' into the network appears to be feasible. Resilient systems are ready for attacks and can maintain some functionality and control while under attack, thus preserving the functions of the organizations. Intrusion tolerance means the intentional capacity to work under degraded conditions, recover quickly, learn to deal effectively in the future, having in place an alternative albeit less efficient process, multiple modes of planned failure and distributed controls. Failures must be made evident as silent failures make adaptation difficult.

ISPs (Internet Service Providers) can play a vital role in controlling virus infections. About 2 per cent of network providers don't attempt to detect outbound or cross-bound attacks, and nearly half of them don't take any action even if detected. About fifty ISPs account for 50 per cent of all infected machines worldwide. In addition to the choke points, the ISP can identify natural and unnatural internet traffic and botnet behaviour without compromising customer privacy. While China is seen as the 'hacking leader' of the world, it's an irony that 70 per cent of the infected machines are located in China. It's said that the Chinese-based ISPs which were responsible for intellectual property thefts in the US.

For organizations, the strategy of defence, resilience and response is likely to yield results. Some of the tests would be penetration testing, which involves red teams from an external pool of professionals attacking the network in a controlled fashion to more virulent attacks without jeopardizing the system, and more exercises simulating traditional war games. Exercises also underline the importance of coordination between technical decisions and business mission. Building security incentives is another strategy. Unfortunately, software professionals are well paid for speed and novelty and not necessarily for safety.

Before we consider the precautions, individuals can take at their level, certain things need to be in place; the government needs to provide standards and to enforce regulations, the industry has the responsibility to meet them, and the individual has to observe them. For instance, think of the rules for wearing seatbelts in a car. Similarly, a few key actions can help solve 85 per cent of cybersecurity problems. One of them is to bring about a shift in attitudes; individually and inside an organization, especially by the leaders, and realizing the need to educate oneself as well as others through colleges, schools and training programmes.

We must update passwords regularly, always using strong passwords—lengthy with a mix of numbers, letters and signs. Never use common words and phrases. Free software tools like Cain and Abel or John the Ripper automate password-cracking. A list of common passwords is also available online. Never share passwords, never use them across several accounts. Hackers can 'daisy chain' passwords and connect them. Keep all your critical software regularly updated. Cyber threats utilize wireless access to gain entry from the same building, parking lots, coffee shops and so on. Use encrypted wireless access. Even SSL is found to be susceptible; hence precautions need to be taken. Vulnerabilities are created by ourselves, and this needs to be checked. Check off options for automatic downloads, never open links from unknown persons, never accept hardware from untrusted sources, reject links sent through texts, and apps and accept such things only from trusted sources and beware of shortened URLs.

Cyber Security Responsibilities for Corporate Directors

In November 2015, the Stanford Law School organized a Cyber Day: Cybersecurity for Directors and C-level Executives, focusing exclusively on cybersecurity for corporates and companies. A presentation by Fenwick & West on 'Cybersecurity and the Board', discussed exact details about cybersecurity in a business and what are the responsibilities of board members. Though the narratives and the illustrations pertain to the US scenario, other countries have a lesson or two here.

The company board members and the top management need to understand what a cybercrime is and the cost to the company if such a crime takes place, measured in terms of money, time and reputation, and also what the saved costs would be if adequate measures are implemented. In several research findings, it all came down to lack of oversight senior management and board.

The common types of cybercrimes against companies are APTs, zero-day exploits, spear phishing, brute-force attacks, DoS and DDoS attacks. Intellectual property thefts are not uncommon. The risks to enterprises and directors include damage to critical business infrastructure and operations, loss of sensitive customer or employee data resulting in class-action-litigation expenses and settlements, regulatory investigations and potential fines, damage to reputation and shareholder value in addition to loss of intellectual property, confidential business information and trade secrets.

Enforcement actions are brought about by various government agencies such as the Federal Trade Commission (FTC), the Federal Communications Commission (FCC), the Securities and Exchange Commission (SEC), the State Attorney General and the US Department of Justice. The actions include fines and penalties, direct suits by plaintiffs such as customers, clients, corporate partners, vendors, unrelated third parties, etc. In 2015, AT&T handed out

$25m penalty, the largest data security enforcement action by the FCC. In 2014, Terracotta Inc. and Your Tel America were fined $10m each. The FTC imposed a fine to the tune of $10m civil penalty on Choice Point in 2006.The ruling handed out to Rock Young (2012) was interesting; a civil penalty of $250,000, and submission to submit to independent third-party audits of its security systems for twenty years. In February 2014, Wyndham Worldwide had a derivative action filed against the CEO and directors for alleged breach of fiduciary duties by allowing the company to suffer three separate security breaches. In the wake of a major breach in 2013, Target was accused that the board failed to comply with the internal security policies and participated in the maintenance of inadequate internal security controls.

From the above instances, it's evident that directors must act in good faith with loyalty and due care when considering the company's cybersecurity management. They should have a clear idea of the order of deliberations, analysis and ongoing monitoring of such risks and prevention procedures. They should also understand the organization's incident response procedures and ensure that they are followed in the event of an attack.

Some of the corporate responsibilities include recognizing the importance of efficient and continuous cybersecurity risk management, understanding organization's level of exposure to cyberattacks. For this, there needs to be an understanding of the categories of data in the organization and reviews carried out of current data protection procedures and practices and awareness of the system and network vulnerabilities. Then comes determining the risk tolerance based on company's industry, business and information systems' maturity level. Agreement on an appropriate budget for cybersecurity is essential.

For exercising oversight, responsibility for data and information protection needs to be assigned to a board committee for cybersecurity. Regular reports should be provided on risk management. Periodic assessments by independent specialists are necessary. Appointment of a chief information security officer should be considered seriously. The board committee should also determine standardized cyber-threat metrics, which is quantitative and generated by a threat analysis and have a clear connection to business value. Next comes the creation of set goals and expectations of management based on cyber-threat metrics, established risk tolerance and data protection priorities. Another important vector is developing an incident response plan, which should include reporting a breach to law enforcement.

The most important aspect for companies in the US is the availability of a legal framework for cybersecurity. The first and the foremost is the executive order no. 136436, which requires the establishment of an extensive public-private cyber-threat information sharing regime and voluntary cybersecurity standards for the private sector. The National Institute of Standards and Technology (NIST) has been given the task of developing and finalizing a risk framework and best practices. Its services are also utilized to assess the adequacy of cybersecurity practices. The department of homeland security and the department of justice have been asked to ensure timely production and dissemination of unclassified cyber threat reports to government agencies. Also, there are SEC disclosure obligations, FTC Act provisions and federal and state laws to be followed.

In India, we need such arrangements, especially the legal framework and a clear policy on cybersecurity. The biggest takeaway for me from these seminars and working groups at Stanford and from books written by luminaries in the field; Marc Goodman, P.W. Singer and Alan Friedman, from whose works I have quoted extensively in this chapter, was the need for learning to share information. The most important aspect of security in all these arrangements is trust and open-mindedness, the internet being a space which defies traditional governance models. For instance, when phishing takes place, banks remove those websites but never share. Similarly, network operators, network hardware/software providers, data owners, security service providers, law enforcement and intelligence agencies, may each have information that can contribute to the detection and understanding of sophisticated intrusions or attacks. Approach to sharing must be related to data, with whom and how—whether centralized or decentralized. One way is to share data collected automatically with a broad audience to strengthen the defence. Above all, sharing should be based on trust. Establishing information sharing and analysis centres (ISAC) is another effective way, though it's necessary to have the necessary legal infrastructure in place for protection for sharing and rigorous enforcement.

On the other hand, the digital disconnect, which is still prevalent, is basically due to the lack of experience with computers among too many world leaders. A cybersecurity expert in Australia never heard of The Onion Router (TOR), which is due, mainly, to the fact that cybersecurity is left only to the IT helpdesk, without realizing that the technical community can fail to appreciate the broader picture of nontechnical aspects of cybersecurity.

Best defences also rely, to a large extent, on coordination. Single organizations building better walls or better detection is fruitless. Attackers invariably adapt. It's essential for the governments to push for collective action among the players where no one private sector can solve the problem, but the danger is that regulations are seen to add to the costs. Government engagement is found to be both appropriate and useful in some cases good enough to provide advice; in other situations it can intervene to alter behaviour. Human incentives for effective defence have been seen to be effective. Vulnerability tests and practice exercises are valuable, whether it is militaries or private companies. These include penetration testing, hiring 'red teams' from outside security experts looking for vulnerabilities to exploit, attacking live networks in a controlled fashion and lay the foundation for more virulent attacks without putting the real system in jeopardy, and more exercises simulating traditional war games. Exercises also underline the importance of coordination between technical decisions and business mission. As for security incentives, the general tendency is to reward software developers with high salaries for speed and novelty and not for making the code more secure. There is a need for setting up proper access control systems (ACS) in organizations with a matrix of subjects and objects that define who can do what to whom. It requires a clear understanding of both organizational roles and the architecture of the information system as well as the ability to anticipate future needs. The Edward Snowden, Wikileaks and Bradley Manning cases highlight lack of such a system. If ACS is weak, organizations lose the protection of their intellectual property under trade secret law in the US. For access control to be effective, compartmentalization of data is recommended, so that, in the event of an attack, not all data will get affected.

PART II

Exploration, Expansion and Integration

Don't live the same year
seventy-five times and call it a life.

—ROBIN SHARMA

9

Faith

Faith is taking the first step even when you don't see the whole staircase.

−MARTIN LUTHER KING JR

Visishtadvaitam, Srivaishnavam, Iyengars

The conclusions I arrived at in life were based on my observations and experiences. But when I reached a certain stage, I halted and pondered about looking within, and working on myself. Since so much work has gone before by the masters over millennia, I thought it prudent to seek help. J. Krishnamurti shaped my basic concepts, who put the seed of an idea about the mind. Osho summarized all religions of the world for me to develop a basic understanding of the religious and philosophical concepts. G outlined his world view in his Fourth Way and suggested concrete steps for working on oneself. His followers Ouspensky, Maurice Nicoll, A.R. Orage and Daly King further elucidated his theory through many of their treatises. G also gave a precise idea about esoteric Christianity. George Bennett, in his Dramatic Universe series, explained western concepts of life. Ramana Maharishi explained the concept of the Self. Velukkudi Krishnan explained the interpretations of the Bhagavad Gita by

Swami Ramanuja's in a very concise way. Reading Eknath Easwaran's works greatly simplified the Upanishads, the Bhagavad Gita and the Dhammapada. Easwaran also gave the practical meditation technique called Passage Meditation, which is so well suited to our time-strapped age. Satguru Subramuniyaswami, in his monumental work on monism and Hinduism's contemporary metaphysics, laid down so many principles of Hinduism that it took me years to comprehend them all. I will be customizing these concepts to devise a method of working on myself, which is best suited to me. But there was a drawback: Most of these philosophers highlighted the importance of a teacher or guide, to follow the methods outlined in their writings. For instance, the breathing techniques or yoga and meditation, in general, are best done under supervision. Similarly, for mantras, you need to learn them from qualified teachers to get the proper pronunciation. Without the sound vibrations, the mantras don't work. The problem I faced was in finding a guru. They say if the disciple is ready, the guru appears.

As a first step, I decided to study my religion and the sub-sect of Visishtadvaitam, which says God is both inside and outside. I take it to mean that he controls my inner as well as my external environment. I have a duty to populate my internal environment with gods and goddesses who represent certain higher qualities and higher levels of beings in this many-layered universe. I don't believe that a human as we see her/him now, is the ultimate in creation. As G said, he/she is only a potentiality and needs to transform to qualify to be called a human. Believing in higher beings gave me hope and motivation for such a transformation.

In my checkered career of shifting between provinces, postings and waiting for assignments, I did find time for other activities. I believed in G's idea of personality development and raising of one's level of being. I also felt a person's life becomes complete if he/she learns philosophy, science, art and religion. I started working on improving my knowledge of all these aspects and thereby my understanding of life. To know one's origins and to understand the patterns which helped shape the future, I went down my memory lane, searched for clues of my past personality to mould my future thought process. I believed all incidents, big or trivial, from childhood onwards held some clues to what was to follow.

A human being is born into a family, society, a religion and a language, all without a choice, including his/her physical attributes and basic psychological make-up. What *is* in his/her hands, is to understand and transcend them if necessary. To this end, I went about meticulously studying my religion, as I did with the other aspects of my life. I was born into the Visishtadvaitam sub-sect of Hinduism. This religious background had significant cultural and behavioural ramifications. I undertook the study of the concepts and rituals attached to Hinduism, and the Srivaishnavam as practised by Srivaishnavites of Tamil Nadu, where I belonged. I went to an accomplished pundit to learn the nuances when I returned from UP in 1987.

Today religion has become a bad word, and a lot of people are turning agnostic. I, too, underwent a similar spiritual conflict. Because of the atrocities committed in the name of worship, forced conversions, internecine wars between sects within religions, religious wars among various faiths, all tempted me to turn my head away from once great religions. When I decided to delve and deeply understand the religion I was born into, it was imperative that I set aside the current conflicts and problems in society and focus on the true essence of Hinduism and all that it stood for and how it was being deeply distorted. If I didn't find any, then I needed to go deeper. I discovered that my aversion for rituals, which represent a form of mental discipline, was one of the causes of not observing religious tenets. I was reluctant to adopt any spiritual training. I came to realize that these activities had arisen in religion primarily to give meaning in and direction to life; after all, faiths in their original form, were all spiritual by nature, but rituals were necessary to discipline the mind to appreciate the meaning of spirituality thoroughly. In modern times, new religious leaders or spiritualists have come on the horizon to teach these age-old practices sans the rituals. I decided to learn those ancient rituals to see how they contributed to my mental discipline, and how they would help me to understand the basic spiritual principles which have been guiding humanity from time immemorial.

Hinduism has three main streams of thought, belief and action. One is advaitam or monism, which means God is the only one truth and there is no division between God and the human soul, dvaita or dualism which says God and the human soul are different and the third is Visishtadvaitam or Srivaishnavam, which means qualified dualism. Advaitam says God and the individual atman or soul are one, but Visishtadvaitam is qualified dualism, saying God is higher and different from the soul, though He is present in all. All the different streams of thought accepted the supremacy of the Vedas, the scriptures, which are said to have their origin five thousand years ago. The Vedas laid down two rules for human life—dharma and karma. If man adheres to what the Vedas prescribed, then he is said to live according to the principle of dharma, and if not, he follows the path of adharma. Adharma creates bad karma which needs to be worked out, either in this birth or future births, as Hinduism believes that life is eternal.

Saivites worshiped Lord Shiva and the Srivaishnavites, Lord Vishnu or Narayana. Saivism found God is within oneself, whereas Srivaishnavam said God manifested primarily in the heavens called Srivaikuntam but also in four other ways including within oneself as antharyami, which means 'one who resides within'. The other three ways God manifested are as Hari of Milky Ocean, who is the creater and saviour, the avatars of Rama, Krishna, etc., and Archa, the form which is worshipped in temples. Saivites believed in working on oneself, observing penance and yoga and meditation techniques to achieve enlightenment, or self-realization, also known as jivanmukti, which means attaining liberation while alive in this body. The Srivaishnavites, on the other hand, believed in complete devotion—bhakti—and total surrender to God. They believe that bhakti will lead one to videha mukti or liberation after death. They called freedom and enlightenment, moksha. The core of the Srivaishnavite philosophy is that the atman or jivatma is Seshan, subservient to Lord, who is the Seshi, the master. It's possible for a Seshan to reach the Lord's abode but can never equal Him. While the jivatma is anurupena (of the size of an atom), the Lord embodies everything He created. It's not possible for the jivatma to witness the Lord in this life and this body, and thus has no access to any of the four; Srivaikuntam, parkadal (Milky Ocean), avatars or the antaryami. But he has access to one form—the Archa avatar, in the form of statues in temples. A true Srivaishnavite, practises bhakti, chants His names and does kainkarya, service to the Lord, which takes care of his karma, and once free of them he relinquishes this mortal body to reach His abode.

The Saivites contemplated on the inner self, but Srivaishnavites worshipped images of God in temples, which according to them, was yet another way God manifested. Another way God manifested was through avatars. Tradition has it that there were ten major avatars of Lord Vishnu. He is believed to have incarnated to save humanity from evil and to reestablish dharma or righteousness whenever evil overcame it. His avatars ranged from a fish, a tortoise and a wild boar—which are animals—to a half-animal, a half-man, such as the lion god Narasimha and then to purely human forms such as Rama and Krishna, representing all living beings. Lord Vishnu also took inanimate forms such as a stone or a log of wood. Vaishnavism believed that working on oneself was tough and was only meaningful in other ancient times such as Krita, Treta and Dvapara yugs and for modern times, Kaliyug, praising the Lord's names through namasankirtan and worship of His avatars in temples could bring salvation and moksha. (A yug is a division of time in Hindu cosmology, which runs for millions of years each.)

I developed my religious attitudes, to a large extent, by choice; my parents were religious enough, but they never compelled their sons in any manner to follow or perform any rituals. The earliest memory I had about religion was when I was very young, probably in my primary school, and my mother used to take me for discourses to a cultural centre called Sri Rama in north Chennai which was within walking distance from home. The discourses were on the epic Ramayana. The Ramanavami festival and lectures went on for about a fortnight, and every night after dinner we left for the venue and returned late at night. The discourses contained speech and songs, and at important places in the story, they sprayed sandalwood in the auditorium to mark the event. I loved the smell and kept guessing when the shower would occur next. At the end of the discourse Sundalprasadam used to be distributed and if I was awake until then, I liked that too. On many days, I slept through the speech on the sands of the auditorium and my mother carried me back home.

During the month of Margazhi, which is the season of gods in Chennai, bhajans, discourses and varieties of other musical and cultural events used to take place and my mother would participate in many of them. She was a good singer and used to sing 'Thiruppavai' hymns early in the morning. I was an early riser and used to run behind her when she was busy heating water for bathing and making coffee. I learned many hymns this way. The family used to visit temples periodically. Later, when I grew up and began working in the bank, I used to make lightning visits to Tirupati, a temple town which was about hundred miles from Chennai. I would take a bus on Saturday afternoons, when the bank closed. There was a long queue for the darshan, after which I would board a bus back home.

For several years after that though, I was completely immersed in my studies and career, which relegated all my spiritual pursuits to the background. When I returned to Chennai after spending ten years in the UP police cadre, I was able to revive my interests in Vaishnavism. I formally learned certain rituals and mantras from a scholar and pundit and performed them at home whenever possible, and never stopped doing them. I learned more about Vaishnavism by reading books and listening to discourses. I prayed every day.

According to the Srivaishnavite tradition, Lord Vishnu also known as Lord Narayana is the supreme God. He has Mahalakshmi as his consort, who appeared from the ocean when devas and asuras were churning the ocean for amrit or nectar, which was supposed to grant immortality to whoever consumed it. The Lord resided in Sri Vaikuntam, the ultimate abode of the gods. And in four other states. The first is the parkadal, the milky ocean, from where He created and responded to the calls of His devotees in distress. The second is in the form of avatars, such as Rama and Krishna. The third and fourth are the Archa, the deities in temples, and as antaryami, the one residing in all beings. In the parkadal, the Lord lay reclined on the Adhiseshan, the snake god with the snake hood providing shelter above his head. Mahalakshmi sat near him, and Brahma took birth from the lotus flower rooted in His navel. In the avatars, Lord Vishnu is said to have already taken nine avatars and the tenth, Kalki, is due sometime during the present Kaliyug. The other nine avatars were Matsya (fish), Kurma (tortoise), Varaha (boar), Narasimha (half-lion, half-human), Vamana (dwarf child), Parasurama (human), Rama (human), Balarama (human) and Krishna (as divine). As deities in temples, the Lord is present in 108 holy temples, which were visited and praised by rishis particularly by sages called Alwars who were twelve in number.

Lord Vishnu had other things on his body, including the Sudarshan chakra, a conch called Panchajanyam. He had Garuda, the bird king, as his vahana or vehicle, Adhiseshan, the snake king as his seat, Vishvaksena as his general, Dhanvantari as his medicine man and scores of others who were called Nitya Suris, the permanent residents of Srivaikuntam. After creating Brahma and the fourteen worlds out of the primordial substance, the Mula Prakriti, and the five essential elements, the Lord bade Brahma create a human. Brahma also created Shiva. He also set guidelines for a proper life through the Veda, which were first memorized (smriti) and then spread by word of mouth, shruti. These concepts were interpreted through various mythological treatises called Itihasa and Puranas. The Lord also had some teachers and gurus such as Narada and Vasishta to spread the Vedas and the Shastras, the divine codes of conduct. There was a line of gurus or acharyas, such as Ramanuja, Swami Desika and Andal. Andal was one of the twelve Tamil saints called the Alwars who sang the praise of the Lord. She was a human child who sought and got direct union with the Lord through her devotion. The Alwars went to various Srivaishnavite temples and sang the praise of the Lord's attributes. These temples are known as Sthalas, and 108 of them are famous. While 106 are on this earth, two are in the heavens and are attainable only after death. Four such important sthalas are the Srirangam temple at Trichirapalli, the Balaji temple at Tirupati, the Varadaraja temple at Kanchipuram and the Chellapillai temple at Melkote. The temples are considered the most sacred and every Vaishnavite strives to visit all 106, or at least the four most important ones. In the present day, Andavan ashram and Ahobila madam represent the guru lineage for Srivaishnavites to follow the dharma prescribed.

A Srivaishnavite believes that the Lord resides in a stone, called the Saligrama, found only in the Gandaki River in Nepal. The rock looks like a pebble, a dark shade of black, and has an opening in the front, which is made by years of work by a kind of insect, Chakravakam, which signifies the entrance to the Lord's abode inside. These pebbles are picked up by Srivaishnavites, brought home and kept in the puja ghar. The Lord residing inside is offered regular pujas, called aaradhana or nityakarma, and pure food cooked at home is offered to Him before being consumed. A true Vaishnavite undergoes rituals like panchakarma and prapatti, to signify his total surrender and follows the tenets laid down for him. Salvation or enlightenment comes to a Srivaishnavite only after death. In his lifetime, his focus should be on bhakti towards the Lord.

The primary texts of Srivaishnavam are the Vedas, Upanishads, the Ramayana, Mahabharata, Bhagavatam and the Bhagavad Gita.

Thus, the entire system is in place, and Srivaishnavites are expected to live their lives according to the tenets laid down. The devotee would be under the sway of three gunas—rajas, tamas and sattva, the three attributes which entangle all created things in Maya or the material word. He is also affected by his karma, his past deeds, which have no beginning but an end for which he needed to work on himself. Only by living a proper life can a human reach the abode of Lord Vishnu. I believe this system and observe and perform the rituals as best as I can.

But I also have unanswered questions; for instance, the role of free will and fate and karma. While individual outcome could be attributed to fate or karma there appear to be no plausible explanation for mass destructions in which even children get killed. For instance, as I was a witness to air crashes during my tenure as the civil aviation professional, I couldn't find an answer to the cruel fate met by unwary passengers. Was it that they all shared the same kind of bad karma? My second question is why the religion focuses largely on the afterlife? Though the scriptures do talk about how to live one's life, even such advice has the ulterior motive of liberation from this life. In my opinion, this has resulted in the thinking that even if he lives his life in any manner, he is assured of liberation if he has devotion. What is not understood is that unless your behaviour changes, you can't get true devotion.

I, however, attribute lack of answers to my questions to a lack of understanding on my part and hope, one day, to find the answers. I also believe that a man should be a Hindu or Muslim or a Christian at home, a real secular citizen when stepping out and a true human being in a global perspective. I tried to play all these three roles. I was a Hindu Tamil Brahmin inside my home, a responsible cop serving my country's security when I put on the uniform and stepped out, and much later, felt like a true global citizen, when I went back to school in America, learning together with Americans, Europeans, African-Americans and Asians. I believed that one should adhere to these boundaries strictly to avoid many unpleasant manifestations such as fundamentalism. I also had a spiritual journey side by side, which too started quite early in my life. Richard Bach's Jonathan Livingston Seagull was the first character which awakened the spirit of the Self in me and showed the possibilities of personal growth. My exposure to J. Krishnamurti and G.I. Gurdjieff strengthened my spiritual quest and answered many of my questions. I don't think religion is incapable of answering such questions, and I allow the possibility that I might not be aware of them.

The issues faced by modern India about religion are many. Though we proudly say that we are a tolerant and secular nation, finding unity in diversity, the reality is far from this claim. Religion deeply divides us, and these differences burst forth frequently, hindering our progress as a nation. We observe many religious holidays, processions and congregations—all of which necessitate elaborate arrangements for security—and spend considerable time and energy on this outward show of religiosity. On the other hand, staggering sums of money are collected by religious and spiritual institutions, which may or may not be for legitimate purposes. It always bothered me as to why a spiritual guru should raise so much money, open branches all over the world and keep travelling to deliver discourses. More than the spiritual power, it is money power, which has resulted in many malpractices including sexual abuses by the so-called gurus. For many religious leaders, it appears to be good news that thousands of people throng temples and participate in religious processions. It only breeds superficial devotion and mass mentality.

In my opinion, we must go back to the original intent of all the religions—for the personal evolution and not for the consumption of the masses. Worship should take place within the four walls of one's home. There shouldn't be a third party involved in this. That means the proliferation of prayer places should stop. Congregations should end. Though ancient texts of the religions recommend going to places of worship, going in search of a guru and collective prayers, these practices may not be suitable in today's day and age of religious fundamentalism and ultra-sensitive attitudes. Moreover, we have unprecedented access to information due to technology, which could be put to better use instead of personal presence in religious activities outside our homes.

I, by no means, suggest an atheistic attitude or agnostic tendencies. We must know and try to implement everything recommended in the scriptures. Temples and churches should have the celebrations and festivals inside the precincts, and perhaps beam it into our homes. If religion is meant for the family within the home, spirituality should be for the person within the family.

10

Mind

Epigenetics: What you are thinking is translated into chemistry that will determine what you become.

−DR BRUCE LIPTON

The Fourth Way

The ideas of G, kindled my curiosity and laid the foundation for my quest for the meaning of life. His Fourth Way (the other three being the ways of the fakir, monk and yogi), encompasses a world view consisting of ideas about esoteric religion, cosmology, philosophy and psychology. It doesn't speak about any religion or sect, but about humanity and the destiny of human beings, and how a person should approach life to evolve. During my days in college, as I had mentioned earlier, I accidentally stumbled upon a lecture by J. Krishnamurti, who gave me the idea of the 'mind'. Before that, I was an organic mess, who took his body, mind, etc., for granted. Again, during my days in UP police, I laid my hands on a book on G by Dr Kenneth Walker. I was fascinated by the ideas put forward in the book. So much so that when I was back in Chennai, I searched for more books by or about G's ideas, but could find none. I did, however, find a series of commentaries on the Fourth Way (FW) by Maurice Nicoll and a book entitled *In Search of the Miraculous*, by P.D. Ouspensky, in the Theosophical Society Library in Adyar. A little later, books on the Fourth Way started appearing in bookshops, and today I find plenty of online resources to read and forums to participate. G's ideas provided the key to understanding scriptures and other spiritual material for me. Much later, I laid my hands on a book, *The Force of Gurdjieff* by C. Daly King, who had worked with both G and Orage, the principal disciple of G in America. Hence, this book is subtitled as the Oragean version. In his foreword, author Adrian Mirel Petrariu has aptly mentioned that 'the form of the information usually becomes a significant third force which supports the coexistence of different levels of reality of knowledge and understanding'. I found this very true because though I was familiar with the ideas; the methodology of the presentation in this book was appealing, showing them in a different light. The 'third force' mentioned here is one of the major ideas of the Fourth Way.

The body of knowledge represented here is 'hidden learning' and requires a scientific approach. The truths are concerned primarily with the destiny of Man and that of individual men. While curiosity brings one into contact with such learning, something more is required to take its place once the interest wanes. The secret knowledge itself is likely to provide such stimuli. The procedure employed is like science; four steps of the accumulation and observation of facts and data, a formation of a theory or hypothesis based on such data, setting up of an experimental technique to test the hypothesis and the resulting proof or disproof of the same. G has based his ideas and procedures on the same fields in which science works, such as physics, chemistry, biology, psychology, sociology, astronomy, cosmogony, religion and philosophy, and many others. Also, they invade fields so far untouched by science such as telepathy, clairvoyance, ESP, astrology and so on; in other words, the entire realm of science covers both actual and potential. For a human being to understand these ideas and concepts, one needs to test these ideas on oneself. Another aspect of science that's applicable here is impartiality. The questions to be answered by this system of FW, are the fundamental issues with which all human beings must confront eventually; what and why is a human being?

Reality consists of both actual and potential. Actual is what exists or takes place, and potential is what might or may exist or happen. Unreality is what can't exist or happen and is synonymous with the impossible. It comprises both the impossible and the incredible potential. These things need to be kept in mind while examining any hypothesis. One such hypothesis based on this definition is that the most interesting thing about man is not what he is, but what he may become. The fact about people is that they are undeveloped; their potentiality lies precisely in the possibility of their fuller, balanced development. Credulity and suggestibility are two sides of the same coin; the latter is a disease, which afflicts masses of men. Agnosticism or scepticism is the real antidote to suggestibility, and these ideas require such attitudes.

The Law of Octaves

In considering the position of man in the universe, we find a series of seven degrees or, in general, seven distinct steps. Think of the galactic systems (the universe), the Milky Way (a single galactic system) and the Sun (a single star in the above galactic system). Then the planetary system (attached to the Sun), Earth (a single planet of the planetary system), organic kingdom (a part of Earth), and humankind (part of the biological kingdom). The law in its manifestation appears in our day-to-day lives as musical notes of the piano. The atomic structures, the spectrum of light and the periodic table of chemical elements are some more examples of this law.

The Law of Three

In every whole phenomenon, there are always three factors present. They are referred to as positive, negative and neutralizing forces. The first two effects are easy to observe, but the third power is incomprehensible as we are 'third-force blind'. With effort, we can see their presence. In an atomic structure, the nucleus is positive and the electrons are negative, with the electromagnetic field serving as the third force. We can see this law at work in all phenomena. For example, in a dispute, the plaintiff and the defendant represent the positive and negative forces and the judge who brings to bear upon the matter his interpretation of the law, takes the position of a neutralizing force; the result is the settlement. In a city or town, the desire to construct is the active force, the act of construction represents the negative and the land itself is the neutralizing force. It's the nature of the land which forced New York to grow upward, and Newark to spread sideways. In the case of man, his subjective experience is positive, the physical, neurological functioning of his body is the negative factor, and it is his consciousness (neutralizing factor) which mediates the transformation of neuron activity into experiential content. If you consider any species, the thermodynamic energies are the first force, the chemical entities are the negative second forces, and the organic electrodynamic field serves as the third neutralizing force. What is necessary for any event is that all three forces are required, with no priority. The law of seven is an operational law and concerns what happens, and the law of three has to do with what is. In this sense, the law of three is more fundamental than the law of seven for any phenomenon to occur.

Another idea central to the FW system is about the neurological equipment (nervous system) of the human body, which puts it into contact with the world outside of the organism. It also mediates the responses of the organism to the volume of internal stimuli arising from within. Its actions are incredibly complex and integrative. Its job is to coordinate and harmonize the external and internal stimuli constantly impinging upon the organism, and to produce an adequate reaction balance consisting of the inner and outer responses of the body. From conception until death, the nervous systems are in control of the body. From the moment the sperm fertilizes the ovum, and cell multiplication commences, the steady-state biological field lays down the human body pattern and the neurosis of the body. It is the mediation of the factor of consciousness, the third or neutralizing factor in the economy of the human being, which transforms the factor of neuron phenomena into the element of subjective experience.

So, when a man thinks, he thinks his response is a personal awareness of an already determined neural event taking place within the limits of the frontal lobes and therefore, the notion of personal control is an illusion. His access to the external world is indirect. Hence his awareness needs to be directed towards the neural points rather than the outside world or phenomenon. This principle will be helpful in explaining why self-observation without being critical is necessary to study a phenomenon. From this standpoint, what is normal is that the organism functions according to its design, and there is nothing like an average or ordinary human being. The average is only a mathematical calculation.

Functions of Humans: The Three Centres

The most obvious features of the humans are thinking, feeling and action. In other words, they can be called mental, emotional and moving functions. Most of the things he does come under one of these essential functions. They are also known as centres, which converge at the base of the spinal column, the solar plexus and the forward portion of the brain. The centre is defined as 'the ganglion of plexus whence issues the nerves controlling a function'. The lower levels of the neurological mechanism of the body are concerned with the involuntary maintenance of the machine, with the processes of metabolism, food digestion, breathing, and with those reflex actions which respond to the stimuli from the external environment that take place *before* we think about them. This kind of activity originates in and is mediated by the spinal cord mechanisms. Emotional responses, although affecting many parts of the organism, have their centre of gravity in the nervous nodes of the upper trunk, the sympathetic nervous system and the celiac plexus is the largest and most complicated as the focus of this emotional activity. The forward portion of the head brain, primarily the cerebral cortex, mediates not only speech but also other functions such as memory, foresight, abstract conceptual processes, perceptions of relationship, recognition and so on. These are all mental faculties and their seat in the body constitutes the centre three. The sequence of their first growth will be that of the moving centre developing first, in conception with the electrodynamic field of the nervous system, followed by the emotional and mental centres.

Heredity and Environment

It is, therefore, evident that the neurosis of the organism comes into being first. The three centres are formed much before birth. Neither the given human being nor the centres themselves have any control or decision over the nature or the sequence of this content. When impressions pass through these centres, they leave traces, forming the basis for memory, which is of three types— sensory-motor, emotional and mental. Their condition is due, in the first place, to heredity and secondly, the environment. The forces we call inheritance, including the steady-state biological field of the organism, completely and finally control the formation of the three primary brain systems and they also determine the degree of efficiency or normality with which the given centres must possess as regarding their functioning structures. After the organism has been laid down and is developing, the environment at once commences to bring to bear its distinct influence but doesn't alter the structural characteristics of the centres. It may, however, either permit or deny their exercise. For example, a man may have the ability and opportunity to run a championship marathon, but if the environment breaks his leg, he can't exercise his ability for the time being. If the environment so injures his leg that amputation becomes necessary, he can never do so. The environmental effect is brought to bear not upon the abilities but their manifestations.

In other words, the heredity provides the equipment and that environment determines its use.

No ordinary man can control these two factors. Of the two, the preponderant element is the organism and not the environment, and environment never transforms the essential characteristics of those persons subjected to it. Thus, structure and function are always dissociable aspects of the same entity. The human organism is designed to manifest the maximum reinforcement and cooperation between and among the three principal subdivisions in its entire response patterns of behaviour. When this type of harmonious functioning takes place, the whole mechanism operates at its highest efficiency. Under these conditions, it may be said to be normal in the full sense. When functioning thus frequently, there are almost no conditions or circumstances on the surface of this planet which it can't meet and successfully overcome. The only condition is that the centres should cooperate and not interfere with each other. The important attribute of the average man is that he comes under the 'Law of Fate', which means he lives according to his true fate. Ordinary people come under the 'Law of Accidents', which subjects them to more accidents and their lives remains accidental by nature. Consider a plane crash in which all the occupants die—do you think they all had a similar fate or did they in fact, come under the law of accidents? A man who cancelled his trip at the last minute due to some reason, and escaped death. What does this mean?

The Permanent 'I'

The question that then arises is how these three aspects of the organism function within us and who controls them? It will be a fallacy if we say we control them by our will. What we call 'I' is expected to be the governor of these functions, provided we had one single I. We have several of them, and to observe this fact, we need to be honest with ourselves. In addition to this, our three centres which interfere with the functions of the other; we are emotional when one is required to be rational, and one is thoughtful when required to act. We don't possess a permanent will, but remain under the delusion that we control our lives with a permanent I. The trouble lies not in the organic factors we have been discussing, but with the element of consciousness. We discussed the threefold analysis of the nature of the human being, in which the three essential elements appeared as the content of experience, end products of neural functioning, and the third-force factor of consciousness as a mediating element, irrespective of what the neural product that it might be mediating is. It is an erroneous assumption that conscious factors interfere with such processes in some inexplicable way, when in fact, the actual role of consciousness is simply and solely the translation of neurology into the terms of subjective experience. Working on yourself to remove the anomalies in the inner workings often end up in repression and result in unexpected consequences.

The Black Sheep and the Moon

One famous parable of the system is that of the only black sheep among the ordinary sheep, and the shepherd. In the cosmogony, everything grows and needs nourishment. The ray of creation, which flows from the Sun to the planets, including the Earth and the Moon, also grows. One day the Moon will be like Earth, which will be like the Sun. The organic life on Earth serves as a layer for the transformation of energy, which goes to the Moon to enrich it. Essentially, when the biological life form dies, or it suffers, the energy released goes to the Moon. Consider the extraordinary men we admire. They have more energy to offer to the Moon than most of us. The path to development for such an individual is from extraordinary through the ordinary to the normal. The more influential the dictator, the more fanatically successful the religionist, the more renowned the philosopher, the more celebrated the actor. By the same token, the more the individual is the Moon's slave.

Therefore, taking the 'black sheep' analogy, the Moon is the shepherd to ensure that it gains the mutton and the wool of the herd. The shepherd feeds and shelters the herd only for this purpose. The black sheep is the one who understands this game and escapes the common fate by disappearing one day. The irony is that Nature conspires with the Moon and is not designed to help man. It supports man's semi-conscious state of being so that he serves this larger purpose. If a person wants to escape this general fate, he has a slim chance of doing so; by serving the Sun instead of the Moon. For this to happen, he must wake up by developing the potentialities present in him.

The Comfort Bed

Adrian Mirel gives another analogy of the Comfort Bed to describe the current situation of ordinary men, which is an old tale from a lost civilization far older than our own, and even more fully equipped with gadgets. It is related that the ultimate triumph of this culture was the production of the 'comfort bed'. It could be purchased at one swoop, and after that, the buyer had no further worries. He lay down on the contrivance and from then on everything was accomplished for him; all his needs were attended to entirely automatically; such as feeding, excretion, an occasional bath, sexual requirements and everything else that could be desired, and in the end, the contraption even gave him a decent burial. His existence thus is entirely passive, without the necessity for any effort whatever, and this ingenious invention permitted its owner to live mechanically in the fullest sense. Depending, of course, upon what is meant by the verb, to 'live'. We can appreciate this situation better in our own time. We are already on our way to achieving the comfort bed for ourselves; electric fans and heaters, buses, trains, cars, dishwashers, washing machines and dryers, air conditioners, stoves with automatic timers, kitchen equipment, power tools and jacks, self-opening garage doors, farming equipment, TV, mobile phones, etc., to name a few.

The answer to all this is not some back-to-nature fad whereby the machines are all scrapped; they are part of our present environment, and the thing to do is not to destroy them but to relegate them to their proper place in our scheme of practical affairs. The crux is that greater the number of such gadgets, the happier the ordinary man. All this is about as humanly abnormal as may be and on sober reflection, it will look less like a fuller life than a negation of any life at all. But not to the ordinary man, for under the conditions he has created for himself, the comfort bed is a serious deal. It saves his labour, but for what? This wild exaggeration of labour-saving desires is far closer to death than life. No corpse does any work at all. Many ordinary men are walking about dead while their physical mechanisms still move. Not only have they never developed emotionally or mentally, but in these two respects, they have died in unconscious atrophy.

The Impediments of Kundalini and Imagination

According to G, the other hurdle that prevents man from development are his mechanisms of bondage in the form of kundalini, the faculty of imagination and the self-calming attitude. It was a shock to me to see such a view about kundalini, a much-celebrated force in yoga philosophy. G refers to this as 'kundabuffer', intentionally planted by Nature at the base of his spine to make him see the truth upside down. This diseased apparatus, however, helps in the process of self-calming. The next is the faculty of imagination, which is further divided into real imagination and phantasy. Real imagination is concerned with real things. For example, consider a lamp; you can imagine how it came into existence, what materials have been used and how many people would have worked to make it a reality. Phantasy is something you indulge in semi-consciously, also known as day-dreaming. It is rooted in unreality and therefore, you gradually lose grip over reality. (This is quite contrary to the Indian philosophy, which considers kundalini as an important factor in the process of enlightenment.)

The system has so far explained the cosmological

arrangements—the place of Earth, organic life and human beings in this grand scheme. It also discusses the functions of natural life, human life, the apparatus provided to him for the purpose of nature, and the difficulties he faces in waking up from the semi-conscious state. The system further goes on to explain the real potentialities awaiting man, provided he makes the necessary efforts. The problem is, in modern times we confuse our actuality with possibilities and term all of them as qualities of humanity already present.

The Potential Centres and the Universal Octave

Man is described as a three-centred or a three-brained being. Since the centres were all in functional operation, they are actualities for him. Moreover, according to the Fourth Way, he has three further potential centres, which are present but not active, and therefore, come under the category of potential. Their operations are not within the field of consciousness nor do they furnish any part of his present context of experience. Only when the potential gets converted into actual, they become his qualities, and for this to happen, he must make efforts. These centres are higher intellectual, emotional and physical. In technical terms, they are the cerebellum (individuality), the heart centre (consciousness) and sex cells (will).

Let us briefly go back to the first three centres. Centre 1 has two parts—the moving centre responsible for external and muscular responses, and the instinctive centre which is meant for the working of the involuntary organs and biological functions within the organism. In other words, to maintain the homeostasis of the body. In ordinary humanity, these two sub-centres are accompanied either by little consciousness or not at all. Centre 2 manifests physically all the emotional states experienced by ordinary men. Some of these states are hate, fear, affection, anger, sentimentality, dominance, compliance, submission, desire, etc. Some of them are negative emotions and some, positive.

Centre 4, the higher intellectual centre mediates a different kind of thought process called realization, indicating that the centre deals with reality, containing the potentialities of formal logic and objective logic. Centre 5 exhibits emotions called awe, ecstasy and reverence. Centre 6 has the real ability to 'do', or genuine action. Organically, these higher centres are represented as the cerebellum, which generally is dysfunctional save some minor functions, and disproportionate to its size. The Center 5 is the heart, which only carries out minor functions of pumping blood, which otherwise has the potential of arousing genuine love but merely arouses sex, lust, lower emotions, etc. Because of dysfunctions and cross-connections, all these centres tend to interfere with each other's functions and misuse the energies. For instance, sexual energy is misused and degenerates into lust, anger, etc.

Food

Food is another potentiality. There are three kinds of food—what is consumed through the mouth, the air taken in through the nostrils and the sensory impressions through the senses and nervous system. The first kind of food enters as a solid, passes through the liquid state and becomes gaseous. Of course, if it is ingested as a liquid, it skips the first stage. Further, it gets transformed into magnetism, emotions, thought and sex, where all its possibilities have been used up. The second kind of food enters as different types of gases and then that too passes through the next stages of magnetism, emotion and thought. The third kind of food take the form of impressions, a cerebral phenomenon known as thought, and that's the state in which it remains. Thus, it will be seen here that these interrelated octaves account for the entire range of metabolic products demanded by the operation of the cellular mechanism in its present condition. Regular food goes through three stages and stops. At this point, the second kind of food is supposed to provide the necessary impetus by joining here and further pushing the transformative process to the third level, where the third kind of food, of sensory input, completes the universal food octave, making the finest energies necessary for the higher functioning of more exceptional thoughts, feelings and actions. This stage has remained as a potentiality only and therefore, the average person's life continues to be mechanical in all the centres, and he remains an automaton. This situation ultimately leads him to an impasse, because, no matter how he struggles and strives, all his efforts turn against him in the outcome. All such efforts go into strengthening one or the other function he already exercises, and not into transformation. How to escape such a trap is the question, and the answer lies in the 'secret'.

The Method in the Fourth Way

The method consists of two parts—open secret and hidden secret. This process is like a science because it is based in observation, hypothesis, experiment and conclusion. In another way, it differs in that it doesn't commit the error of affirming the consequent. The open secret is 'open' because it can be revealed by very ordinary means. The degree of such knowledge as 'know thyself', that can be acquired by normal, though careful, means constitutes the open secret. There are difficulties in this, but there are none which require more than the usual amount of tenacity, intelligence and courage. The first difficulty is the delusion that we already do know ourselves. But the first step towards knowing oneself is the realized admission that one does not in fact, know oneself. The key requirement is a rational objectivity. The possibility of knowing oneself can arise only when a man is prepared to investigate his attributes and characteristics, and his behaviour, as he would do in case of a stranger. Once he starts doing this sincerely and impartially, he will discover that at every turn, his image of himself distorts what is plainly in front of his eyes.

The Investigations

It's important to organize one's work in the sense that the boat needs to be propelled by you if you want to go somewhere. The first thing required is self-knowledge, and if you do it sincerely, it will start of by being painful, because the image you have of yourself doesn't change so easily. Over a period, you gather observable data about yourself, upon which you build a hypothesis. The hypothesis or the judgement is the second step, after which arises the possibility of experimental confirmation or refutation. Other types of investigations are also possible—a nightly review is one of them. When you go to bed, review the day and note down all that you did. Another exercise that can be undertaken is referred to as motion picture. Here, you gradually relax your body and achieve emotional relaxation by reinstating images from the past when you felt most comfortable, not by feeling alone but trying to recapture the sensory inputs. You can achieve mental relaxation by counting a series of numbers, which also involves a little effort. For example, counting 1-2-3-4, 4-3-2-1, 2-3-4-5, 5-4-3-2, etc.

Thus, the threefold relaxation forms the basis of the motion-picture exercise. Imagine a moment, for instance, rising from the bed in the morning, and allow this 'video' to run while you're still in bed. The video will frequently break in the beginning but will become steady as you practise. With the kind of self-knowledge you manage with the previous exercises, you can manage to make a decent movie of yourself. Then, watch the effect.

There are still further investigations can be made by using ordinary methods. For that, we need to understand the distinction between essence and personality. When a baby is born, it possesses certain qualities and characteristics of essence, which are an undeveloped and infantile condition. These essential qualities begin to get overlaid and hidden by the inputs from the environment, family, parents, etc., which is called personality. As the child grows into an adult, this overlaying keeps happening, and the essence gets buried deeper and deeper. Finally, it's an exterior personality hiding an essential core, long unconscious and very different from the presented appearance. Only an extreme emergency brings out the essence into play. Essence is not wrong but undeveloped. For instance, the essential fear later becomes clairvoyance. Astrology is another science, related to the essence of man, but in modern times, it is erroneously related to the personality. The planetary influences work on the embryo and the just-born infant as prenatal and perinatal influences but not later, when they are interpreted as 'fate' of the child; this is, in reality, far from the truth. In the present context, astrology could be a useful way to study one's essence. (This interpretation of astrology as an excellent science and a tool for self-observation influenced me to such an extent that I learned the rudiments of astrology with keen interest.)

The Chief Feature

Closely related to the essence is a man's chief feature, also called his main weakness, of which he is deeply ashamed. Most of his activities, mannerisms and efforts would be towards masking this feature of his essence. For instance, an army man's primary function may be cowardice and his joining the army would have been to hide his main feature and prove to the world and himself that he is not a coward. A direct struggle against one's primary function will not yield any result, but genuine self-observation will gradually change it over a period. Until then, the main feature will remain the secret mainspring of behaviour in everything. We can even observe ourselves, as to which animal or bird type we belong to, in terms of our behaviour patterns. Self-knowledge comes about with such life reviews and motion pictures. As a result, we may gradually unravel the kind of person we are and what sort of habitual patterns are recurring in our lives endlessly. Thus, impartiality towards oneself is the fundamental crux of the open secret activity. It is the indispensable demand of the next work known as the 'hidden secret', if calamity is to be avoided.

The Four States of Consciousness

Modern psychology recognizes two primary states or levels of consciousness—waking and sleeping states. There are two more, which are self-consciousness and cosmic consciousness. Self-consciousness is that state of consciousness in which the subject is currently and accurately aware of all the operations of his organic body. The cosmological consciousness is characterized by an awareness of cosmological phenomena and is, at best, a pathological state which man undergoes, however briefly, which he is neither able to comprehend nor communicate later. Entering or exiting the state is not under his control. The result of self-observation and self-consciousness is that it is an impartial, detached awareness of one's body, as also distinguished from the 'I', which is making the observation. On the other hand, the ordinary understanding of the state of self-consciousness is an awkward condition of the body and attitudes, which is baseless.

Coming to the two normal states of waking and sleeping, waking is a subjective state, hypnotic in kind, characterized objectively by daydreaming and delusion. Sleep is usually characterized by unconsciousness, usually an experience marked by one lacking in 'logical' connection and consistency due to the general exclusion of sensory input to the brain. According to this system, all states except the waking state are healthy.

When a normal man sleeps, he sleeps without dreams because his life is balanced among the threefold aspect of experiential content, neural end products and the neutralizing factor of consciousness, with the last one transforming the objectivity of neural experiences into personal ones. The three elements constitute his being, and behind them all stands the I. For ordinary men like most of us, the passivity of consciousness in the waking state is what mainly characterizes that level of consciousness and renders the state an unusual one for an adult man. Thus, the keynote of the self-conscious state is the activity of the conscious or neutralizing factor. Another aspect of this state is that it can be entered only deliberately and purposefully by the subject.

To sum it up, in sleep, a man is not conscious of external phenomena, in the self-conscious state he is aware accurately and clearly of internal phenomena, and in cosmic consciousness, he knows precisely—though indirectly—of external events and their reality-relations.

Self-Observation, Participation and Experiment

The first is the technique of self-observation. Its purpose is to reach the self-conscious state gradually and healthily. It's a psychological activity that is completely unique. Ask yourself what it is that a human being can do, which is neither thinking and feeling, nor moving, all of which are his standard functions? The fourth type of activity is the act of self-observation, in which the both, the observer and the observed are you yourself, making a clear distinction between the two—the 'I' the observer, and the 'it', the body and its actions. So far, we registered all events passively, but now, through the act of self-observation, we start recording actively. When a passive act becomes active, it's called awareness. Hence, self-awareness is the fundamental requirement of self-observation.

To achieve the ability to see the distinction, we may use a 'mantra'. According to this system, a mantra is not a word or series of words, but a series of experiences so joined that their sum becomes a force. The psychological activity of self-observation is defined by seven limiting characteristics. In case of an absence of any one of them, accurate self-observation does not take place. These features are: without criticism, tutorials or analysis but with non-identification, within the prescribed area, about all available sensations and with confinement to no line or place.

Similar steps are required for participation, which is likened to learning to drive an automobile. First, you only sit in front of the car and observe how the car is driven, which is comparable to self-observation. Then, before assuming the driver's seat, you place your hands on the steering wheel and the gearshift lever and your feet next to the accelerator and the brake. You are not yet controlling the act, but are participating in the operation being carried out by someone else. Thus, participation is more active than self-observation.

The third and final step in the first stage of the method is known as the experiment. After successfully practising self-observation and participation, the experiment is with our habits, good or bad, and which brings about the alteration in behaviour. The real purpose of this type of operation is to live less mechanically and more consciously. If you are accustomed to wearing the shoe on the left foot first, then change it to the right first and see. After some time, when this becomes the altered habit, change back to the left foot, or consciously alternate between the right and left feet every other day. Gradually, when a certain degree of mastery is achieved, bigger habits like smoking or drinking can be included in the experiments to get rid of them. Experimentation can proceed with simple physical habits before moving on to complex patterns involving the whole organism, with simple roles to more complex functions.

The Effects of Self-observation on the Organism

The results are twofold—one has to do with the 'digestion' of the three kinds of food we take. The second aspect is activation of different organic centres. The primary feature of metabolism is that it is an active process. It can't be pushed down the throat. One needs to eat food, followed by procedures like masticating and swallowing down the alimentary canal. Similarly, for air, hundreds of muscles work in tandem to draw it into the lungs, where an active interchange takes place between the gaseous and the chemical substances in the blood. All these proceed automatically without interference from us. At the place where the first category of food gets stalled, the air that we breathe provides the necessary boost to take that energy to the next level. For the air power, however, help is not provided automatically by the next level of mental food—the impressions. We must create this help by learning to process impressions consciously. By the same token, the food of impressions also gets stuck because of lack of proper digestion. Just as we keep eating more and more, without bothering about proper digestion, we keep accumulating mental and sensory impressions without processing them consciously, resulting in passive registration, which is the reason for the semi-conscious waking state of humanity.

The activity of self-observation is similar to the eating and digestion of sensory impressions, continually arriving from without and within the body itself. With a conscious intake of impressions, the mental energy increases by about 50 per cent, while the emotional and sexual energies triple. When the sexual energies of two individual beings are combined, it results in the birth of a child, and can help the individual in developing further organisms or subtle bodies within himself. Much greater energy is made available to the person for more creative pursuits. Voluntary suffering (suppression of manifestations of negative emotions) and conscious labour (pondering about higher subjects) begin to produce the second conscious shock or boost, which permits the food octave of impressions to progress through its own obstacles and complete its evolution, the result of which is the formation of the third or mental body.

The Three-storied Factory

The human body is a three-story factory which receives supplies at each of its levels. The ground-floor supplies are used and one-half of the materials entering the second storey. The other half of the latter and the entire storage of the third are lying where it was delivered, and they rot, and this clutters up the space, necessitating a clean-up. At this point, the operations of the factory are just sufficient to maintain the plant and carry out the repairs, with practically no output achieved. Just as such an enterprise will be treated as unsuccessful, the human enterprise becomes a futile endeavour. With proper utilization of its delivered materials, all this can change. There is now a conversion of supplies into finished products of higher mental and emotional activities, and those energies permit the use of genuine will and the consequent ability to 'do'. Doing or consciously directed action is precisely the final output which the factory is designed to produce and in no way, does it resemble the automated movements and actions of the 'factory' during its just-maintenance phase.

The Concept of Sub-centres

We were so far discussing the centres of the cellular machine called the human body with its three centres. There is a larger system in which the human body is the first centre, and the three storeys become its sub-centres. If you are equating this with the three primary universal positive, negative and neutralizing forces, then the intellectual sub-centre becomes the positive force, the emotional sub-centre, the neutralizing and the instinctive sub-centres negative. If the human body is the first centre, then the second and third also consist of bodies just as physical and material as the first—the gross body. They are called the astral body or psychic body and the mental or psychological body. These are, of course, potentialities for ordinary men. A function of the physical body, or first centre, is to ingest matter of given vibration rates and to transform such substances by raising their vibration rates to permit of the construction within itself of the second centre and the initiation of the third. Thus, the real significance of the digestive processes is simply that in this respect, one continues to live actively and consciously instead of passively and unconsciously. A recurring theme is a warning that no individual should try the hidden secret methods alone. Either he needs an instructor or a group, which is accustomed to the ways of the method.

When speaking of objective morality, the system says that the first principle of morality is to keep the physical body in its highest degree of health, which is the first duty of a normal human being. I took this as a starting point for my investigations into my life. I decided to devote more time to understand my body, be sensitive to its real needs instead of just feeding and keeping it comfortable. Getting proper exercises and learning about modern medicines and the art of keeping it in healthy balance, and application of therapy whenever needed became one of my primary goals. At the emotional and intellectual levels, I felt the need to understand my religion and the cosmos better, while keeping the Fourth Way ideas as the bedrock of my investigations.

11

Body

*The secret to living well and longer is: Eat half, walk double,
laugh triple and love without measure.*

–TIBETAN PROVERB

Rolfing

I became body-conscious very late in my life, around the age of
fifty. Until then, I had enough running about in my career and
family life, but that was no excuse to neglect the body. Luckily
it didn't result in any serious illness, except diabetes and mild
hypertension, which remain under control with proper medication,
diet and exercise. But on a different level, I regret that I did not
pay enough attention to my body and wasn't more sensitive to its
needs. I was always preoccupied, either with career or reading about
philosophy, spirituality or religion. But my reading *The Protean Body*
by Don Johnson proved to be a revelation and the game changer.
It's interesting how I came to know about Don. One day, I was
sitting with Robert McDermott, the head of department for religion
and consciousness studies, CIIS. He had a friend who retired as a
police officer too and lived in New York. When we were discussing
the kind of experiences I had in my tenure as an officer—murder,

crimes and other forms of violence—Robert said I must try Rolfing, as all these experiences would have manifested in some form or the other on my body and muscles. He also mentioned that his friend would to do this for relief from stress. Then he went on to describe what Rolfing was—a form of deep-tissue massage therapy, which principally worked on the fascia, which is a band of connective tissue beneath the skin which separates and encloses muscles and internal organs. Rolfing helped to take the rigidity away so that the body tissues and muscles had more space to operate without constriction. It was essentially a therapy aimed at restoring the structural integration of the body and restore normal health. Robert also recommended that I meet Don Johnson, the head of the somatic department, to know more about Rolfing. So I met Don, and he presented me with his book at the end of a pleasant and informative chat. After reading it, I was so impressed that I wanted to try the massage. Back home in India, I used to go for ayurvedic oil massages; I wanted to try rolfing and see how it differed. I found a good rolfer in my neighbourhood—Michael Murphy, who had over forty years of experience. The therapy is done over ten sessions, covers the entire body and emphasizes its connectedness rather than looking at it as separate body parts. It was an unforgettable experience.

There were some compelling ideas in the book that transformed my attitude towards the body. In his book, Johnson says that our bodies are three-dimensional projections of energy from many sources. We are like Homer's Proteus, the ancient god of the seas who could change into water, fire or anything on the face of the earth. Solidity and fixity are myths. The human body is not a given thing or substance, but a continuous creation and an energy system, which is never a complete structure, never static, is in perpetual inner self-construction and self-destruction; we destroy it to make it new. The body is a fluid energy field that is in the process of change from the moment of conception until the time of death. The flesh is not a solid, dense mass; it is filled with life, consciousness and energy. Unfortunately, most people experience their bodies as opaque, solid masses that, except for deterioration due to age and accident, are fixed.

Many of us will readily accept the notion that our functioning in the world—our emotions, feelings, our health, the shape of our body, its ease—changes from day to day. But only a rare person lives his life with the feeling that his *structure* is changeable. There is a bleakness in human life stemming from the assumption that body structure is fixed. Despite exercise, healthy eating, psychotherapy and meditation, many of us find ourselves still trapped in old pains, both physical and emotional. Some of us have discovered that the trap often lies in body structure—in the tipped pelvis, the forward neck, the twisted lumbar spine. A young woman had open-heart surgery when she was five. Though she enjoyed a good life, she was in psychotherapy for a long time for unspecific pain and sorrow. When she was rolfed, it seemed her entire body was wrapped around the large scar between her sixth and seventh ribs where the surgical incision had been made. During the ten sessions of rolfing, the scar-wrapping, which extended up to the soles of her feet, was undone and her endless sorrow rolled out of her.

It is liberating to know the extent to which our physical behaviour is programmed. The action does not necessarily come only from our inner sense of rightness and ease, but from the way we are taught to use the body and the ways others would like us to use it. What is sacrificed in the process is the virtually unlimited adaptability. We are capable of many responses to any particular stimulus or a group of stimuli, but our adaptive capacity is limited, starting in our early months, and our responses become rigid and predictable over a period. From a world of primates, nature has worked to create a dancer or an artist; our consciousness has warred with nature to make the dancer-artist into a machine. But instead, we would like to think of ourselves as warm, loving, free and creative beings and not machines. Everybody knows that the body changes; if you overeat, your pants get tighter. Blood circulation increases when you improve your diet or take up a new exercise programme. Your height changes during adulthood, usually shortening as you grow older, but sometimes increasing when you come out of severe depression. Even as you know these things yourself, the idea is to tell you that the body changes more than you ever suspected.

Your body represents your personal history, including the way your parents taught you to use your body by the way they learned to use their bodies. It also includes birth experiences—often traumatic—accidents, illnesses and your emotional history in the context to your flesh. Your unique form is the clear realization of universal patterns from society, which themselves are in an almost imperceptible state of change. For instance, the image of female beauty is communicated from the earliest years through movie stars, fashion models and singers. The same goes for men—the athletic male, the Marlboro man, etc., in comparison to which we either feel happy or sad. Another surprising factor is the gravity which affects our body by putting a strain on them and the form our body has at any time is a function of those static and dynamic force vectors. But what we intend to do with ourselves shapes us; how we choose to deal with our environment, our fears, and other emotions, the types of activity, the lifestyle, the food we eat, our exercise regimen and what we do for stress reduction.

Structure refers to the relatively stable connection of large body segments (head, torso, pelvis, legs, and feet) into one another. The relations are a function of the length and tone of the muscles, fasciae, tendons, ligaments, cartilage and bones. Structure and posture are related—position feeds into structure just as structure dictates posture. For example, a tennis player will, over the years, find his right shoulder becoming significantly different from his left. A person who spends a good deal of her childhood slouching on a couch and goes on to become a scholar later, will develop stooped shoulders, sunken chest and drooping head. As our perception of our original physical being becomes more flexible and differentiated, our perception of larger areas of human concern also changes, such as the impact our experience of body structure has on politics, spirituality and intimate personal relationships.

A general goal of the first seven sessions of rolfing is to modify your present body structure; to remove old stress patterns, old postures, old ways of bodily relating to the world. But whatever happens on one level of personal existence is reflected on all levels. During early sessions of rolfing, people frequently report feeling disoriented, freaked out, unfamiliar in their world and unable to relate to people as they did in the past. Some refer this 'taken-apartness' to their body—they fall a lot or throw out their backs doing heavy work in old ways. They often report feeling like newborn babies. Three qualitatively different self-experiences are available to each of us for analysis and understanding.

1) In what are, for most of us, extraordinary experiences, we are aware of ourselves as connected with the universe, as appropriate, as fitting and worthwhile, as we are. It has traditionally been called our essential self that undergoes 'peak experiences'—mystical states and moments of artistic insight and creativity. At the precise body level, it is feeling good, comfortable, mobile, with full use of our energy.

2) Another level of self-experience is the awareness of our profound inadequacy; self-doubt, depression and despair. In the body, it is the level of the deepest hurt, distortions and scars.

3) A more typical level of experience is the self we show to the world. It is constructed to hide the self-hating feelings of the second tier, which themselves are born of forgetfulness of our essential selves. At this level, we pretend that we are okay. We hide our anger and hostility. We are polite and manipulative. In the body, it is the level of muscular imbalances used to shield us from experiencing the deeper discomforts.

The levels are reflected directly in the body and in what happens during the rolfing process. It proceeds by stripping the veil of muscular compensations to get to the real misery so that we can finally reach a level of physical existence where there is ease and maximum of energy without effort. The threefold division is not intended as a picture of the individual, but as a tool to unlock the doors of our experience. There are many alternative viewpoints to the modern view of the body as an incredible machine made up of many parts. The Chinese system of acupuncture meridians and the Indian system with its chakras are based on centuries of observations of regular channels of energy flow throughout the body. In the West, there is an alchemical model of the body based on the principle of harmony between microcosm and macrocosm. This aspect led me to study the Indian chakra system in detail.

The matrix for the phenomenon of the science of the body in rolfing is that which arises from the mesoderm, the first layer of cells that occurs in one of the earliest differentiations of the fertilized ovum. It includes fasciae, muscles, tendons, ligaments, cartilage and bones. The relationship among these elements forms the structure of the body. They determine how a person's body is and how he functions, and the relative positioning and functioning of the elements of the body—the nervous, circulatory, digestive, lymphatics and respiratory systems. Except for muscle tissues, all tissues are composed of the same basic stuff; protein fibres called collagen, elastic fibres, reticular fibres and a gelatinous medium. One type of tissue, say a tendon, differs from another, say, a bone, in the relative proportion of these components.

Fascia is the forgotten organ of the body. It starts just below the surface of the skin to form an inner covering for the entire body. At certain points where the body function demands it, it thickens to form bracelets to stabilize tendons at joints such as the ankles and wrists, or to create large sheets called aponeuroses. In the embryo, individual muscle fibres develop within the bed of fascia, such that a muscle bundle appears within a single fascial sheath as a group of fibres. Fascia is the primary vehicle for change in the body—for good as well as ill. A severe leg fracture, for example, will cause the fascia in that area to become like gristle. This knot inhibits the free movement of the neighbouring muscles. In other places, lack of use or poor posture will give rise to shortening of fascial planes and adhesions of those planes to muscles and bones, also limiting body movements and the flow of fluids through the body. In many places, such as the bottom of the buttocks, the fascial covering of one muscle group (the gluteal muscles) will become confused and enmeshed with the covering of another group (the hamstrings), resulting in restricted movement through the area. The fascial planes of fasciae indeed constitute, in the non-dissected condition, a sheet of connective tissue varying in thickness and density according to locality. Fascia is the unifying organ of the body. It is the matrix for the flow of metabolites, for circulation and even nervous flow. Shortening and thickening of fascia distort the whole body. By loosening and moving the fascia, you can radically alter the body.

The divisive kind of thinking that is a Western heritage from Descartes and his followers goes into our marrows. When we make distinctions between various parts of the body, just as it is helpful to make distinctions between emotions and physiological phenomena, errors occur when we think of those differences as pictures of reality. Because of the language we use, we believe there is a thing called emotion, another thing called the nervous system and a third thing called the tightness of muscle. The very stuff we are made of is highly elastic. The composition of all connective tissues is the same, and the bones are not dry bones. A person is like a plant whose fibrils, nearly indistinguishable from their nourishing soil, flow into the roots that flow into the trunk that differentiates into branches and leaves and flowers and beyond into the electrical field surrounding it. Spiritual consciousness, emotions and feelings, intelligence, physiochemical functioning, the musculoskeletal systems, are all only viewpoints from which we can examine the sole reality we are.

Personal History

At this moment, your physical form is the unique result of your history: parents, gestation and birth, home environments, accidents, illnesses, the ways you learned to use your body. Your flesh is your family album, your diary. The personal history starts from the womb, as the newborn is not at all the unconscious little thing we have assumed it to be. A baby has a wide-open consciousness that is not conditioned. We do have a womb-history. The way a baby keeps its legs in the womb, the environment of the mother, her diet, breathing, her ways of moving, her emotional reactions—all create the foetus's environment. So, much of the uniqueness of your present bodily form goes back to your very earliest days. You might have had a difficult delivery in which your skull was slightly distorted. Early intrauterine or birth experiences may have put tension in your body that has continued to grow throughout the years, so that your chest, which has always been tight, is tighter now than ever. Then comes the series of accidents and illnesses which leave a mark on the body, to make the person you are today. Adulthood—whether in mind, spirit, emotion or body—is something to be attained, something to be developed. Adulthood in the body has to do with balance and length: lengthening the germinal muscles of childhood; adjusting the front and the back, right and left, top and bottom. It involves allowing the body its full expansion outwards and upwards. But in older people, we frequently see a child's body with wrinkles and aged skin.

Rolfing is about the radical changeability of the ground of our being, the understanding of which leads to exciting new possibilities for life. The deepest block to this kind of knowledge is the world view that you developed so far back you have forgotten it was a viewpoint and came to confuse it with reality. Unfortunately, we have invested so much into that viewpoint that we are more interested in proving that it's right than in experiencing the possibility of a more satisfying existence. One of the essential programmes that direct our life is the notion that our body except for patchwork here and there, changes only in the direction of deterioration. Another typical picture of the body is that many of us think it is made of an outer muscular shell covering inner glandular and organic contents. We are myofascial beings all the way through. Psychological and spiritual depth has a physical component. A physical aspect of becoming an adult is learning to use the entire body, evoking movements at all depths of our physical being. Your body is also the history of your unique path of avoiding pain. It also has a component of the emotional history of your life, your relationships with parents and others and their relationships with each other.

Every single factor that has contributed to your physical being at this time can be changed, reversed and alleviated—once it is recognized simply as a variable in your personal history and not part of a permanent structure. The tragedy is to view your here-and-now body as the inevitable result of a history that has become concrete in the flesh. There is no concrete in the flesh; it's all moving, breathing, changing tissue, always ready with the least bit of support to rid itself of all the poisons from the past.

The Culture and the Body

Our personal history takes place within the larger context of culture. The social body constrains the way the physical body is perceived. As a result of this interaction, the body itself is a highly restricted medium of expression. The bodily ideals of a culture are creative—in their light, we shape our bodies either in imitation of them or in rebellion against them. We feel either right or wrong about those ideals. Appearance and function are confused. The images of male and female beauty projected in our culture do not provide the best functioning for the body. Most of us are confronted with a choice between having a body that looks good, as dictated by what is propagated by the media, or a body that functions well. Neither the *Vogue* model nor the *Playboy* bunny nor the mighty hero enjoys optimal breathing. Their pelvis is extremely tight, and at the very least, they are prime candidates for sexual, digestive and respiratory problems.

The back has become a forgotten, or oft-neglected part of the body in our culture. It has been allowed to atrophy, becoming an immovable wood-like thing 'somewhere back there'. In many people, the soft tissue of the upper back becomes overextended and is creeping around the sides toward the front. You can often feel long strands of hard atrophied tissue running the entire length of the back. When we breathe, there is little movement in those muscles. The back sometimes awakens us out of our forgetfulness by expressing its presence through chronic pain, which is rooted in our forgetfulness. The psoas muscle located on the side of the lumbar region, when tight and in proper working condition, contributes significantly to proper visceral functioning and full sexual responsiveness. Hiking, swimming, yoga, meditation, lovemaking or defecating can be done through trying and effort, or through the opening and lengthening the body. The activities done in the former way increase tension and restriction in the body and in a latter way, nourish the body, allowing more energy to flow through the system in the form of oxygen, blood, metabolites, nervous currents and sensory data. The plasticity of the body allows many different responses to pain. There are ways of breathing, sitting and walking, that can significantly ease pain, just as there are many ways to intensify it. You don't stop playing because you are old; you grow old because you stop playing.

One of the most significant body programmes communicated to us through our culture and made concrete in our families has to do with the predominant attitude towards ageing. A general pattern goes like this—the body grows, matures and ripens until its prime somewhere in the twenties, then gradually deteriorates until death. The mind programming can be even more drastic—that body is a pain, a burden or even a dangerous thing, specifically from some religious point of view, because it has the potential to be the medium of sin that could lead us to hell. The cultural norms for beauty are directly related to our attitude toward ageing. Both men and women are affected by the first signs of grey hair, wrinkles, flabbiness and baldness. What concerns most of us is not the deterioration in the internal functioning of our bodies, but the change in appearance, which is interpreted as deterioration. Pain is another factor, which becomes pronounced in old age because the imbalances of the earlier years have become more intense.

Gravity, Body and the Earth

The way your body is right now demonstrates the history of your relationship to the field of gravity. The body, like any other physical structure, is subject to the laws of physics. The human form is designed to be vertical, in the sense that its systems—circulatory, respiratory, digestive, sexual, lymphatic, nervous—function at their optimum when the body's structure is comfortably balanced in the gravitational field. It contrasts with the animals such as a cat or dog whose structures are designed to operate best with their spines in a horizontal plane with the earth. We are talking about the structure and not posture, and whether a person is sitting, standing or lying down, his structure can be such that it is comfortable or uncomfortable in the vertical plane. Gravity is a constant teacher, always giving clues about our being. If we do not learn to dance with it, it will slowly destroy us. But in learning to dance, we derive new energy that can change our lives.

Ida Rolf, the founder of the rolfing movement in the US, had a simple insight into the human body. Consider the body as an aggregate of large masses of head, shoulder, trunk, belly, pelvis, legs and feet travelling through the field of gravity. Realize that the relationship between those masses can be changed because of the plasticity of connective tissue. Notice that the body functions best at every level (physiologically, mechanically, emotionally, spiritually) when the centres of gravity of the segments are aligned with the plumb line of gravity, balanced front to back and side to side. As more energy is available to the body, external circumstances and internal crises have less power over one's life. The pure energy of the body feeds into the need for energy at the emotional and spiritual levels.

When we think of rolfing, we often envision pain. Many people who have neither witnessed nor experienced the process see it as a violent tearing apart of the body. The process is a slow, sensitive and gentle moving of tissue according to the rhythms of the flesh. The pain comes both from the depth of the work and from the conflict within the person. There is, in most of us, a tension between wanting to be free and the fear of being free. In the flesh, it manifests itself as a conflict between the tissue's moving with the hands of the rolfer, and its resisting them. The resistance and the tightening are the primary sources of pain. There is also an everyday experience of pain that is the reliving, and more fully experiencing, of a past repressed injury. A person will experience, for example, the exact kind of pain one experienced fifteen years before when one was hit in the head by a falling board. What many of us discover is that the primary source of pain in our lives is a failure to experience an event that is painful, whether it be an actual accident or the rolfer's fingers. In either instance, the pain lessens when we allow ourselves to experience the stimulus fully.

Who's Responsible for Your Body?

The central idea is that the body structure is a function of at least four variables—the events of personal history, cultural forms, the body's relation to the gravitational field and one's intentions. Consider your body and think about what you're doing with it now, in this period of your life. The form of your body will correspond to your chosen directions. For example, if you are a dancer, you will have long, slender waist, lifted chest and highly developed thighs. If you are a tennis player, a golfer or a guitar player, you might find your right shoulder developed much differently than your left. If you are a middle-aged officegoer who leads a sedentary life, you will probably find yourself sagging in the middle, with your flesh losing its former tone and your height a little shorter. A nurse might find chronic pain in her calves and the soles of her feet. A scholar may find herself hunched over with the head forward.

Meditate on this fundamental question—what have your goals in life been? We each have several goals, and they all have some effect on our body structure. There are deeper layers of our aims. Some of us may have the intention of living outside our body. Some may like to live in a world of fantasy, daydreams, books, philosophy or movies (sounds like Don is describing me!). That intention may form a body that is dense, insensitive and extremely armoured in the pelvis. If that purpose changes to living in the body and experiencing it, confronting the pain in it and learning to use it, then that intention will produce a different body structure. Your present body reflects your current lifestyle, which, in turn, reflects your purpose, life goals and values. It is not about mind over matter, which has the connotation that things are wrong in my life because my thinking is wrong since I have negative thoughts. If I clear up my thinking, my life and my body will also improve. It is an attitude that perceives the material world as unreal or, at least, insignificant. People with such philosophies shun forms of body therapies and even psychotherapies because they believe that indulgence in such therapies perpetuates the illusion that the physical body and emotions are real when, in fact, they are creations of the mind.

On the other hand, the intention is meant to bridge the gap between mind and matter. Intentions are always embodied; they are always a unity of mental attitude and physical activity. The 'intention' to get well, for instance, includes not only the handling of negative thoughts but also the implementation of those means one considers necessary to renew the flesh, including changes in diet or exercise. For example, both negative and positive thoughts have their tangible manifestations. Thought and body patterns are not two separate interacting things but two aspects of a single pattern of behaviour. If you think of yourself as a victim, you engender feelings of anger, hostility, resentment and uptightness. It is the 'it's their fault' attitude—parents, wife, the government, even world history'.

The body is the fundamental matrix within which we experience the world. By our experience, we participate with others in creating the larger structures of the world: social, economic, political, artistic. When the structure of my body changes, my experience changes, thus changing my relationship to the other structures. Between the body and the body politic lies the world of experience. My immediate experience (so omnipresent that it usually goes unnoticed) is of my body: hot and cold, hard and soft, right and left, balance and imbalance, pleasurable and painful, satisfying or disturbing, fearful or peaceful. By those initial experiences, I assess my world. As I do so, I act, rejecting certain forms of activity and supporting others.

The Body and the Body Politic

Practical and valuable political action has, at the minimum level, some fundamental requirements—it must proceed from knowledge and, it must proceed. Both are functions of the body structure. The precise understanding of what kind of political structures are of service to the human community is rooted in the fundamental experience each of us has within the society. The microcosmic body is a political system. Your body is a political system that works or doesn't work, or works relatively well or poorly. We have an immediate experience of how various parts interact to produce a healthy or sickly organism. And by developing the kinds of consciousness suggested here, you can gain direct experience of the mechanisms of increased or decreased functioning within the whole, as well as what constitutes optimum operation. Clearheaded knowledge of what 'ought to be' is not enough. Such knowledge must be able to proceed into the world of effective actions. That is, for many of us, a major problem. Our energies are locked up inside our bodies. We are in such conflict that we are unable to participate with other like-minded people in constructing a more harmonious society. The blocks to our energy can be found in the tight pectoral muscles, the atrophied extensors of the back, chronically contracted neck muscles or short psoas.

Talking of boundaries, where does your body end and mine begin? Where does the air which enters your lung end and you begin? Are you different from the food and the waste products in your system? What are the boundaries between you, your smells and those who smell you? Although the skin is a convenient boundary for ordinary discourse and action, is it any more real than the border constructed by a surveyor around your plot of land?

The commonsense notion of the body is that of a thing in space and time. The notion is an instant of the traditional tendency to split mind and matter. To conceive of the body as an energy system is to conceive of it as interrelated with other systems. The interaction of body, atmosphere and food; the interaction of the central nervous system with sound, colour, light and gestalt; the interactions of memory, appetite and instinct with the environment. The spiritual is experienced when all the boundaries are experienced as arbitrary. Some of the boundaries are obviously human constructions—property lines, national or state borders, the delineation between physics and chemistry. Some people, however, are seduced into thinking of these boundaries as natural or even divine. The boundaries we are concerned with here are the ones within the flesh. The walls we have constructed to protect ourselves from the dangers outside our skin; the compensatory hardening in muscle groups to protect ourselves from feeling the pain of imbalance; the hardening of fascia that obscures the perceptual centres by setting up boundaries between the sensory receptors and the stimuli.

The spiritual refers to the level which makes sense out of all the other levels. When all the boundaries used to shape our world are experienced as arbitrary, we can experience the total system of interrelationships itself, the only unity that is not arbitrary. There are many parodies at this level; a distraction from 'true' spirituality by notions that suggest spirituality means withdrawing from the illusory world of matter, time and history. In this view, the goal of being spiritual is attaining a bliss that can never be had in the hurly-burly world of economics, sex and hunger. In this view, several boundaries are left still standing—the spiritual and the unspiritual, matter and spirit, and an authentic world of eternal bliss and the illusion of hungry people in Africa.

The practice of centring differentiates spiritual consciousness from sheer psychosis. The breaking down of boundaries that characterize spiritual disciplines, as well as many emotional and body disciplines, is done in the context of maintaining an awareness of one's being. For example, in the midst of an utterly chaotic flood of images and fantasies, you are taught to sit quietly and breathe. Thus, the ability to centre is a function of the body structure. Breathing exercises, hatha yoga, sophisticated postures and meditation, are all means to prepare the body to be centred during the dissolution of its ego-world. A central goal of rolfing is to awaken the physiological centre of the body, including the structures deep in the belly and the pelvis.

The body is of no ultimate importance. What is, is the love among us all. There are lifelong cripples and people with twisted bodies who are filled with love and whose lives have served humanity. There are people with balanced, flexible and energetic bodies who are selfish and cruel.

With so much onslaught on my laziness and lack of body consciousness, I decided to pay more attention to my body. The first step was to become more fit and to know what the principles of cure are in the event of a disease or illness. I have been using allopathy medicines for a long time, and I will continue to do so unless I find dramatic cures in Ayurveda or alternative systems. I do have a fascination to study Ayurveda, which I propose to fulfil sometime in the future.

Health, Fitness and Healing

As I have said earlier, my consciousness about bodily health was dismally low. I always lived in my mind and concentrated on developing my thoughts and ideas, but my body was not there. It was taken for granted. I started becoming health conscious around the age of fifty, which was unfortunately ironic, considering that as a member of the police department, I should have been more concerned with fitness! I never did regular exercises before I became diabetic and my blood-pressure levels were hovering around hypertension. Soon after beginning my work with CISF, I developed a sore throat that wouldn't go away with conventional medication. The doctor suggested a lab test and found that the blood sugar was high. He prescribed medicines and thus began my life as a person with diabetes. First, I was in denial; it simply couldn't be diabetes, because I had always been thin. It was this feeling that I was healthy enough that kept me away from exercises. I consulted several doctors, took different tests in different labs, bought self-check machines, which I kept checking at various times of the day and rejoiced at slight variations in readings to justify to myself that it was not diabetes. I took some time to accept it and start doing the right things to keep it under control. Today, the average glucose levels in the blood are considered normal, but there is a catch. The experts keep revising the standards.

The first impediment to health is a lack of consciousness. I have written a lot of details to contribute to such awareness in the following sections. I have used many abbreviations and technical terms without elaborating them too much because if I start explaining them, it would be a medical treatise by itself and that is not the intention of this book. The purpose would have been served if the reader's curiosity is aroused and he gets interested to know more by himself.

The time has come for each of us to be proactive about our healthcare. It should no longer be about giving the reigns of your health to the doctor; going to him when you fall sick, undergo certain tests and swallow the pill he gives, all without a question. I found that many doctors don't care to explain the cause of the illness and what are the effects or side effects of the treatment proposed. More importantly, we don't ask questions. That's because we don't have the knowledge or consciousness to ask the right questions. Above all, neither the doctor nor we have the time to go into specifics, especially in India where the population density is high, and there may be a ratio of one doctor for thousands of patients. But all that must change; we need to take charge of our health, in addition to having health insurance and healthcare providers.

Having said that though, I have to say that health consciousness has improved considerably in the last ten years among the general population. So much is being written about health that more and more people have come to follow health regimen at a comparatively young age. I found that personal awareness depended much on that of the society as a whole. Back in the eighties and nineties, the awareness was simply not there. For instance, with the help of the new knowledge I have gained, I can say with certainty that my habit of consuming soft drinks was solely responsible for my diabetes. I had long journeys to perform by road, in hot summers, in the line of duty and Coke and Fanta came in handy during those trips. Added to that, in the meetings, big bottles of different types of cola were kept in front of you, just as mineral water bottles are kept nowadays. Only recently, in the last decade or so, people were shocked to learn how much sugar the aerated drinks contained. But then it was too late for me. I was a confirmed diabetic, and once I accepted this, it became easier to do what's needed.

So, I embarked upon a diet-exercise-medication regime. I stopped adding sugar in my coffee and tea, completely stopped the cold drinks and drastically reduced my consumption of sweets. I hired a physical trainer to come home and teach me weight training. The circuit-training he taught fifteen years ago is still followed strictly. I used to go for long walks in the Theosophical Society,

Adyar, which was right across the road from my house. Luckily, I was flexible enough to run and so mixed my walks with short bursts of intensive running. After going to the US, I had regular access to the gym and added cardio and weight training routines to walks. Through the libraries, I also had access to books on health and the latest information on health-related research. And now, the internet is exploding with information about health and fitness. In fact, now the amount of information is enough to make you feel overwhelmed. The plethora of dos and don'ts and rights and wrongs is enough to consume your whole day if you tried to follow even a few of them! I also found many of the research findings were motivated to promote certain products and one needs to be wary of such traps. I realized that I had to balance health with life because after all, good health is necessary to live a good life.

Dr Krishnapriyan, my healthcare professional at that time, gave me a new way of looking at health. Once, while carrying out a regular checkup, she mentioned 'there is money' in the bodily organs. What she meant made excellent sense. If you don't pay attention to these organs, then that will lead to a lot of expenditure later in repairing them or doing without them. What you earn and accumulate, you spend on health in later years. I had to filter my knowledge and stick to only what was relevant to my health. Accordingly, I formulated certain principles for myself which I will be sharing in the following paragraphs.

The books which appealed to me are Dr Comite's *Keep It Up: The Power of Precision Medicine to Conquer Low T and Revitalize Your Life* and Dr David B Agus' *The End of Illness* and *The Lucky Years*. *The Protean Body* by Don Johnson really helped me in getting a perspective on the human body. I was conditioned to think that the body is not me and I should care more for the self. In my studies of Hinduism mention is made as to how the body is the temple of God. Ayurveda is a Vedic medical science entirely devoted to holistic health. But I hardly heard about these medicines in my day-to-day life.

Otherwise, I thought a whole lot of emphasis was given to working on your mind; the concepts of higher levels of being, levels of consciousness, etc. Then slowly I began to pay close attention to my body; to its well-being and what it's trying to tell me when I was happy or sad, in pain or agony. I started paying close attention to the four aspects of fitness—diet, exercise, medication, and stretching and relaxation. I realized the importance of drinking enough water and to moderate on three whites—refined salt, sugar and rice, the need to balance protein, fat and carbohydrates, and the requirements of replenishing the body with supplements for vitamins and minerals. When it came to exercise I balanced between walking, jogging, weight training and cardio workouts. Most importantly, there is a need to measure everything and keep a record; what's not measured can't be controlled and measuring includes the entire gamut—weight, body-mass index (BMI), blood pressure, blood sugar, cholesterol, daily exercise details and much more. There are many apps these days which help you do this.

There is a battle within the body—between muscle and fat; muscles store energy from protein as glycogen, cells store energy as mitochondria. Excess sugar and carbohydrates are stored as fat and as it increases, the muscle vanishes. Proteins help build muscles and sugar, fat. Watch out for sugar in liquids, as this form is quick to enter the blood stream and cause damage. Reduce your calorie intake and keep a watch on the base metabolic rate (BMR). Avoid fried items and binge eating. The requirement of protein is 1 gm of protein per pound of body weight per day, half-an-hour before workout, for optimum results. In addition to multivitamins, consider flaxseed oil for Omega-3 fatty acids for heart health and green tea for antioxidants.

As for exercises, an aggregate of 7.5 hours per week is recommended by experts. It should include weights and cardio workouts. Interval or burst training is most effective as a cardio workout. The most important thing is pushing yourself to the limit—the maximum heart rate to aim at is calculated by the formula: 220 minus your age. We should remember that in the first fifteen minutes of a workout, the body uses glycogen stored in the muscle and then the muscle starts burning fat for energy. The index of health and success is good sleep, how you look and how you feel. For occasional help use a melatonin supplement for sleep and not sleeping pill.

Why exercise?

The benefits of exercising appear to be numerous; strengthening of the cardiovascular system, regulating fuel, reducing obesity, elevating the stress threshold, mood enhancement, boosting the immune system, fortifying bones, heightening motivation, fostering neuroplasticity and unleashing the Human Growth Hormone (HGH), among others. Reduce weight, strengthen bones and muscles, push the heart rate to its maximum limit with aerobics, muscle to the limit with weights and nerves to the limit by stretching. Walk for light, jog for moderate and sprint for high intensity. In other words, run for fitness, weights for strength, squat for growth and do 'surya namaskar' for overall well-being and energy. Even if you do regular exercise, don't sit in one spot for more than an hour. Get up between bouts of work and move around for five minutes at least.

The traditional way of thinking about health would be regarding the body and mind. In the last decade, the health of a third factor has come into much sharper focus—the brain. It is exceptional in many ways. It consumes 20-30 per cent of the glucose the body needs and has a body-brain barrier, which doesn't permit everything in the blood stream to enter except glucose.

Research is showing that many illnesses are connected to the way our brains are wired. To have better health, we need to have better brain health and exercises were found to promote exactly this. Life, according to new thinking, is body, mind and brain. Modern life has changed and given us a modern mind, and the body has also adapted to some extent, but the brain has not, because those changes are slow to come. While evolution gave the frontal cortex, it has not taken away the old wiring, which is still present. For growth, the body and the mind need stress up to a point. When stress arises a human has two choices; fight or flight. To combat it, do either or both. Seen in terms of a workout, weight training is a 'fight' response and running or cardio is 'flight'! By exercising, we satisfy both the reactions of the brain and aid in relaxing the mind.

Our aim should be to increase growth hormones, the neurogenesis and neuroplasticity of the brain. The intent behind any form of exercise is to build and condition the brain in addition to the body. There is a biological relationship between the three. Exercise helps at three levels—it improves the mindset by increasing alertness and attention, prepares nerves to bind and aids in the development of new cells. The neurotransmitters serotonin, norepinephrine and dopamine increase with exercise. Its role in improving the Brain Derived Neurotropic Factor (BDNF)—which helps in learning, connecting thought, emotion and movement—is significant. Exercise balances the neurotransmitters and other chemicals in the brain. It spawns neurons and stimulation of environmental enrichment help those cells and neurons survive. More stress means you need to increase the duration of the exercise to keep the brain running smoothly. Skill acquisition and aerobics combined improve executive function. While aerobics create new blood vessels that pipe in growth factors and spawn new cells. A complex activity puts all that material to use by strengthening and expanding networks. For example, playing the piano is shown to improve one's mathematical skills.

Dr Comite's Precision Medicine

Precision medicine appears to be the future of Western medicine and the next stage of evolution in healthcare. Dr Comite's book *Keep It Up* has focused on men's health, though many issues can be related to women too. I had a consultation with Dr Comite, who took elaborate tests and helped me put together my health and medication regime in a more focused way. The concepts of Dr Comite are as follows.

Ageing is fiercely individual, yet inevitably universal. Medicine should be personalized and integrated. Health should be based on the person who is unique, and not on averages or the 'evidence-based medicine'. There is no such thing as normal or average, and the bell-shaped curve which shows where you fall. Average about the mean is likely not normal for you. Good health is more than a series of numbers. You need to focus on extending your *health span* to keep up with your extended *life span*. Healthy longevity means being vibrant, active, happy and pain-free well into your nineties.

You can also get clued in to the state of your body. Gather details of your habits, your health, your family's medical history and combine this with the numbers from your lab data. Observation and tracking changes over time are the key. The only way to do this is to take a holistic view of your health, and monitoring metabolism and hormones is a critical part of that approach. Changes in the body functions occur very slowly over the years. For a long time, the body keeps adapting. You're usually not aware of the shift in health until it all adds up and becomes a visible symptom or disease. You don't pay attention because you take it for granted that your body will continue to do its job. The general model has been to try to repair the body's malfunctioning systems and parts with medicine, which commonly shuts down any remaining functionality, creating a lifelong dependency on pharmaceuticals.

Invert the old model of intervention after breakdown, and identify risk before the doctor is forced to take heroic and immediate action, to prevent the truck that nobody saw coming, from ploughing you down in the form of a heart attack, diabetes, cancer or kidney disease. That metaphorical truck didn't just appear out of nowhere. It started its journey towards you, hundreds of miles away. That accident waiting to happen was possibly laced into your DNA, brought about by lifestyle. Human is a complex being, the result of the somewhat random combination of many factors. That complexity goes all the way down to the molecular instructions for the expression of your genes, your DNA. There is a physiological explanation for how you're feeling, and you can do something about it. You can change how you look and feel by taking ownership of your health.

Medical history includes baseline family history and lifestyle. All of us can alter the expression of our DNA and genes and neutralize the disease. Genetics tells you what genes you have. Epigenetics tells you how your genes are turned on or off by how you live. But it may be truly the intangible that makes the biggest difference of all—it may be optimism, faith, a sense of purpose, a fight in the personality or daily decisions of what to consume and how to live.

The body's functioning depends upon the programming within the double helix structure of DNA. The RNA—the mirror-image messenger triggered by DNA—produces specific proteins, hormones, neurotransmitters and performs other tasks given to it. In essence, the DNA and protein production in conjunction with the switches that modify them, are likely responsible for the way you operate and your functional quality, such as whether or not you will have arthritis or a heart attack. In effect, we all carry a regulation system within the very DNA that decides how to behave and is highly influenced by our decisions. Genetics offer clues, but it's up to you to connect the dots and make choices. Lifestyle choices directly affect the way the genes express themselves. We can choose not to become victims of our genes and intrinsic ageing held hostage to switches that might pay attention if only you adjust what you eat or optimize your protein intake. We can pull one over Mother Nature by modifying our behaviour. Nature plus nurture, along with other events of life and the choices made shape who you are and what you do. Genetics, epigenetics, your life experience, your lab data—all of it makes a diffcrence.

Ageing in a male is the slowing down of male hormones, primarily testosterone (T), the main sex hormone and the 'rocket fuel' that powers men's health, energy, sexuality and state of mind.

In women, this manifests itself as menopause. Andropause for men begins eventually when the testosterone levels remain low even if the brain is producing the hormones. High levels of the luteinizing hormone (LH) and gonadotropin-releasing hormone (GnRH), and low testosterone constitute andropause. These two processes are the winding down of operations which started in puberty. By bolstering the body's hormonal balance, we can defeat this design of nature. It's presumed that by increasing hormone levels—except cortisol and insulin in which case it is the lower the better—you are going to have better functionality. We don't have to sit back and accept Nature's plan; we don't have to give up or give in. We can intervene. You can take advantage of new insights and technologies to evaluate your state of health and take charge of rest of your life to prevent the diseases that put the face on what we see as ageing. Clinical studies are just beginning to show correlations between the drop in testosterone levels and the onset of age-related problems like heart disease, cancer, diabetes, kidney disease and more. Caught early enough, many of these conditions can be reversed through hormone and metabolic interventions combined with lifestyle changes, supplements and medications when clinically indicated. The aim is to complement lifestyle changes with a right blend of supplements and cutting-edge interventions.

One key area in maintaining health is the critical role of hormones, especially testosterone in men. Messengers that allow the various systems to work synergistically to carry out body processes in an ideal setting. Communications throughout the body happen through the interaction of hormones and proteins; these agents determine much of how we think and feel. Hormones increase and decrease throughout life and even over an hour. Paired with other bio-markers, they offer insights into the disorders of ageing such as heart attacks, strokes, diabetes and osteoporosis. We may stop growing upwards, but the body and mind keep evolving and hormones shape these changes. There's a relationship between the decline in hormones of various types and diseases such as diabetes, heart disease, reduced bone density, depression, etc. Hormones such as testosterone, thyroid, insulin, cortisol, or any number of others affect your drive, energy, attitude and emotion. They influence every system in your body, regulating how you metabolize food, how your arteries expand to circulate blood, how your brain functions, how you focus; whether you want to have sex, eat, sleep or exercise. As hormones diminish along with signals from the brain to produce them, you begin to slow down. As hormone levels decline, the hypothalamus releases the gonadotropin-releasing hormone (GnRH) and the pituitary releases luteinizing hormone (LH) urging the testes to produce more testosterone. However, many a time the brain is desensitized to lower testosterone levels and fails to act, like a team coach not paying attention when the team is failing, leading to all three hormones—testosterone, the luteinizing hormone and gonadotropin-releasing hormone—all fall below desired levels.

Testosterone is not all about sex. Its levels directly impact a man's metabolism, muscles, and major organs, and is also associated with fatigue, depression, reduced muscle mass and strength and osteoporosis. As one loses testosterone, it becomes harder to lose fat, especially around the midsection. One of the most noticeable signs of low testosterone is the loss of morning erections. The dehydroepiandrosterone hormone (DHEA), responsible for testosterone synthesis, also reduces with age. A man passes from a less androgenic state to one that includes more estrogen. Estrogen undermines male sexual function because estrogen competes with testosterone at the receptor binding sites. There is also an increase in the sex-hormone-binding globulin (SHBG) secreted by the liver. It binds to the testosterone, and makes it difficult for it to target its receptor sites to perform its function. As fat increases, the enzyme, aromatase, is produced by fat which in turn converts testosterone into estradiol (E2), which is a type of estrogen. An overweight individual has elevated levels of aromatase.

An elevation of dihydrotestosterone (DHT), a breakdown product of testosterone, means too much of the hormone is being broken down. The high levels of DHT also raise prostate-specific antigens (PSA) levels indicating a prostate disorder.

The therapy for reduced testosterone levels is also not without risks such as breast tingling, breast enlargement, testicular shrinkage, a decrease in HDL cholesterol, increased red blood cell count and reduced sperm count. Correctly balanced, the benefits of treatment well outweigh the risks. Testosterone injections are most efficient, and there is no danger of transference to others via skin contact. For men who are yet to go through andropause, human chorionic gonadotropin (hCG) is used to stimulate testes to produce testosterone. The breakdown products of the hormone, estradiol and DHT, also needs to be managed with medication.

Poor food choices, overeating and inadequate physical activity along with hormone levels and genetic makeup conspire to increase the odds of poor sugar metabolism. When insulin is present in the blood, you don't burn fat; you are in fat-storing mode. For carbohydrate metabolism, integrate information about fasting blood sugar, insulin, haemoglobin A1C, with facts about your diet, exercise, genetics and hormones, urine analysis and lipids. Elevated triglycerides have nothing or little to do with the fat or cholesterol you consume and more to do with your sugar intake and your activity levels.

The cardiac C-reactive protein (CRP) and homocysteine are critical, and common denominators to disease. Inflammation is the common denominator that links many factors such as cholesterol, diabetes, dietary issues, and more. Inflammation signifies damage, injury or change in the body. Our bodies are producing free radicals continuously, whether it's from eating or working out, activities that are critical to existence. These free radicals ping around our system, damaging our DNA and causing inflammation. At a cellular level, inflammation may prevent you from combating the disease. High levels of cortisol, the stress hormone secreted by adrenal glands, lead to increased storage of body fat in the abdominal region. This visceral fat surrounding vital organs secretes a hormone-like chemical, cytokine, which causes an inflammatory response. It can also result in metabolic syndrome, a cluster of symptoms including blood pressure, sugar, etc.

The changes you need to make to position yourself in that sweet spot is not the gym or the kitchen, but the bed; sleep well. The levels of cortisol play a significant role in determining the quality and quantity of sleep. Since all systems are interconnected, if you can't sleep well and your stress levels are high, the efforts you make by eating well, exercising regularly and taking nutritional supplements may not yield maximum results. The combination of quality sleep and lower stress levels will help you to be healthier. The natural rhythm of sleep and wakefulness is determined by the cycle of hormones that are released by the brain. Increased or high cortisol, whether from sleep deprivation or stress, is a major factor in carbohydrate metabolism leading to the development of insulin resistance and diabetes. Poor sleep and cortisol overload are a recipe for packing on the pounds, not just from overeating but also because you will begin to store fat around the middle. Insulin-like growth factor (IGF-1) and the human growth hormone (HGH), which is secreted during sleep will be unable to bind to receptors if insulin levels are high. The activation of genes in the liver related to carbohydrate metabolism and the growth hormone may be suppressed with inadequate sleep. Sleep deprivation interrupts production of the thyroid-stimulating hormone (TSH), reducing the level needed for its proper functioning. Hormones such as progesterone and neurotransmitters such as dopamine, tryptophan and serotonin all play a vital role in brain function, sleep and mood. One week of sleep deprivation results in men's testosterone levels going down by 10-15 per cent, thus impacting bone strength, heart, energy, libido, muscle mass, vitality and sense of well-being. Because of inflammation, the autonomic nervous system (ANS), the sympathetic nervous system and the enteric nervous systems, all get affected.

To build a high-performance body, food and nutrition are vital. Food is your fuel. If you don't properly give your body the right kind of nutrients, you won't feel healthy and energetic, lose weight or build muscle. Type-2 diabetes occurs over time at the cellular level. Blood sugar spikes if you eat successive carbohydrate-heavy meals, raising insulin levels continually higher, and thus causing insulin resistance. Contrary to popular belief, insulin resistance is a process, and it doesn't happen suddenly. The glycemic index (GI) indicates how quickly the food raises your blood sugar. Glycemic load (GL) shows the level of insulin released to digest the food. In most cases, the higher the index, the higher will be the load, which will drive up the insulin. Intelligent eating means choosing foods that keep you feeling full and satisfied. That's why a high-protein diet is so effective at helping people lose weight. Protein tells the body not to store energy as fat but to burn fat stores it already has. Protein takes longer to digest, lowers the glycemic load and provides raw material to repair tissue damage in addition to muscle building. However, the downside is that excess protein is stored as fat, thus defeating the purpose. It is believed that the body can't process more than 35 gm in one sitting, and consuming 1.2 gm to 1.4 gm per kilogram weight is ideal. Protein metabolism is hard on kidneys, so it is important to hydrate adequately. It's advised not to eat carbohydrates in the night, which drives up insulin levels and prevents IGF-1 from binding to the receptor sites. Similarly, fruit juices are to be avoided but combining protein with fruit is good. Vegetable juices, however, are permissible.

As for the workout, doing cardiovascular in the morning before breakfast is good. Ramping up the intensity of exercise and not necessarily the volume, is advised. Going short and intense, not long and slow, is advised for a more productive workout. Performance will increase with the amount of interval training done. Most importantly, the resting heart rate will decrease.

Eating nutritious food and taking food supplements is

another vital suggestion. Recommendations are, however, made based on personal health metrics, the aim being to lower the systemic inflammation. Supplements for reducing oxidative stress and boosting immunity: L-Arginine supplements paired with L-Citrulline combat oxidative stress which shortens the telomeres. B-Complex vitamins are for controlling inflammation and keeping down homocysteine levels, high levels of which indicate damage to arteries. Vitamins C and E remove free radicals from cells and improve the immune system. Omega-3 fatty acids help metabolic and hormonal optimization. Another way to balance inflammation is to balance Omega-3 and 6. Vitamin D is for bone maintenance and metabolic function. Dark chocolate (75 per cent and above) provides antioxidants, blood thinner for protection from heart disease, slowing the ageing process and some cancers. Green tea extract, melatonin, resveratrol and selenium help to produce sperm and prevent prostate cancer.

Supplements for metabolic and hormonal optimization, by which your body turns chemical energy into mechanical energy, are also necessary, and hormones drive this process. These supplements may assist both functions for optimal results. CLA or conjugated linoleic acid for weight loss, coronary artery risks, vitamin D, which in addition to optimizing metabolic, hormonal optimization, and immunity boosting, it also helps in increasing insulin sensitivity, bones, and regulate calcium and phosphorus, probiotics help digestive enzymes to improve nutrient absorption, Supplements for mental, physical and sexual performance include L-arginine for oxidative stress and immunity, relaxing blood vessels and vasodilation helps in erectile function, improves libido, for a great workout, L-citrulline in combination replenishes L-arginine, rids the body of lactic acid, L-ornithine to keep up replacing arginine in the night while sleeping, B-complex vitamins and coenzyme Q10 (CoQ10) which helps in mitochondrial functioning, Curcumin is a potent anti-inflammatory agent found in turmeric, DHEA for testosterone and balancing Omega-3 and 6 to combat inflammation, protein powders and multivitamins to optimize performance.

Dr Agus

Dr Agus believes that the secret to reversing aging organs is lying asleep inside each of us. In his landmark books, *End of Illness* and *The Lucky Years*, he explains various concepts of health and disease in a new way. He refers to the times as 'lucky years', given the cutting-edge technological advancements being made in the field, which give the sense that humanity is on the cusp of a health revolution. He is referring to the stem cells, the mother all cells, with the potential to become any cell in the body, from those that allow your heart to beat to brain cells that make you smart, and have the power to renew themselves or multiply. Human trials are said to be underway for plasma transfusions. Blood transfusions contain only red blood cells but not plasma. If they are successful, then transfusion of young blood plasma in older people will then become possible to combat many diseases such as dementia or cancer.

Just as in technology, we have reached an inflection point in healthcare, and we are expected to adapt to the shift and use those emerging technologies which are wildly successful; if we don't, we fail. We need to abide by three things—believe that ageing is optional, think about our future and act on it today. We, as a society, stand at a historic crossroads. Only those who learn how to think, act and behave in certain ways will reap the benefits of the tremendous opportunities afforded to us through the power of these medical revolutions. We need to bring technology into the food and drug realms. Healthcare is not a right; it's a responsibility. And the first step to take for the sake of our health and that of the society requires an important tool in understanding our context.

The difference between you throwing a lit match into a dewy wet forest or a parched, dry bush is the same as in healthcare. In one case it gets extinguished, and in the other, it becomes a moving fire. Similarly, we need to understand our DNA and genetic makeup to make lifestyle changes accordingly. Not all people who smoke get lung cancer and not all who drink alcohol spoil their livers. While this is certainly not meant to encourage either, it is a yardstick that speaks to the importance of an individual's DNA, and reiterates the significance of context. In my case, I probably had a framework in the form of genes prone to diabetes, which was provided by the matchstick of an overdose of soft drinks. *Science* published a paper in 2015 calling attention to the fact that healthy skin taken from normal people's eyelids—a common site vulnerable for cancer-causing ultraviolet (UV) exposure from the Sun—is already full of potential drivers or mutations for cancer. So, while gene alterations that point to the disease are already there, these people didn't have cancer, probably because the context wasn't right despite these mutations. Ultraviolet radiation causes so many mutations that we would all have skin cancer if there were an absolute and linear path between these mutations and the development of skin cancer.

How do we know what our context is? So far, we had little information in this matter, which served vested interests of all sorts. Pharmaceutical companies sold their drugs based on generalized principles such as smoking causes lung cancer, tobacco causes mouth cancer, etc., but now it's possible to know our contexts and adjust our lifestyles accordingly. Actor Angelina Jolie tested and found out her propensity to develop breast cancer, which was prevalent in her family, and had a mastectomy done. The concept of context cuts in multiple ways; your body won't be the same five, ten or twenty years from now. Even during the day, the body is different in the morning, noon or night. Accordingly, the DNA behaviour changes. That explains how lifestyle habits are important. We go by one-size-fits-all health recommendations that don't necessarily consider our context. Hence, knowledge about our specific needs is essential. In olden days money mattered, and only those who could afford could have expensive surgeries and therapies. Dr Agus now believes that the game has changed now. Money is not the differentiator; the treatments are the privilege of the prepared and the knowledgeable.

However, it is also important to know that diseases can't be predicted by genes alone, because our genes don't work in a vacuum. Our diet, behaviour, stress, attitude, medicines we consume and the environment are some of the factors which affect our genes. The condition is likely to be the result of an elaborate network of forces interacting within the complex human body. Ultimately, individual genes get on or off, triggering pathways whose end points are an illness. 'The nature vs nurture debate has been clarified by the science of epigenetics—the science of controlling genes through environmental forces such as diet and exercise.' Most of the conditions commonly diagnosed today are those that result from the intricate relationship between genes and the body's contextualized environment. The DNA differences do not cause the disease, but they are markers of the relative risk of the disease. That brings us to the question of genome editing, possible through a tool called the Clustered Regularly Interspaced Short Palindromic Repeats (CRISPR). But it raises questions—while it can be used to cure diseases inherited from birth or acquired we don't know what other things get affected by this editing. It is about a decade since our genome has been read. We may as well exercise caution before we begin to rewrite it.

Another interesting finding Dr Agus talks about is understanding the code to the TGF-beta (transforming growth factor beta) pathway, that's essentially a conversation between molecules through which cells signal one another to stop multiplying, among other actions. The TGF-beta, a protein secreted by the cells, has many functions apart from the proliferation part. It plays a role in cancer cell multiplication, immunity and a spectrum of illnesses, from something that is relatively mild, like asthma and diabetes, to the more severe, such as the heart disease, Parkinson's, multiple sclerosis and AIDS. Metastasis is another process by which cancer cells proliferate by leaving the mother cell and invading other cells. The whole point of chemotherapy and radiation after surgery is mostly to avoid or treat metastasis. As said earlier, the cures for many of our maladies are already inside us, and stem cells are part of such cures. Female longevity, compared to men, is due to the abundance of these cells, signalled by estrogen. Another find, reported by Dr Agus, is about the length of the telomeres, a structure that is present at the end of every chromosome. So far it was believed that shortening telomeres indicated reduced life. Now they say that longer they are, the higher the risk of lung cancer!

Near-infrared spectroscopy (NIR) have been around for a while. They help detect the profile of chemicals and other components in substance. For instance, it will compare the image of a pill with the cloud database and identify the material as 'ibuprofen, brand Advil'. It not only eliminates fake drugs but also brings peace of mind by preventing a mix-up of medicines. It can look at a plate of food and tell you how much carb or protein or fats it contains. It could analyse urine and tell you how much you're dehydrated. The possibilities are endless. Proteomics is the study of body proteins and helps to explore how proteins shape the body's language and ultimately form the language of health. A recently discovered inexpensive test called VirScan contributes to identifying all the viruses the body had been exposed to all through one's life. It may sound like a cliché, but holding on to optimism about the world and even the future of medicine is the key to health. Optimism will help you choose how you age, but to fully enjoy the current advancements in medicine depends much on how we learn to use technology that will contribute to control our health. It also helps in aggregating our health data, which will go to improve the big data of the society, paving the way for more research and better cure. Unless we, as individuals help change the system, we won't see a vast improvement in our own system. Reading and lecturing provide knowledge, but they often lack valuable context to make those lessons come to life and be truly useful. That is why defining your meaning in your own context will help you reap the benefits of modern technology and live better.

Dr Agus' take on precision medicine is the same as that of Dr Comite's—it will be the future of medicine. The difference between the ancient science of Ayurveda and the early theories of Hippocrates—the father of modern medicine—and precision medicine is that the latter has a molecular standpoint. It focuses chiefly on DNA, single-nucleotide polymorphism (SNPs) and environmental factors that influence an individual's biology and risk for the disease. SNPs are variations in DNA sequences that are thought to provide the genetic markers for our response to illness and drugs. For example, a change in a gene may indicate a predisposition for high cholesterol.

The mitochondria, the energy source for the cells, were once free-living bacteria in the environment that somehow ended up getting incorporated into physiology to power life. It turns out that we owe our life and health to more microbes than we ever imagined before—they outnumber our cells by a factor of ten and include more than eight million genes, which is three hundred times the number of genes we contain in our DNA. You find microbes everywhere—they cloak our mouth, nose, ears, intestines, genitalia and skin. New technologies are emerging to identify about 35,000 species of bacteria in our body. Most of these species make our guts their home and support our health. Even our DNA has codes of viral origin. Throughout our evolution viruses have inserted themselves into the human genome. The takeaway is that we are an intricate web of microbial components that have a say in our lifelong biology, in addition to that of human cells.

The body is an incredible self-regulating machine. Our goal should not only maximize our lifespans but also delay the onset of chronic diseases, so we can make the last years or decades of life as fulfilling as possible. Dr Agus gives three pieces of advice—record your body features, measure yourselves and automate your life. The biggest hurdle, according to him, is a lack of honesty on our part to accept and record the facts truthfully, without deceiving ourselves that everything is okay with us. It's possible that there is a huge gap between how much sugar people think they consume and the reality.

The body loves rhythm, pattern and predictability to maintain homeostasis. So, maintaining regular habits places less stress on the body. The flow of genetic information in a cell is from DNA through RNA to protein. Therefore, studying the RNA of a species can show which genes are turned on or off. In a particular study, researchers identified three genetic pathways that seemed to be involved in these gene expression changes—the TCP-1 ring complex chaperonin, which helps proteins fold; the mitochondrial electron transport chain complexes (mETC), which relate to the energy cycle of a cell; and a collection of genes in charge of the body's circadian rhythm. These trials showed how time-restricted feeding helped to keep in check the tendency to obesity and other cardiovascular diseases.

Mental health gets very little attention, which is a huge issue. Prescriptions for antidepressants are more common, especially among women aged fifty to sixty-four than men, and about 25 per cent of women take these drugs. There are cases in which mental trauma manifests through physical conditions, and once the context of such an injury is understood, the disease vanishes. For instance, elbow pain is often linked to refusal to let go of the past, and once this context is understood and reconciled, the pain may vanish.

Putting it all together, Dr Agus recommends the following measures: Fasting lipid profile, with total cholesterol levels between 120–200 mg/dl, HDL level greater than 60, LDL levels less than 100, triglyceride level less than 150, high-sensitivity C-reactive protein (CRP) between 0–2 mg/dl, hemoglobin A1C of 4.2–5.6 per cent, a comprehensive metabolic panel (CMP) is necessary to assess your liver, kidneys, electrolyte and acid/base balance, seven hours of sleep for everyone to get the optimum level of performance, and overlay all the results and see the pattern, to understand how the body functions, start storing your plasma, as labs can freeze the plasma for twenty years, and take baby aspirin and statin daily to keep inflammation under control.

Like Dr Comite, Dr Agus also lays great importance on controlling inflammation in the body as it's the single most dominant factor underlying most diseases, including cancer. The same goes for anything that continually irritates the body and its immune system; high blood sugar, diabetes, obesity, tobacco use, to name a few.

Life is a genetic gamble. We must play the cards dealt to us, but we can stack the odds in our favour by controlling our exposure to environmental and lifestyle factors (not smoking, eating well, regular exercise, using technologies to stay on top of our health status, etc.) Most medical studies are, in a way, wrong for various reasons—studies with small sizes, tiny effects, invalid exploratory analyses and blatant conflicts of interests combine with an obsession for pursuing contemporary trends of dubious importance. The need for scepticism has never been greater. We need to seek multiple sources that arrive at the same answer. Until we have better curators of medical wisdom for the benefit of all, each one of us must play the curator role in our individual lives.

According to a study by Louisiana Pennington Biomedical Research Center, in a week, we spend an average of sixty-four hours sitting, twenty-eight hours standing and eleven hours moving and walking in ways that don't count as exercise. That means no matter how active we are otherwise, most of us are sitting for more than nine hours a day. The individual who exercised the most didn't spend less time sitting. So, in addition to the workout, we need to get up every hour and take a five-minute stroll. Extended periods of sitting result in increased risk of both breast and colon cancer. If you keep sitting idly, the circulation drops with less blood sugar getting used and less fat being burnt, thus increasing the risk of heart disease and diabetes. When looked at the risk factors for mortality, physical inactivity stood at 6 per cent, compared to high blood pressure, at 13 per cent, tobacco use at 9 per cent, high blood glucose at 6 per cent and obesity at 5 per cent. Dr Agus says it's better to be physically fit and slightly overweight than to have a healthy weight but a sedentary lifestyle.

Muscle mass and bone strength are among the most under-appreciated and unrecognized aspects of health. Loss of muscle can lead to loss of life. Just as fat stores extra energy as reserve, muscles store amino acids, so we need to build tissues and biological substances. This is because the body doesn't store amino acids as well as it does fat and carbs; if there aren't enough coming from the diet, the body will take them from the tissue by breaking down its protein sources, usually muscle. That is partly why the loss of muscle can lead to loss of life. Recovering from illness or trauma relies a lot on muscle mass, strength and function. Consider how advanced heart disease and cancer, both of which are often associated with rapid loss of muscle mass and metabolic function and survival, can depend on the extent of muscle loss. Ageing is responsible for the loss of muscle mass and function, a condition known as sarcopenia, and it can erode one's quality of life over time.

Sleep hygiene cannot be overemphasized. In addition to balancing the hormones in the body, sleep helps us manage stress, replenish cells, heal and fight infections. It also helps utilize energy efficiently, control weight, renew skin and bones, lower risk factors for heart disease and strokes, sharpen our planning and memory skills, improve concentration, and revitalize organ and tissue function. If you think your body is powered down for the night when the lights go out, think again. It's catching its breath. A legion of neurons springs into action as soon as you surrender to sleep. The brain starts going through all the information you took in during the day and organizes it so that you can take in more and learn more the following day. It goes through its checklist to ensure your hormones, enzymes and proteins are balanced and in sync.

Meanwhile, the 'brains janitor's (glymphatic system) are at work to sweep out any toxic debris that can gum up its systems if left to build up. Periods of sleep loss, even if they are brief, can be damaging; cells fail to make enough antioxidants to counter the build-up of free radicals. Most organs sweep away their garbage with the help of an efficient system, such as by recruiting specialized immune cells that can chew up the trash like a disposal. Some organs are tied into a mesh of vessels that are part of the lymph system, the body's drainage pipes. The glial cells, which help neurons expand and work during the day, assist them to shrink during sleep. The wakeful state resembles a busy airport, swelling with the cumulative activity of individual messages travelling from one neuron to another. This inflates the size of the brain cells by a whopping 86 per cent. In the sleep state, the neurons are low-firing or not firing, depending on the stage of sleep. Meanwhile, the brain cells shrink to make room for the fluid in-between them to cleanse the system. The biggest takeaways from Dr Agus are that, inflammation is the most significant cause of many illnesses, and we need to measure and control it. For those above forty, a daily dose of baby aspirin and a statin, for control of inflammation and better cardiovascular health. In complete contrast to what Dr Comite says, Dr Agus believes supplements are unregulated and backed by little research. He says, vitamin D supplements are entirely unnecessary. The deficiency of D is more a consequence of poor health and not the cause of it. Moving and hydrating are two important activities in addition to all other activities of diet, exercise, and relaxation and stretching. The optimum level of workout activity is 450 minutes per week with 30 per cent of it being the intensive, heart-accelerating kind.

These facts are quite fascinating, though it looks, at the outset, too much information to take in all at once. Nevertheless, the point here is to understand just how complex our lives have become and how we need to be conscious of this complexity. Expansion of consciousness and assuming more and more responsibility for our bodily and mental health seem to be the demand of the times. At the same time, I had doubts about the experiments conducted by the Western countries. They were tested either on the mice or select groups of people from the population embedded in the Western ethos and environment. It got me wondering if such tests would also hold good for entirely different cultures and populations, such as the East? The fact remains that we have adopted the medicine of the West in a big way, without knowing whether such trials have been conducted in our country or not. The question is—do we go back to our traditional medicines, such as Ayurveda, which is said to be suited to our body physiology and constitution? Is it possible to do it at all? How are we going to deal with the mammoth information related to health and fitness being discussed over the Net, periodicals and magazines, without considering core issues such as the above? The ultimate decision could at best, be left to our individual intuition, which again is a part of our consciousness and therefore, the need to work on our consciousness and awareness can't be overemphasized.

12

Energy

If you want to find the secret of the universe,
think in terms of energy, frequency and vibration.

−NICOLA TESLA

Since the body consciousness, health, fitness and well-being depended on energy at various levels, I thought it necessary to study energy systems, as well as the role of the transformation of energy as the fundamental function of ecology/organic life in general, and human life in particular, contributing to the expansion of consciousness. I was also interested in studying how philosophy and religion function as tools for such transformation, as examined in the context of Indian, Asian and Western thought. The fundamental questions of 'who am I' and 'what's the purpose of life' have different answers depending upon the state of consciousness of who is asking these questions. For a Hindu Brahmin of the Visishtadvaita tradition, for instance, the answers would be simple— that he/she is a jivatma and God is Paramatma. This life and separation from God are the consequences of past karma. Through karma, dhyana, bhakti or yoga, one tends to wash off karma and attain His feet, which is the ultimate purpose of life.

According to Hinduism, mahat is the primordial energy out of which God created the universe. The core aspects of creation such as the panchabhutas of air, water, earth, fire and space and the three aspects of creation, sustenance and destruction illustrate the point further. The feminine and masculine energies as complementary to each other are yet another point of energy, which is fundamental to life. In Visishtadvaitam, the Almighty Sriman Narayana is considered incomplete without Shri, the feminine energy aspect. Similarly, Shiva and Shakti unite as Ardhanariswara to illustrate the dependence of consciousness on energy. Aurobindo became Sri Aurobindo only after Mother joined him. The roles of Durga and Kali in Hindu mythology, both representing the extreme forms of energy required to destroy evil, is well known. Different times demanded different forms of worship. In the Satya Yuga, yoga worked. In the Treta Yuga that followed, yajna and yaga were relevant, while in the Dvapara Yuga, offering archana to idols was the ideal thing to do. In the current Kali Yuga, the mere recital of God's name works wonders, according to the Upanishads. The idea behind this seems to be focusing on different types of energy and their transformation in different epochs.

Spirituality is integral to religion. William A. Richard, in his book, *Sacred Knowledge* quotes William James from his book *The Varieties of Religious Experiences*, where he makes a distinction between primary and secondary experiences. The main are the ones that happen directly to you, and the secondary religious experience refers to those of others, some of whom taught humanity about beliefs and wrote them down which subsequently became enshrined as scriptures. According to Richard, there are four pillars to religious experience, including the above. Of the remaining three, one is sacred scriptures such as Torah, the Bible, Vedas, Upanishads, the Koran, Buddhist Sutras. The second is theological formulations such as those found in Hebrew Talmud, Christian Creeds and lectures of Sankara and Ramanuja. The third pillar is the social expressions of religious belief in compassionate service to others, the examples of which are Buddhist bodhicitta or tonglen, Jewish tzedakah and chesed, Muslim islaah or da'wah or Sikh langar and Christian soup kitchens. All the four pillars are equally important, but the primary experience may well provide wisdom and vitality that may illuminate and strengthen these other pillars. It would be interesting to examine these two ways of life regarding energy and how work on oneself (transformation of energies) makes it possible to experience them.

Yoga explains the energy aspect of life and consciousness regarding the kundalini shakti and its ascent through the seven chakras, which represent the various levels of consciousness. The scope of work lies in transforming and balancing the Sun and the Moon energies of the nadis, ida and pingala respectively, and facilitating the rise of the kundalini or consciousness through the sushumna. Tirumular, the Siddha sage of Tamil origin, as interpreted by Satguru Subramuniyaswami, a proponent of Saiva Siddhantha of Kuvei, had identified twenty-one worlds, fourteen in addition to the seven represented by the chakras. He also speaks about three planes of existence—instinctive, intellectual and intuitive and five states of consciousness—conscious, subconscious, sub- subconscious, sub-superconscious and superconscious. Ramana Maharishi, a Tamil sage, explained states of mind as waking, sleep and dreaming. B.K.S. Iyengar, the contemporary yoga guru, speaks about five koshas or bodies—the annamaya, pranamaya, manomaya, vijnanamaya and anandamaya koshas. These roughly translate into the physical, astral, mental, intellectual and causal bodies or energies.

Western philosopher G calls energy as force. He identifies, in his theory of cosmology, seven levels of creation akin to the seven musical notes. According to this theory, the power from the absolute at level one descends in the involutionary process to the next levels. He says the organic life, including humans, continually transforms energies, and these energies, when not utilized for self-transformation, go elsewhere, as energy doesn't go waste. Plants always change the energy received from sunlight into chlorophyll. If humans want to use force or energy for their progress, they need to work on themselves. The waking-up process is like a plant growing; first, the seeds are buried in the darkness, then they crack, grow and transform. By a complicated process these energies, according to G, are transformed, which go into making subtle bodies and minds. It is proposed to examine the theories of philosophers such as Steiner to verify correlations between energy and consciousness.

In this regard, the observations of J.G. Bennett, a disciple of G, are significant. He defines 'energy' as the power to do work, and each kind of work requires the appropriate kind of energy. Energies differ in quality, quantity and intensity. According to him, our destinies depend upon our ability to make the right use of the powers available to us. The capacity for work and enjoyment depends on the availability of the right energies in the right place. Nearly all the emotional and mental suffering to which humankind is subject is due to the failure to use psychic powers rightly. For a better understanding, he classifies energies into twelve categories and humans can understand and control to some extent some types of those life energies. He categorizes consciousness as a finer form of energy along with universal and cosmic energies and thinks that there are strengths such as creativity over and above consciousness. Unitive and transcendent energies are the other categories well beyond consciousness. He makes a significant observation that in the ordinary human, the sensitive and conscious energies remain stuck with each other and therefore, the work lies in freeing consciousness from sensitivity. The transpersonal aspect is about separating these two and liberating awareness.

In ancient times various religious concepts found expression in rituals, which were basically at the instinctive level. The ceremonies slowly gave way to the intellectual pursuits in the form of text, where you can find God in scriptures, philosophies and written accounts of mystical experiences of saints and sages. The third transition, which humanity is yet to witness, except, perhaps, in rare cases, is primary, direct, religious experiences at the intuitive level. It would be interesting to examine how this transition is going to occur and what universal factors such as energy and its transformation would catalyze such a transition.

I also joined various yoga and meditation groups after my return to Chennai from UP in 1987. For instance, I went for kriya yoga practices, which are based on Paramahansa Yogananda's teachings, the Art of Living yoga classes taught by Sri Sri Ravi Shankar, the meditation techniques taught by Sri Aurobindo and the Mother of Sri Aurobindo Ashram at Puducherry, the meditations classes organized by Osho, and many others. I also read with interest, the translated version of the *Patanjali Yoga Sutra*, BKS Iyengar's *Light on Life*, *Merging with Siva* by Satguru Subramuniyaswami and *Yoga and Psychotherapy*, which were authored jointly by Swami Rama, Dr Rudolf Ballentine and Swami Ajaya from Himalayan Institute. For some time I was a member of a Gurdjieff study circle in Berkeley, California.

The mind is a thought-producing machine and controller of senses, turned outwards. Life is like a beautiful garden with plants, trees and flowers, fountains and retreats, but we live like we have lost the keys to the garden, which is the mind. Meditation is the key. Nowadays, we hear people making all sorts of claims, about how meditation helps find our true self, and helps us find God. Many believe it is a means of relaxing and de-stressing and enhancing one's health. It can best be a catalyst for all these. It's a mind trainer, just as we train our body for a marathon. Starting on meditation as early as possible helps train the mind from a young age.

Yoga and Meditation

Patt Lind-Kyle, in her ground-breaking book, *Heal Your Mind, Rewire Your Brain*, explains meditation combined with brain science. Our great brain has evolved to teach us how to survive, relate to each other, dream and achieve success in our lives. To survive, human beings developed the old brain (the brain stem and the thalamus) of 'fight or flight', also called the reptilian brain. To experience feelings, emotions and family connections, we developed the emotional or mammalian or limbic part of the brain. To create and imagine new worlds we evolved the neocortex or new brain, which also integrates the functions of other layers of brain. We developed the frontal lobes that integrate these functions and offer the possibilities of compassion and success and the creation of a positive future for ourselves. The neural networking connects all three layers or centres of the brain, which is the means for the brain-mind, that part of the mind closely associated with the brain, to continue to evolve even today. Each structure of the brain has a brainwave pattern; beta, alpha, theta and delta, and each of them is connected with the neurotransmitters dopamine, acetylcholine, gamma-aminobutyric acid (GABA) and serotonin. While beta helps us with our day-to-day work, alpha and other neurotransmitters bring on meditative states.

Meditation is a form of mind training. It helps us to focus our attention, quietens the scattered mind and brings flexibility and clarity. Meditation is seen to increase the size of the brain area concerned. We can mentally challenge our brain structure, increase brain cells and modify neural pathways through our life experiences. Meditation and mind training is at the heart of making positive changes in every area of life.

In the esoteric traditions, the mind is said to be the mansion with three floors and a basement. The first floor is instinctive—living characterized by activities such as eating, sleeping, sex, recreation, money, buying things, partying, travelling, going to temples, reading literature, etc. The second floor is intellectual living—intellect, intelligence, reasoning ability, rationalizing, knowledge and understanding. The third floor is intuitive living where instincts and intelligence take a back seat, and a whole new way of life opens up. We need to know how to combine these disparate areas and bring forth the right response at the right time. There is a basement too, the subconscious or the unconscious, which is the foundation of life and a storehouse of knowledge and power. Unfortunately, we use it as a junkyard.

Now, compare this with the modern scientific theories of reptilian, limbic and cortex brains, which correspond to the three floors and the basement to the subconscious mind. It will also be clear how breathing connects these three floors like an elevator, and it is possible to ascend to higher levels of consciousness with the help of breath work. Meditation does just that.

Yoga is not necessarily postures and mudras only. That is just one aspect of the eightfold yoga disciplines. Knowledge, understanding and practising the principles of yoga will lead to the much-desired art of mind control and unity of body, mind and self or soul. There are hundreds of books providing various explanations and interpretations of yoga principles, out of which the treatise, *Yoga and Psychotherapy* interested me because of the psychology and therapy angle it explored.

Yoga has attracted particular attention in part because it is one of the oldest continuous disciplines studying voluntary physical and mental control and the induction of the altered states of consciousness (ASC), somewhat akin to the Sanskrit word *thuria*. One of the first practices of yoga is self-observation. It is a systematic study of mental states and their corresponding physical sensations, as well as a method of studying one's internal organs and physiological processes. In the typical sequence of scientific events, observation leads to the ability to predict, and this ultimately leads to control. The control over physiological processes enables you to control your metabolism and induce changes that would serve to alter the state of consciousness further.

Yoga Psychology

Yoga psychology proposes the concept that there are various levels of functioning beyond the body and mind and each one has its own specific organization and function. Each, as we are aware of it and think accordingly, gives a certain quality to our consciousness. While we feel comfortable to think of our body being used by us, we seldom think that we also use our minds, that part of us which observes our thoughts, can also learn to regulate them, control them and use them as we deem fit.

In yoga psychology, this idea of different levels of being, with each one capable of observing and controlling the one below, is central and fundamental. The systematic exploration, development and experimentation with these higher levels are the work of yoga and meditation. Five such levels are described as 'sheaths' in the ancient texts on yoga since the more evolved level is existing within. Each sheath covers the subtle awareness that's interior to it. These five levels or sheaths span the whole spectrum of human nature. The continuum they form make up a sort of stepwise ladder that is the basis of all growth and evolution. Within this framework fits the developmental theory, the therapeutic process, and all the aspects of philosophy, religion and art that focus on the unfolding of man's higher potentials. Growth is a unitary process—the biological evolution from protozoan to man, the psychological evolution from child to adult, the therapeutic evolution from mental illness to health and the development of universal consciousness in the mystic, are all included in this process of growth. The concept of sheaths provides the only framework within which one can compare such diverse subjects as yoga, biofeedback, sleep research, medicine and psychotherapy.

The first level deals with the physical body and working with yoga postures, bioenergetics and rolfing, a deep tissue massage method that has been described in a previous chapter. We look at biofeedback as a means of teaching people to tune into and control that internal part of the body which is ordinarily considered involuntary. It is basically meant to cultivate awareness of internal states. When you become aware of this experience, you unfold sheath two, which deals with breath and energy, and provides the intimate connection between the mind and body. This aspect is concerned with breathing patterns and their effect on internal processes and the mind. In yoga science, concentration, the build-up and controlled release of subtle, latent energy provide the key to integration and achievement of higher states of consciousness.

The third level or sheath deals with the mind. Unlike the Western ways that believe that the mind can be observed through behaviour, yoga teaches the method of studying it through the direct experience of introspection using meditational techniques. In yoga, the ego is only a stepping stone to further evolution. The fourth level comes into being with the refining of a non-verbal discriminative faculty in the form of imagery. The next sheath shows how further growth of the power of discrimination achieved in level four and passive volition (will) is related to the development of a yogic state of bliss, which is the natural state of human consciousness. Within these five sheaths lies the pure consciousness.

There is another dimension to this uncovering of pure consciousness—the chakra system, the seven centres of consciousness which come into prominence during the process of meditation. They constitute the structure of inner reality, and their framework provides a sort of workshop within which one operates to explore oneself and evolve a higher consciousness.

Many people primarily associate yoga with complicated contortions of the body, but yoga has much more to do with cultivating your self-awareness and your relationship to the world. It's a complete system of therapy, which includes developing awareness and control of the physical body, emotions, mind and interpersonal relationships. There are many aspects to yoga—the physical (hatha), the devotional (bhakti), service or action (karma) and philosophical (dhyana) yoga. The most comprehensive and scientific yogic system for developing awareness is Raja Yoga, or the royal path. It is also called the Ashtanga Yoga, which define yogic practice as having eight aspects to it. Mastery of each step leads to work on a subtle aspect of our being, beginning with habits and behaviour, then proceeding to work on the body and breath and then mental functioning. The physical postures are essential as one of the early phases of yoga training. After learning to discipline the body, the student becomes supple, healthy and relaxed so that the central aspect of yoga—which involves mental work and introspection—can be pursued. But this is more than mere physical preparation, for the discipline involved in training the body serves as a model for later work on other levels of functioning.

Although the body is worked with intensively, the actual goal is to become less bound up in the body, distance yourself from it and gain perspective on its functioning. Working properly in this way cultivates an objectivity and detachment which permits the neutral observation of the body as it assumes such yogic posture and gradually leads to increased control. The default posture reflects one's state of mind, i.e., the physical state is the embodiment of a mental state. Posture is a stance from which we face the world physically and mentally. For instance, when we are angry, the breathing becomes fast and shallow; under strain, the brows knit, the muscles of the forehead tense and the stomach is pulled in and rigid. A posture which becomes habitual, beginning as a reaction to a mental state, may come to sustain and perpetuate that state. Usually, yoga combines the regular practice of asanas (postures) and the introspective study of meditation to produce a well-integrated improvement in bodily functions and mental attitude. Hatha yoga includes a series of poses to stretch and strengthen each of the muscles and tendons that may have become shortened and contracted due to mental tension and incorrect posture.

By assuming certain asanas and mudras (gestures), one can learn to create the desired mental states. Relaxation is also important because when the voluntary muscles become quiet, you gain a clearer awareness of internal states. Random static from postural tension no longer drowns out subtle signals from within. There is a tendency to ignore information from inside the body until it becomes painful or uncomfortable and ultimately manifests itself as illness. The surface of the body, instead, receives most of our attention. There is less concern with possible internal disturbances which might be manifesting themselves physically. This attitude is responsible for the conviction that most of the illnesses result from invading microorganisms. We look for causes of discomfort outside of us.

Various aspects of an individual must be trained and gradually integrated to achieve the degree of consciousness that will allow some level of control. The body, mind and the consciousness which goes beyond the usual mental states should be in harmonious coordination. Such a comprehensive approach is a traditional characteristic of yoga.

Prana

The preliminary steps in yoga involve the body as a preparation for a deeper exploration of the self. The physical postures should leave the body supple and calm, free from nervous movement or muscular tension. However, even when the body is relaxed, one is not completely still because the circulation of the breath breaks the silence. Therefore, once the body is under control, the attention needs to turn to the breath. It is the link between the gross material body and the subtle realm of the mind. The key to proper breathing lies in the realms of consciousness, beyond the mind. Breathing is the only physiological function which is both voluntary and involuntary. We can either control it or allow it to carry on mechanically: breath becomes agitated in anger, stops momentarily in fear, gasps with amazement, chokes with sadness, sighs with relief, etc. Though emotional and mental states are difficult to control, we can indirectly control them with breathing as these states are closely connected. The act of breathing connects one with the environment and the energy pool of the universe. Proper breathing could induce relaxation and states of higher consciousness. When the use of the diaphragm replaces the utilization of the rib cage and other chest muscles, much more movement is involved, and much more effort becomes necessary.

Besides depth and rhythm, breath shows another quality—alternating between the two nostrils controls the left and the right hemispheres of the brain and the connected activities. When we have a cold, the breath is not even but alternates between the nostrils. When the right nostril is clear, the right side of the body and the left hemisphere of the brain get prominent, and the subject becomes active. More passive tasks need to be carried out with the left nostril open. In Sanskrit, the right and left currents are Pingala and Ida, respectively. The channels of energy which carry the breath to various parts are called nadi. Again, the right side is identified with warmth or heat and therefore the Sun, while the left is cold and thus associated with the Moon. In hatha, 'Ha' means Sun and 'Tha', the Moon. Hence hatha yoga is a discipline which leads to the integration of these two. There is yet another way of describing this: there are three gunas—rajas, tamas and sattva, in Sanskrit, particularly in the ayurvedic tradition of healthcare. Rajas indicate activity, aggression, etc., and therefore the Pingala nostril is identified with this. Similarly, the left is tamasic and the central nadi, sushumna, represents the sattvic forces.

There is a hierarchy in yogic levels, forming a continuum. At each level, there is more consciousness than in the previous. On the lowest level exists the physical body, the next level is the cumulative energy of the individual concerned and on the level above is called the mental plane. Since these levels are interconnected, it's possible to do something physically to raise the standard of energy and something mentally in the thought form can contribute to this effect. Mental exercises can have desirable effects on the energy level or physical health. Good thoughts induce high energy and a healthy body. As prana enters with the breath, it becomes divided into five subsidiaries with functions of their own—prana vayu, apanavayu, vyana vayu, samana vayu and udana vayu. Their functions are respectively, respiration, excretion, coordination and integration, digestion and providing body heat, and speech and communication. Thus, the current of prana is the currency of the psycho-physiological system and the medium of interchange between physical and mental worlds. When the energy starts flowing through the sushumna, the central nadi, the energies are balanced, and creativity and meditation ensue. The fusion of physical and mental powers creates that level of existence known in yoga as the 'pranic' sheath or the energy body. The energy pathways in the body, cross and converge at certain points located along the axis of the body, which is approximately the spinal cord. Chakras are nothing but these energy centres.

I have often wondered why I was not able to meditate or do yoga. I subsequently learned that my energies are probably dissipated or entangled in wrong places in body and mind. In physical tensions and bad postures, the energy gets trapped in muscles and tissues. Secondly, mental energy also gets entangled with stress, depression, etc. More energy gets spent on keeping these leakages out of the consciousness and awareness, resulting in enormous quantities of energy getting spent. It dawned on me that I needed to find ways and means of therapies to get the energies flowing back to continue my inner journey. As mind seemed to play a major part in this aspect, ever fluctuating and restless, I decided to study the mental field further.

As mentioned before, just as calming the body helps in getting the quietness required for the study of breath and energy, meditation brings the mind into focus. Through meditation, one develops a capacity for observing the functioning of the mind. An untrained mind becomes part of what it's trying to follow. To train the mind, one needs to understand how it functions. There are two ways for this purpose—raja yoga by Patanjali and the Vedanta tradition of Shankaracharya.

Instincts are the behaviour patterns developed by lower forms of existence like animals. Lacking choice, flexibility and the capacity to anticipate, the animals are wholly dependent on the demands of the environment. For sheer survival, therefore, animals developed a set pattern of behaviour which was then passed on through generations through their DNA. In the case of mammals, the instinctual urge becomes less necessary for organizing action and is important during emergencies. They are semi, but can change. Habits gradually replace instincts. Despite all the progress, the survival and base instincts lie dormant at the bottom of the mind. These instincts are food, sex, sleep and self-protection. Choice, freedom and control, and a new level of awareness, all belong to the stratum of being called the mind, which has the capacity for self-awareness and the anticipation of the future.

While the physical and energy bodies are external instruments, the mind body is internal. Yoga speaks about four kinds of mind—the lower mind or mana, which produces thoughts and calculations; ahamkara or the sense of I; chitta or memory, and the inner, discriminative mind called buddhi. The mana is the gateway for impressions coming from outside through the senses, and coordinates motor responses. The ahamkara converts the experience into a personal one relating them to individual identity. When the sensory motor mind functions, a rose is seen. When ahamkara gets involved, I see a rose. When the incoming impression flashes on the screen of the lower mind, buddhi decides a suitable action plan. The interrelatedness of these three aspects constitutes what's called the normal waking consciousness. They are not separate compartments but an organic whole, which is known as the internal instrument. What lies beyond the outer and inner tools is variously referred to as the self, atman, purusha, brahman or jiva. It is the attainment of this level of consciousness is the grand scheme of yoga psychology.

The dhyana yoga of Vedanta philosophy is based on experiences of others to some extent. It is organized around teachings and concepts framed by someone else. Raja yoga of Patanjali contrasts with this, in the sense that it is based on personal experience.

Patanjali calls thoughts and other machinations of the mind as vritti, modifications of the mind. He advocates Ashtanga Yoga, as a part of Raja Yoga, consisting of eight steps of yama, niyama, asana, pranayama, pratyahara, dharana, dhyana and samadhi. The first four stages coincide with hatha yoga and the next four with raja yoga.

Chakras, the Seven Centres of Consciousness

Yoga includes the science of the body, an understanding of the energy level which governs the body's functions, a study of the mind and higher states of consciousness as well as a whole philosophy of the structure and nature of the universe. The point here is that while yoga has integrated all these principles, it will, perhaps take many disciplines and studies from the Western system to deal with such a vast scope. Yoga is based on an individual's inner experience and not an amalgam of disparate ideas. If you must explore the world of spiritual experiences, thoughts and emotions and learn about yourself, you must have some basis within which to do this. The structure of the seven centres of consciousness does just that.

In every experience, we have these three components. Underlying them is a more fundamental principle, which is called consciousness. The sheaths or bodies don't function independently. There is a connection between them. For instance, if you focus your thoughts on the solar plexus, it increases the concentration of the energy in that level. The solar plexus, in the physical body, serves as a focal point between three bodies or sheaths corresponding to points in the other bodies.

There are seven such centres, which are called chakras. In the physical body, their positions correspond to points along the spinal cord. The first chakra called Muladhara, is located at the base of the spine at the lowest extreme of the vertebral column (coccyx). The second one, called Swadhishtana is just a few inches above that at the level of the genitals (the sacrum). The third, Manipura is located at the navel and is associated with the solar plexus. The fourth centre, Anahata, is near the heart, the fifth, Vishuddhi, at the throat, the sixth, Ajna, between the eyebrows, while the seventh and the last, the Sahasrara is at the top most point of the skull, at the crown of the head. While the Sahasrara Chakra is associated with the highest state of consciousness, the lower ones get closer and closer to the level of animals or instinct-based side of human nature. Developing the capacity to concentrate more energy, attention and awareness at the higher centres is one aspect of what happens with the evolution of the consciousness.

The word 'chakra' means wheel in Sanskrit. At the outer circumference of the wheel, there is more space, more material and diversity and more movement; in other words, it is material phenomena relating to the gross body. The fundamental aspects of the chakra correspond to the higher sheaths or bodies. At the centre of the system is the centre of consciousness—purusha or the self. Recent medical research has established that the endocrine glands serve as strategic points of interaction between physiological, emotional and psychological functioning.

Each of the chakras is associated with one of the primary elements, which are known as bhutas. Each contains a certain proportion of the matter (prakriti) and consciousness (purusha), which endow the centres with qualities of solidity (earth), liquidity (water), combustion (fire), gaseousness (air) and spaciousness, that which constitutes the space in which the other elements exist (ether). For example, the first centre, the Muladhara Chakra is associated with earth, the dense awareness of physical body and physical plane, and given its location, near the anus region, is anatomically related with the excretion of solid matter from the body. If the centre is weak, the person may develop bowel problems and other related illnesses. Similarly, all other centres can be explained in practical ways.

Another treatise I read with immense interest is called *Merging with Siva* by Satguru Subramuniyaswami of Hawaii. This work is probably meant for Hindus outside of India, to understand the concepts of Hinduism better. The work is based on the aphorisms of a Tamil siddha saint and mystic, Tirumular and his monumental work, *Thirumandhiram*. I will refer only to two of the concepts put forward by Satguru Subramuniyaswami on the mind, consciousness and chakras.

The mind is vast. There are three planes through which the awareness moves, the instinctive, intellectual and intuitive. There are five states in which the mind manifests—conscious (jagarachitta), subconscious (samskarachitta), sub-subconscious (vasanachitta), sub-superconscious (anukaranachitta) and superconscious (karanachitta). The conscious mind is the one which comes to the fore in our day-to-day working. When our awareness lies in this state, we are externalized. We take our directions from our memory, past life and experiences. The second is the subconscious mind, the 'grand storehouse' of the mind. It registers all experiences, thoughts and feelings passing through the conscious mind. What's interesting is the next category, the sub-subconscious mind, which is the distillation of all actions and reactions in life. It's very subtle, and any two experiences—of action and reaction—mingle and produce the third vibration. For example, we have an experience and react to it. We have a similar experience again and respond to that too. These two reactions merge in the sub-subconscious to produce a hybrid response, which stays with us until we neutralize the responses properly. A good example of this state is cooking, where different ingredients go into forming an entirely different dish, where the components become inseparable. The fourth one is the sub-superconscious, which is deep, refined and powerful and filters the flashes of intuition from the superconscious to suit the subconscious grid. Finding solutions to challenging problems through flashes of insight and intuition is a good example of its working. The fifth is the superconscious mind. When you are super consciously alive, you feel joyous and blissful physically, emotionally and mentally.

To live positively in the conscious mind, one needs to exercise every day, follow a vegetarian diet and live joyously. Society and other external phenomena shape the conscious mind. If one happens to be alone in a desert, there won't be much of the conscious mind. One will live in the inner minds. The conscious mind arises once a city comes up around, and are surrounded by people and life is filled with experiences and interactions.

For a long time, humans remain enmeshed in the trappings of the conscious mind, and they need attention and concentration to regain access to the inner minds. The subconscious mind stores everything which passes through the conscious mind and gets embedded even in the DNA (karma). It can serve well or otherwise, depending on what kind of subconscious one carries. Hence, the need to clean up the subconscious with understanding and fearlessly facing the contents of the subconscious without any reaction to neutralize the issues. Intuition travels through a pure subconscious. Elements of a problem have a way of coming together coherently when it can relax. One effective way of cleaning up the subconscious is to write down the experience or emotion which causes turmoil on a piece of paper and burn it. Burning is a powerful message to the subconscious, says the author. Another way is to write it down on a paper and let it float away from you in running water (he calls it Ganga Sadhana), sending a powerful message to the subconscious to wash the negativity off. The sub- subconscious mind is the one which attracts the kind of life akin to its content. If one has ill will and negative emotions, one will invariably face an adverse life until the sub-conscious is neutralized. A meditative state and clear instructions in the form of affirmations can be given to the sub-subconscious to clean it.

Another interesting aspect of Satguru's teachings is the description of twenty-one chakras, seven above and seven below the seven chakras we know. The worlds or planes above our world—known as the Bhuloka—are Bhuvarloka, Svarloka, Maharloka, Janaloka, Tapoloka and Satyaloka. The seven below-the-root chakras—otherwise called talas—are Atala, Vitala, Sutala, Talatala, Rasatala, Mahatala and Patala. While the chakras above-the-crown chakra are higher realms belonging to subtle beings, the talas below root chakra belong to grosser and negative beings. For instance, the two talas just below-the-root chakra are fear and anger. When fear grips you, you feel an uneasy stirring in your lower stomach, and when anger arises in you, you feel the heat in your lower abdomen. The successive talas below the Muladhar Chakra situated in the thighs, calves and soles depict various stages of depravity, which explains what goes to make a psychopath or an assassin. These talas affect the normal functioning of the regular chakras. For example, the atala in combination with the Muladhara Chakra affects appetite and feeling of safety; in conjunction with the Swadishthana Chakra, affects happiness and enjoyment, together with Manipur Chakra, affects will power, and so on. At the time of death, a soul exits into the chakra, loka or tala in which he was active during his life, to work out the excess energy which was responsible for the activity. To me, it appears that the concepts of heaven and hell originated from this idea.

The explanations, as above for yoga, meditation and chakras provided by the authors of the book, *Yoga and Psychotherapy*, are among the best I have read on the subject. While many books dwelt on the specific characteristics, properties, and the nature of yoga or the chakras, this book deals with their psychological aspects and their structure, which appealed to me. Since my larger scheme was to find the meaning of life in general and my life, I found the explanations served that purpose considerably well. I wandered into many subjects and aspects of life as described in the previous chapters and only finally turned my attention to the treasures from our ancient culture. Significantly, these explanations come from foreigners, who seemed to have had a good grip on what is in our scriptures, and more significantly, the ability to express their ideas lucidly. I don't regret the fact that I started my spiritual journey with another Western philosophy, The Fourth Way by G. In fact, it is doubtful I would have been able to grasp many of the principles of our literature better without the help of the Fourth Way, as it served as a key and laid the foundation for my understanding. Without them, the Ramayana and Mahabharata would have been just another couple of mythological stories, which either evoked belief or otherwise. Now, I know that these are myths beyond the duality of belief and disbelief, belonging to an entirely different dimension.

Astrology

Astrology is a study of planetary energy affecting human life. I had considerable interest in astrology. The idea was to learn the basic things so that I was armed with the necessary knowledge in case I ever consulted an astrologer for some purpose. After learning certain basic principles, I thought astrology was a real science and if approached scientifically, could prove to be useful for getting some guidance, if not predictions for future events. I also found that many of the famous astrologers were found to be more accurate in telling you about your past, but when it came to future predictions, they often slipped. I found the Krishnamurti Paddhati (KP), a system of calculations based on birth-star positions was excellent, but there were not enough practitioners who could give accurate predictions based on this system.

There are nine planets (grahas)—Jupiter, Saturn, Sun, Moon, Mars, Venus and Mercury. The nodes, Rahu and Ketu, are also treated as planets for calculations and predictions. The Zodiac divides into twelve houses, Aries, Taurus, Gemini, Cancer, Leo, Virgo, Libra, Scorpio, Sagittarius, Capricorn, Aquarius and Pisces. A planet owns a house, and it is called the 'Lord' (ruler) of the House. Mars rules Aries and Scorpio, Taurus and Libra belong to Venus and Mercury rules Gemini and Virgo, Saturn controls Capricorn and Aquarius, and Jupiter holds Sagittarius and Pisces. The nodes Rahu and Ketu don't own any (they are only mathematical points, which nevertheless weild considerable influence) but take on the properties of either the houses they are in or in conjunction with the other planets. The Sun and the Moon each own one house, Leo and Cancer respectively. Each house represents certain aspects of life, such as the sixth and tenth houses represent career and work, the eighth house longevity, the second house, family and wealth, and so on. Similarly, planets also symbolize certain aspects of life. Venus is associated with love and pleasure, Saturn with hard work, Mars with career, and so on. Each rashi houses 2.25 stars, and each star is divided into four pada. Where the Moon resides in your birth chart is called the rashi, and where the 'ascendant' falls, the lagna. The ascendant is a node which rises at the time of birth and changes every twenty minutes and hence, is considered more accurate for prediction purposes. The Moon represents the mind. There are twenty-seven stars in the Zodiac which are considered for calculations. Every individual is born under a sign, a lagna and a star.

There is yet another factor called 'dasa and bukti' which is used to predict events and major trends in one's life. There are many systems for dasa calculations, but the most common one is the 'vimsothari', which is calculated based on the Moon's position in the birth chart, also known as the kundli, at the time of birth. If a clock represents the Zodiac, the hour hand is the dasa, the minute hand, the bukti and the seconds hand the 'anthra'. Each planet either causes or participates in dasa and bukti, the latter being the subdivision of the former. For instance, Sani Dasa ran for a terrible nineteen years and Sukra (Venus) Dasa ran for a delightful twenty years!

If the calculations are correct and accurate, things happen in the individual's life as the 'dasa-bukti-antra' juggernaut rolls. One's karma, which is supposed to be responsible for the events in one's life, can be equated to the battery of the clock. Without the battery or the power source, the clock stops ticking.

To prepare the kundli, the astrologer requires the name of the individual, the place and time of birth. The location and time of birth decide the latitude and longitude for calculation purposes. Other factors considered for calculations are ayanamsa (sidereal time), etc. For instance, we in India consider the ayanamsa for calculating the ascendant, but the Western methods don't. We base our calculations on the Moon's position whereas the Western systems are based on Sun's. It is the reason why your rashi in case of the latter would be ahead of your rashi as per the Vedic system. Each planet rules three of the twenty-seven stars, which, again reflect the properties of the planet concerned. The chart thus prepared at the time of birth is called a kundli (natal chart) and the positions of planets on a day-to-day basis are referred to as transit positions or gochara. Therefore, to make predictions, you consider the relative positions, strength and weakness of the planets in the houses in the natal chart, the dasa-bukti operating at the time of prediction, and the current positions of planets.

You require a calculator and an almanac to sit down and calculate the kundli, and predictions need to be given considering several factors, over and above the ones mentioned. You can imagine why so many predictions go wrong! Fortunately, these days with the advent of computers, software is available for ready-made calculations. You just need to key in the name and the date and time of birth to get instant estimates. Still, you should have the expertise and instinct needed to make correct predictions. It is where charlatans enter and make tall claims for accurate predictions.

I developed a full passion for learning the art and science of astrology in 1991 (in-between postings), sat with scores of professionals, travelling long distances to meet them, and poured over several volumes on astrology written by renowned astrologers such as B.V. Raman, Krishnamurthy and others. When I went to Delhi, I went in search of software available in the market and bought them along with palmtops, which was prohibitively expensive during those days. I made my kundli and tried my hand at making prediction, some of which did come true. My friends would chalk it down to beginner's luck, though. For instance, seeing my friend's face—its shape and size—I predicted that his rashi must be Aries. It seemed likely, given that the goat is the symbol of Aries, and my friend looked like a goat! I didn't, of course, tell him the basis of my prediction, so my friend was suitably impressed that I got it right.

The readings of nadi astrology also fall in the same category. In a place called Vaitheeswaran Koil in Tamil Nadu, ancient records on palm leaves in scripts unknown are said to contain accurate details of life and death of everyone on this planet. I tried all this on an experimental basis and found them to be not very satisfactory. After gathering as much information as I could on astrology, including nadi astrology and horoscope predictions, I noticed that the rate of successful predictions was little, but camouflaged in elaborate demands for 'pariharam', which meant propitiating the Gods to ward off the evil effects of planetary positions. There were claims of completely offsetting the ill effects by doing some rituals while some others argued that the planetary periods will run their course, and we could at the most mitigate the harmful effects. I willingly went along with some of the astrologers to observe how things operated. Soon I discovered a network of astrologers, pujaris and temples. One refers you to the other, and the other takes you to the third one. I could see that it was more of a business than a genuine science. I always believed in experimenting and not condemning anything until I tried it out myself and discovered the pros and cons. My interest in astrology slowly faded with increased commitments at work, travel and other preoccupation. The main reason for this waning interest though, could have been that the outcome was not worth the trouble as there were too many factors to be considered before making predictions. Moreover, my life appeared to defy all the planets and dasa bukti periods and remained stubborn in its course, irrespective of what the stars foretold! But still, I have astrologer friends and keep chatting with them occasionally. I still believe, with proper predicting techniques, astrology can deliver accurate results.

Psychedelics—Future of Healing the Mind

At the outset, I would like to mention that the discussions below are only for academic interests. It is certainly not meant to encourage the use of such substances, which have been declared illegal in many parts of the world, including the US and India.

The question is, am I going to go on reading about consciousness, awareness, mind, body, enlightenment, Vedas and Puranas, etc., or am I going to have a mystical experience in my lifetime? When I read about rishis and munis doing penance and tapasya in the forests and hills for thousands of years, I always got the impression that such things are beyond me, because I am not even able to meditate for five minutes. Several modern-day spiritual gurus of modern times give an impression that they have had mystical experiences. This posturing gives them millions of followers, billions of dollars, ashrams all over the country and the world. They coin some aphorisms, have the power of speech and use social media extensively. While this certainly holds no appeal for me, I have always desired one thing—the mystical experience they boast of, and the enlightenment the great grand masters of the past are supposed to have attained. What if I didn't have the power of expression they had or the bhakti, knowledge or understanding they achieved? What if I succeeded in meditating for one hour and it is not enough? How much more is enough? In short, can an ordinary man have mystical experiences or enlightenment?

Isn't it possible for me to achieve enlightenment and have a mystical experience just as I am? Why are such experiences the preserve of the privileged few, or require insurmountable efforts to achieve? After reading with fascination the history and potential of psychedelics, it appeared that for mystical experiences, you don't have to go to the Himalayas; you may get them in scientific laboratories. As I have mentioned elsewhere, there was an epoch of time when rituals dominated the scene. Then came spoken words (mantras) passed by word of mouth, and the next one is the written word in the form of scriptures and accounts of other seers' experiences. Then came the epoch of bhakti. Has the time come for our own direct and more authentic mystical experience? I wanted an answer for this quest. I had read about soma, the celestial drink of the Gods, which gave such experiences in the distant past even to meditators subsequently. I have also read about plant medicines of siddhas, the Tamil saints of ancient lore. When I read Carlos Castaneda for the first time, years ago, I wondered about the magical plant which Don Juan ingested to alter his state of consciousness. When I came to the US, while studying consciousness, I stumbled upon certain interesting facts in this direction. One day, Janis Phelps, the director of psychedelic research and therapies, CIIS, invited me to attend a seminar on the subject. I was curious and made it a point to visit. I listened to fascinating lectures by the speakers, including Anthony Bossis and Jeffrey Guss (New York University); Karen Cooper, Nicholas Cozzi and Dan Muller (University of Wisconsin); Rick Doblin, Michael Mithoefer and Annie Mithoefer (Multidisciplinary Association for Psychedelic Studies, MAPS), Betsy Gordon, George Greer and David Nichols (Heffter Research Institute); Roland Griffiths and William Richards (Johns Hopkins University); Charles Grob (University of California, Los Angeles); Stanislav Grof and Ralph Metzner.

After listening to them and reading a few books, it appeared that I had hit upon a new hope of finding mystical experiences for myself. Psychedelics could be catalysts for such experiences, if used responsibly—have the right mindset and proper setting with qualified guides. There was plenty of research done on these substances with laboratory experiments conducted on humans to study the effects of such substances on human consciousness. Everything came to a standstill until the 90s when slowly, institutions like Johns Hopkins University came forward to investigate further. In the first decade of the twenty-first century, progress was made with these schools receiving further grants for research, particularly in the fields of treating depression and post-traumatic stress disorders (PTSD).

In fact, in the US, things are moving in the direction of getting governmental approval for the use of MDMA, another psychedelic, for similar treatments.

The biggest impediment in India, in addition to legality, is the fact that we don't think much of healing and therapy. These are prohibited words for us because we equate mental healing with mental ill health and would like to believe that we don't need such 'treatments', so we don't pay much attention to healing. There is another view that our ordinary consciousness is not as 'normal' as we would like to imagine. Elsewhere, we have seen that an 'extraordinary' person needs to become 'ordinary' before becoming 'normal'. I hope that psychedelic substances, if permitted for use, may help in this direction. Some overenthusiastic authors claim that such substances were banned because, if they cure many illnesses, the big pharma may suffer! The governments, on the other hand, argue that the materials are misused as party drugs. Because of lack of proper guidance and mindsets and settings, some cases of psychosis and damage to brain functions came to notice, but there were possibly other reasons such as the use of wrong and contaminated stuff available on the streets.

So, what is the right mindset? A genuine passion for knowledge and understanding and a desire to expand your consciousness and achieve a mystical state of experience. It requires study and expertise. Religions and spirituality strive to create such mindsets. Great ideas were aimed at this state of mind. The 'setting' refers to the circumstances of ingestion of such substances including dosages and the kind of material to be used for a particular type of experience. It is not the bars and discos but the laboratories, natural surroundings or a pleasant environment where higher energy fields are available. The third factor is the presence of a guide or counsellor who can be with you when you are 'voyaging' in the inner recesses, to keep you grounded and facilitate easy return to your ordinary consciousness and later integrate your subjective experiences into your life. It is critical because the revelations of such trips should be understood and followed in our lives.

The 'new science' of psychedelics claims to hold promise for a direct primary religious experience. Researchers in this field, such as William A. Richards, Thomas B. Roberts, and David Jay Brown make an impassioned plea that psychedelics or entheogen need to be distinguished from drugs and hallucinogens, which are toxic. All such substances have been clubbed together and remain banned in most parts of the world. According to some definitions, 'psychedelic' means 'mind-revealing' and 'entheogen' means 'generating God within'. The advocates of psychedelics claim that entheogen such as ayahuasca, psilocybin and LSD, if consumed under proper conditions of 'set and setting', and under the watchful guidance of qualified personnel, could result in immense benefits in religious and sacred experiences including experiences of unitive consciousness. Advocates of these substances claim that they release the energies of the mind, working through the personality accumulations of years of living, before affording the deeper experiences.

Some of the salient points from the book, *Sacred Knowledge: Psychedelics and Religious Experiences*, by William A. Richards, are as follows:

These substances (psychedelic) are regarded especially highly by many people, not simply because busy Westerners may tend to be impatient in their spiritual quests, but also because entheogen, wisely ingested, are noted for their power and effectiveness, thereby potentially supplementing other psychological and spiritual disciplines. The use of psychedelic substances is also an art that requires some skills. There are principles of navigation in the inner world that can be taught and learned.

Mystical Consciousness

The core idea is the nature and relevance of mystical consciousness and the visionary experiences that sometimes precede, follow or accompany this unspeakably vast, dynamic, magnificent and profoundly meaningful state of awareness. The term 'mystical' denotes a form of consciousness that vividly remains in the memory banks of those who witness it (or claim to die in it and be reborn afterwards) that goes by many names: ultimate reality, cosmic consciousness, the eternal core of being or the source of the perennial philosophy. All the great religions of the world have words that point towards this highly desired and valued state of the spiritual awareness—samadhi in Hinduism, nirvana in Buddhism, sekel mufla in Judaism, the beatific vision in Christianity, baqawafana in Islam and wuwei in Taoism.

The major psychedelic substances employed in research include psilocybin, LSD (d-lysergic acid diethyl), DPT (dipropyltryptamine), MDA (methylenedioxyamphetamine) and DMT (dimethyltryptamine). These descriptions are not about the 'drug experiences' these substances induce, but rather about the profoundly important states of consciousness that they may occasion when employed with knowledge and skill. Richards concludes that these incredibly beautiful, awe-inspiring and for some, terrifying experiences are best understood not as being 'within the drugs', but rather as being within our minds. These exciting and unique states of consciousness can also be facilitated by many non-drug approaches, though sometimes yielding experiential discoveries that may appear to be less vivid in intensity or completeness. It includes a plethora of meditative techniques from different religious traditions, many of which include focused attention coupled with changes in breathing patterns that alter the balance of oxygen and carbon dioxide in the body. Some people prefer sensory isolation, sitting in a perfectly quiet place or being suspended in dark tanks of saltwater at body temperature. Others may opt for sensory flooding or overload while immersing themselves in the music of rock bands and symphony orchestras.

No longer is the study of mysticism limited to the scholarly scrutiny of historical documents, such as the beautifully expressive writings of Ramanuja, Sankara, Rumi, St Teresa of Avila or Meister

Eckhart. Nor is it limited to the noble attempts to express the subtle shifts of awareness encountered in meditative disciplines within the structural limitations of human language. Profoundly sacred experiences are now occurring in the laboratories of medical professionals and social scientists.

The Mystery

Expanded into a larger perspective, the issue of the relationship of these particular molecular compounds to inner experiential content fades into the enigmatic question of the relationship of the human nervous system to consciousness, and perhaps, still further into the mystery of matter itself—those atomic and sub-atomic energies that form the cells of our bodies and brains and dance within and between them. Pierre Teilhard de Chardin, a French philosopher, suggested that we are spiritual beings who are currently undergoing physical or human experiences, and called matter 'the divine milieu'.

It is important to realize that a substantial number of people have ingested psychedelic substances on many occasions without experiencing the profound states of consciousness described here. These substances, especially when they are ingested in low dosage without understanding important factors such as trust, honesty, courage and open environments not conducive to safe introspection, can provide changes in sensory perception and mild forms of mental imagery may be experienced as either delightful or frightening. They can also trigger personal psychological experiences, such as regression to childhood traumas or confrontation with unresolved grief, fear, anger or guilt. Such experiences may well have potentially significant value in accelerating psychotherapy and personal growth, whether they are viewed as having religious import. Further, especially if one is unprepared and seeks to control or escape from emerging inner experiences, the flow of unique mental adventures facilitated by psychedelic substances can culminate in episodes of panic, paranoia, confusion and physical distress and perhaps a trip to the emergency room for psychiatric care. None of these are visionary or mystical in the real sense. There is no general state of consciousness following the ingestion of these compounds that could be labelled 'the psychedelic experience', just as we know there is no single meditation, religious or psychotherapeutic experience.

As skilfully portrayed by Hermann Hesse in his short novel, *Journey to the East,* it is often hard to recognize the enlightened minds around us. Sometimes, instead of being highly credentialled academic or religious leaders, they may well turn out to be your sanitation worker, a cleaning lady or the checkout clerk at the supermarket. Those who have known these profoundly important states of consciousness have often shared them with no one, or only with those most intimately trusted, for fear of being misunderstood, called crazy or weird, or viewed as mentally ill. Many religiously-oriented people have looked sceptically at psychedelics, concerned that they might foster hedonistic indulgence rather than spiritual revelations. Similarly, those dedicated to addressing drug abuse in our culture (a regular police officer like me)—a social concern of critical importance—have tended to lump all drugs together in their anti-drug rhetoric, not even distinguishing between narcotics, sedatives, stimulants and psychedelics. In the words of an opiate addict treated with LSD-assisted psychotherapy, 'as far as the comparison of heroin and LSD, there is none. LSD helps you to find yourself; heroin helps you to hide from all kinds of responsibilities and from life itself and LSD has more reality because when you find yourself in it, you can live life better.' It's a proven fact that the psychedelics are not addiction forming but addiction treating. It's now understood that the benefits of a well-planned psychedelic experience come not from the substance itself, but rather from the integration of the enduring memories of the state of consciousness that were experienced during the period of drug action. That is why those who encounter profoundly important states of mind express little interest in repetitive ingestions shortly.

The terms entheogen and psychedelic substances also

include Mescaline, the active ingredient in the peyote cactus used sacramentally by members of the Native American Church. Next is DMT, a substance active in the incredible brew called Ayahuasca, sometimes administered weekly to the members of at least three religions in Brazil and neighbouring countries. Psilocybin, the active ingredient in a mushroom variety called magic mushrooms, is capable of doing magic with your consciousness. And then the LSD, the molecule that the Swiss chemist Albert Hoffman synthesized in 1938 and accidentally ingested in 1943 that still evokes such irrational responses, for and against that many researchers today hesitate even to mention it.

Another term used for these substances is the frequent reference to 'altered state of consciousness' (ASC). When people in psychotherapy wanted to be 'normal', the therapist asked them why they would like to be normal. When the norm is the average in the society, and unfortunately normal behaviour for many tends to be compulsively acquiring worldly goods, mindlessly watching television and drinking beer—not necessarily an ideal which we all should aspire for. Some of the states of consciousness discussed deviate from this norm, but that does not imply psychopathology. It is not that Moses, Isaiah, Ezekiel, St Paul, Ramanuja, Sankara or Madhvacharya suffered from any mental illnesses when they experienced their vision. In this sense, we may as well call these states as 'alternate' and 'non-ordinary', neither of which sounds extraordinarily judgmental. Similarly, the terms 'mind' and 'consciousness' are used synonymously, referring directly to our inner fields of awareness, including the totality of our perceptions, thoughts, mental images, emotions, intentions and memories. The terms refer to what we observe, experience and recall, whether with open or closed eyes, on a vast continuum between unconsciousness or dreamless sleep, and that state of being acutely aware that some seers would call enlightenment.

The Place of Religious Experience in Religion

A primary religious experience refers to the experience that happens directly to the individual. Secondary refers to those you have heard or read about and which subsequently became enshrined as scriptures. Primary forms of religious experience may also include personal devotion, the experiential sense of entrusting your life to, and perhaps communing with, a sacred dimension greater than what you may encounter every day, as is manifested in bhakti and other forms of worship and prayer. As precious as such primary states of mind are for those fortunate enough to experience them, regardless of completeness or intensity, they constitute but one pillar of what many would consider a balanced and mature religious life.

There are three other components, each of which bears its significance. First, there are sacred scriptures. Second, there are theological formulations—fundamentally rational in nature and unique historical or institutional traditions. They may change over time (as they are transmitted through word of mouth or by way of commentaries), as found in the Hebrew Talmud, Christian Creeds, and the lectures of Shankara (the Advaita or non-dualist seer from the eighth century CE) or Ramanuja (a Visishtadvaitan or qualified dualist Hindu philosopher from the eleventh century CE). Third, there are social expressions of religious belief in compassionate service to others, both within religious congregations and in the world as a whole. Primary religious experiences may well provide wisdom and vitality, but they do not render others less relevant. Entheogen is said to facilitate forms of significant experiences of religion, among other states of consciousness. Some of the substances which are said to promote the altered states of consciousness are as follows.

Psilocybin (Magic Mushrooms)

Research is on regarding the various effects psychedelics can have on brain functions. It is said to work on the mind in unusual ways to breed new insights and break from negativity and intransigence. It frees the mind from set patterns and ego-driven assumptions and allows the user to look at the world—and him or herself—from a whole new perspective. Waves of real feelings and psychedelic visions of sound and colour attend the consumption of psilocybin mushrooms. Research published in 2015 in the *Journal of the Royal Society* found that psilocybin changes the brain's organizational framework and allows information to pass from section to section in new or underused neural networks, bypassing the old, well-trodden pathways. It relaxes the constraints on brain function, ascribing cognition a more flexible quality. The brain doesn't simply become a random system after psilocybin injection, but instead retains some organizational features, albeit different from the normal state. In short, the study found that 'the psychedelic state is associated with a less constrained and more intercommunication mode of brain function, which is consistent with descriptions of the nature of consciousness in the psychedelic state'. These results build on other evidence about how psilocybin can rewire the brain. A previous study at the Imperial College London showed that 'brain activity diminished in certain areas when the subjects took the substance, particularly on the part of the brain responsible for the sense of self'. Another study showed that 'more activity occurred in the hippocampus and anterior cingulate cortex, areas associated with memory and emotion'. The result was a brain pattern similar to the dream state. The new pathways help explain why psilocybin is useful in combating mental disorders like depression and PTSD. By building new pathways across the brain, the chemical allows people to shake lose their old assumptions and stimulus-response reactions. In effect, it allows you to reset your brain. Individuals who get into depressive thinking have over-connected brains. Dampening down of that circuit allows one to escape from being chained to that thought process. A Johns Hopkins study says the effects are long-lasting as well, with the personality changes on the tested populations lasting for over a year. A core feature of these mystical experiences is the profound sense of the interconnectedness of all things. Where there is a growing sense of not only self-confidence and clarity, but of communal responsibility—altruism and social justice—and a 'felt' sense of the golden rule: To do unto others as you would have them do unto you. Understanding the nature of these effects, and their consequences may be critical to the survival of our species.

According to another study at Johns Hopkins, psilocybin mushrooms provoke mystical experiences and spiritual journeys when the body breaks the chemical down into a compound that is very similar to serotonin, a natural neurotransmitter in the brain, but psilocybin and serotonin are not the same. What seems to happen in a psychedelic state is that when something is positive, it has the potential to be incredibly positive, to the extent of being euphoric or ecstatic. Similarly, if something is negative, it has the potential to be hellish and dysphoric and frightening. Our brains are biologically hardwired for mystical experiences. It's not special to mystics spending years of meditation in a cave. It is part of the human biology to have these kinds of integrative experiences that can set the stage and platform for remarkable personal change.

Conventional treatments for depression seek to normalize the overactivity in the frontal cortex; the mushrooms have the same effects, and do so very rapidly and perhaps, with much fewer side effects. Mushrooms are being studied for effects in cancer patients who suffer from anxiety and depression from a life-threatening diagnosis. The research conducted by the Heffter Research Institute confirms the fact that psilocybin can help alleviate anxiety and depression in terminally ill cancer patients, helping them to come to terms with their mortality. The other areas where this can be of help are in cases of obsessive compulsive disorders (OCD) and addictions including cocaine, tobacco and alcohol. This healing power seems to arise from the way psychedelics shift consciousness, allowing hitherto unconscious material to enter conscious awareness. It means one can reflect deeply upon life issues and gain insights by seeing things from a new perspective. Dennis McKenna, Heffter's director of ethnopharmacology, points out that mystical experience was always thought of as something of a gift. It happens to you if you're lucky. Many people strive for it their entire lives and don't get the benefit of a mystical experience. But now, with 30 milligrams of psilocybin and under controlled supervision, we can reliably induce mystical experiences, and they are among the most meaningful experiences that people have. In psilocybin, we have a tool that we can use to study that state of mind.

It was indeed what I was looking for and one of the fundamental aims of my quest. As it stands now, according to Heffter, psilocybin is classified as schedule-1 substance in the US and class-A in the UK. It implies that it is one of the most harmful and pernicious drugs we know of—with the ability to devastate people's lives and in the same category as crack cocaine. You can even be arrested and charged for picking naturally occurring psilocybin mushrooms. This distinctively oppressive state intervention is despite the fact that psilocybin is non-addictive, non-lethal and is even considered sacred by native Mexicans who have safely used it in its fungal form for thousands of years.

LSD (lysergic acid diethylamide)

LSD is not a plant medicine but synthesized and regarded as a psychedelic. In 1938, Albert Hoffman, a chemist, developed a molecule based on a fungus called ergot, while trying to create a respiratory stimulant. Five years later he accidentally 'tasted' the substance and thus had the first acid trip in the world. For the next two decades, scientists all over the world experimented with the chemical, trying it on disorders like alcoholism and autism and using it as a tool to break through tricky scientific and engineering problems. Soon, LSD leaked out to the general public and impacted the music, literature and culture of the 1960s. Soon, reports of insanity, suicide and even murder among users followed, and the US government shut down the labs in 1965. It was banned outright in 1970, and research was closed for the next four decades. Now after forty years, research has started picking up. A Johns Hopkins survey found that psychedelics like LSD had more success at stopping cluster headaches than prescription drugs. David Nichols, a professor at Purdue University, says the molecule activates what is called a serotonin 2A receptor in the brain's frontal cortex, which helps visualize and interpret the signals that our senses collect. It is as if the filters that we normally have to function are lowered so that more can be taken in. James Fadiman of the Institute of Transpersonal Psychology says more sensory emotional and visual impressions and more access to the parts of the mind are made available.

Scientists do remember the dark side of LSD, as well, which, in some circumstances, can bring on bad trips, paranoia and delusions with some people even entering psychotic states. To orchestrate a single, profound transformative experience that then results in an unfolding of behavioural change over time depends on three things—mindset, settings of the place where experiment is conducted and guidance. Set refers to mindsets and the controlled environment, like that of a laboratory, or a peaceful setting with good energy under the watchful guidance of qualified personnel who administer right quantities and closely monitor.

Ayahuasca (DMT)

Like psilocybin, ayahuasca is also a plant-based substance. Originating from the Amazon, this mixture is made from a vine called *Banisteriopsis caapi*, a shrub *Psychotria viridis*, which includes large amounts of dimethyltryptamine (DMT), a psychedelic substance. The material has been used for shamanic ceremonies for centuries in the Amazon jungles, and more recently, it has caught the attention of modern media and is fast gaining popularity.

It sends those who consume it on a mystical journey, leaving their ego behind as they experience visions and self-revelations. Ayahuasca's therapeutic benefits are coming to light with numerous people saying that it helped them conquer depression, addiction, PTSD and even saved their lives. Way back in 2007, the *Journal of Ethnopharmacology* published a paper that found the drink to have a significant effect in relieving feelings of anxiety, hopelessness and panic in a group of study participants. Ayahuasca was also believed to be non-addictive and in fact, helped fight addictions of other things like alcohol, tobacco and cocaine. The Sigma-1R receptors found in various tissues such as the brain, retina, liver, lung, heart and immune system, are essential in managing intracellular stress. DMT naturally binds to these receptors and elicit cell-protective effects. It also balances the neurotransmitters, such as 5-HT and dopamine and helps make new neural connections leading to processing repressed traumas and promoting positive outcomes. Increased body awareness, reduced drug cravings, triggering a catharsis, increased inner resources for coping with emotions and increased abilities of introspection are said to be some of the other benefits.

Micro-Dosing

A micro-dose is about a tenth of the standard dose—around 10 micrograms of LSD or 0.2–0.5 grams of mushrooms. Rick Doblin, founder and executive director of the Multidisciplinary Association for Psychedelic Studies says the dose is sub-perceptual—enough to feel a little bit of energy lift and a little bit of insight, but not so much that you are tripping. James Fadiman, the author of *The Psychedelic Explorer's Guide*, introduced the concept of micro-dosing by publishing the results of his surveys and experiments. Those personalities who openly credit psychedelics for their creativity include Cary Grant, Steve Jobs, Frances McDormand, Karry Mullis, Jack Nicholson, Susan Sarandon and Francis Crick.

Ecology and the Pursuit of Energy

Life happens on four levels for everyone—the physical level, the emotional level, the mental and intuitive levels, and finally, the higher consciousness levels. While our senses keep us glued to the first, thoughts keep us busy at the mental level. The energies which we seek and spend should be evenly spread among these four levels. While the energies we expend at other levels are subjective, the physical energy we need are objective and part of the world we share with each other. And it is this relentless pursuit of energy on the material level is causing concerns not only to us, but also for the health of the planet.

As our economies are largely oil-based, we need more and more oil to continue to do all our activities. The results of such ravaging of the planet for over two hundred years are showing right now, in terms of climate change. The lack of well-thought-out ecological principles has been responsible for such a change. Continued destruction of Earth and its resources threatens to end life on all the four levels we were talking about. There is no point in spirituality or religion if the planet is heading towards inevitable destruction, and humanity is going to perish.

I needed to see what, and who, was responsible for our present, what brought us to the brink of destruction and despair, and where does all that I have mentioned in this book up to this point stand, in the face of this grim reality.

13

Climate Change

'How sad to think that nature speaks,
and mankind doesn't listen.'

–VICTOR HUGO

Consequences of a Fading World View

The studies about body, mind, psychology, philosophy, cosmology and consciousness have all led me to this moment. The realization dawned on me that the basis of all my experiences is this earth and in this body. If our experiences lie only in our mind and ideas and imaginations, then it would be enough if we were disembodied beings; the state to which we return when we die. The very idea of creation is to give a body and mind and make us experience life. All scriptures and spiritual teachings focus on human life and its potentialities and how to convert them into reality. And the state of such a body and the earth, which supports the body and all living beings, is in danger of extinction.

During the spring of 2017 at CIIS, we had an intensive workshop called Active Hope dealing with these issues. I have had considerable exposure to Hindu and Vedic ideas and some familiarity with Buddhist philosophy. After coming to the US for consciousness studies, I am getting an idea of Western thought and world view, not only to the political and cultural implications but also global and ecological consequences of the present times and the urgent need to transform them to avoid the impending collapse of our civilization. I questioned the nature of my current world view to be able to contribute to its change. I also preferred a scientific point of view of complex concepts such as consciousness, spirituality and religion.

Both ways, the losers were the body and the cosmos. Neglected and exploited to the core, both are falling in disease. The body catches diseases because it was unable to withstand the pressures and the pain. The illness of the earth is evident in the bleeding of oil and gas and the raging fevers of forest fires. Just as we treat our physical sickness by popping pills and treating only the symptoms, we are looking to find solutions to the woes of the earth in technology. We blame each other for the current crises of the earth. We want to wait it out, exploit to the hilt until the proverbial last straw. What we refuse to see is that the last straw is already here.

We need to change our world view from unlimited progress to progress that has respect for the ecosystem. Climate change is only a symptom. The core sickness of indiscriminate, sometimes destructible, growth is the cause of climate change.

I recall the Gurdjieffian world view that in the scheme of things, organic life on earth spreads like a thin layer all around it, acting as a mechanism to transform the energies coming from stars above and sending them to the Moon for their evolution. The mechanical humanity along with the other forms of organic life serves as a conduit for the evolution of energy on a larger scale. Humanity needs to become more conscious to overcome the mechanicalness of our present-day living, and get help from the Sun by following a different path. In my view, the reasons for the ills of the planet are psychological, in the same way that the state of one's mental health manifests physically.

In his work, *The Systems View of Life: A Unifying Vision*, Professor Fritjof Capra explains how the mechanistic world view came into being with the industrial revolution and how a holistic and systems view of life is now taking shape. The only problem appears to be time. There is no time for a gradual transformation. It needs to happen now. I am choosing a few aspects of the above book which was part of the workshop at CIIS, to discuss here. I approach this subject under two broad categories of thought—the traditional world views over the centuries and how they contributed to the modern dominant world view of humanity, and how the current crisis of climate change reflects this.

Capra, in his book says, 'The biggest problems of our times can't be understood in isolation.' They are systemic problems, interconnected and interdependent. The problems involve crises of perception. It seems that most people in modern society, especially our larger institutions subscribe to the inadequate concepts of an outdated world view and a perception of reality with our overpopulated, globally interconnected world. There may be simpler solutions, but they require a radical shift in our perception, our thinking, and our values. With the emphasis on complexity, networks, and patterns of organization, a new science of qualities is slowly emerging.

These studies by Capra take a broad sweep through the history of Western ideas across scientific disciplines beginning with Renaissance, the scientific revolution, and the rise of the Cartesian mechanism, from seventeenth to the twentieth centuries. And also through systems thinking, the development of complexity theory, the recent discoveries in biology, the emergence of the new conception of life at the turn of the century, and its implications in economics, political, spiritual and ecological fronts. Before 1500 BC, the dominant world view was organic. The scientific framework of it rested in Aristotelian thought and the values of the Church. Thomas Aquinas studied and combined Aristotle's comprehensive system of nature and Christian theology and ethics. In the sixteenth and seventeenth centuries, the medieval outlook changed radically. The idea of the world as a machine replaced the notion of organic living and a spiritual universe. A mechanistic conception of reality became the basis of this new world view. Revolutionary discoveries brought about changes in physics and astronomy, culminating in the achievements of Nicolaus Copernicus, Galileo Galilei and Isaac Newton. The empirical method of enquiry advocated by Francis Bacon formed the basis of seventeenth-century science. Added to this was the mathematical description of nature, and the analytical method of reasoning conceived by René Descartes.

Copernicus (1473–1543) overthrew the geocentric world view of Ptolemy and what has been propounded by Bible. Earth was no longer the centre of the universe. Johannes Kepler (1571–1630) formulated empirically validated laws of planetary motion, supporting the Copernican system. Galileo made scientific observations of celestial phenomena with his telescope, which further confirmed the Copernican theory. After Leonardo da Vinci, Galileo was the first to combine scientific experimentation with mathematical language and therefore, considered the father of modern science. While he studied shapes and numbers and movement, he left out properties of colour, taste, and smell of matter. Francis Bacon advocated the domination of nature. The idea of the world as a machine replaced the pagan view. The goal of science became knowledge that can be used to dominate and control nature. Descartes separated mind and matter thereby alienating the body and the mind. This alienation stayed with the world for the next 300 years.

The rise of the Cartesian-Newtonian science during the scientific revolution has dominated Western culture for three centuries, though there existed alternative, holistic views of reality during that era—those of the Romantic and the Renaissance movements being perhaps the most powerful ones. In Descartes's mechanistic conception of the material world, all of nature works according to mechanical laws. Constituent parts of complex structures reveal their nature, which position is known as Cartesian Reductionism.

At the end of the nineteenth century, Newtonian mechanics had lost its role as the fundamental theory of natural phenomena, partly due to James Clerk Maxwell's electrodynamics and Darwin's theory of evolution, which went much beyond the mechanistic world view. The theories of relativity and quantum mechanics shattered all the principal concepts of the Cartesian world view and Newtonian mechanics. The notion of absolute space and time, elementary solid particles, the idea of a basic material substance, the causal nature of physical phenomena and the objective description of nature, none of these could be extended into the realm into which physics was progressing, according to Capra.

The Rise of Systems Thinking

Emergent properties are an essential part of a living system; features that are not found in any of the parts but emerge at the level of the whole. These emergent properties arise from specific patterns of the organization—that is, from the configuration of ordered relationships among the parts, which is the central insight of the systems view of life. Aristotle, the first biologist, distinguished between four causes as interdependent sources of all phenomena: the material cause, the formal cause, the efficient cause and the final cause. The first two refer to the two perspectives of substance and pattern, or in other words, the aspects of matter and form. Aristotle organized the entire scientific knowledge of antiquity in a scheme that would remain the foundation of Western science for two thousand years.

The Current World View

The central theme of the world view today is that of the global economy, which comes with the illusion of unlimited growth, in three different forms—economic, corporate and population growth. The proponents of unlimited growth in a limited planet refuse to consider the social and environmental costs, which has resulted in an unethical network of financial flows. Added to this are the overconsumption in advanced countries—and consequent piling up of waste—and poverty and population growth in developing countries exerting severe pressures on our natural resources, leading to overgrazing, deforestation and overfishing. The results are devastating—falling water levels, rivers running dry, lakes disappearing, shrinking forests, collapsing fisheries, eroding soil, grasslands turning barren—all of which are severe threats to food security. Added to this are mass extinctions. Climate change has exacerbated all these environmental problems caused by our energy-intensive and fossil-fuel-based technologies.

The excessive dependence on fossil fuels not only caused global warming but also brought us closer to 'peak oil', which means that after reaching peak levels, oil production will decrease and extraction costs will go higher. Most affected will be the oil-intensive segments like automobile, airline industries and industrial agriculture. The search for alternative sources of energy such as biogas has led to increased production of ethanol and other biofuels. Also, this has resulted in the diversion of food much needed to feed the poor for biofuel production, thus raising costs.

When we think according to systems theory, we understand how all processes are interrelated, and realize that the transport we drive, and other consumer choices we make, have an impact on the food supply in other parts of the world. Another barrier to perpetual growth is the financial obstacle. We have created a global monetary system that requires non-stop growth. Money drives economic activities, and these loans can be serviced only by further growth. When economic growth clashes with the other two biggest obstacles of peak oil and climate collapse, the present economic system based on the concept of unlimited and perpetual growth are bound to fail, leading to massive unpaid debts, unemployment, chain reactions of defaults and bankruptcies, all of which we are already witnessing. What we forget is that the problem of growth can also be harmful or pathological like the growth of cancer.

It is evident that undifferentiated economic growth is the cause of our mountains of solid waste, our polluted cities, the depletion of natural resources and the energy crisis. The only alternative to this concept of unlimited growth is the idea of growth which enhances life. In living organisms, ecosystems and societies, qualitative growth includes an increase in complexity, sophistication and maturity. Qualities arise from processes and patterns of relationships among the parts. We can't understand the nature of complex systems such as organisms, ecosystems, societies and economies if we try to describe them purely regarding quantities. Quantities can be measured, but qualities need to be mapped. In the human realm, the question of quality always arose, which is primarily subjective, and therefore, presented the 'hard problem' of consciousness studies.

Sustaining the Web of Life

According to Gaia theory, 'the evolution of the first living organisms went hand in hand with the transformation of the planetary surface from an artificial environment to the self-regulating biosphere.' In that sense, according to Morowitz, it is a property of the planets rather than of individual organisms. The basic ecological unit is the ecosystem, defined as a community of different species in a particular area, interacting with its non-living, or abiotic environment such as water, minerals, sunlight, etc. And with its living, or the biotic environment, that is, with other members of the community. The ecosystem, then, consists of a biotic community and its physical environment. A fundamental principle of ecology is the recognition that ecosystems, like all living systems, help form multilevel structures of systems nestling within other systems. Systems biology is concerned with the ecosystem as an integrated and interactive system of biological and physical components.

Estimates of current extinction rates, due to deforestation and the destruction of other habitats indicate that the earth is now in the midst of a sixth mass extinction. The current extinction event, however, is unique. Homo sapiens may be the reason of the likely current mass extinction, while natural phenomena caused all previous ones. We need to build and nurture sustainable communities and societies. A sustainable human community is designed in such a manner that its ways of life, businesses, economy, physical structures and technologies do not interfere with nature's inherent ability to sustain life. Being eco-literate means understanding the basic principles of ecology, or principles of sustainability, and living accordingly.

The Indian Tradition

My religion inculcates a world view that makes a classification of all creation into three categories—chit, achit and Iswara. Chit includes all living beings, achit represents all non-living things. Iswara, the God, who created both these categories and therefore, He is the ultimate owner. We are all His slaves, and He is our master. Our job is to live and eat frugally in His name, working out our karma in the process, never getting attached to neither this body nor the earth. It implies that the rest will be taken care of by Him.

Lord Rama's consort Sita is said to be a reincarnation of Mother Earth. Her father King Janaka found her when he was ploughing the fields. She grew up and married Rama, an incarnation of Lord Vishnu, representing the marriage between heaven and earth, God and humankind. She lived happily for a short while, before heading to the forest to live a hermit's life for fourteen years. She gets abducted by Ravana, the king of Lanka, the island kingdom. What ensues is a battle between Rama and Ravana, and finally, after the defeat and death of Ravana, Sita is retrieved and returns to Ayodhya. The story goes on to have twists and turns where again she is subjected to trials and tribulations and finally takes a plunge into the fire to prove her purity. A few thousand years later in another incarnation, she was again born as the daughter of Mother Earth, when a Srivaishnavite saint called Periyazwar found the baby under a tulsi plant and named her Andal, who eventually married Lord Vishnu, again a marriage between heaven and earth.

Indian mythology abounds in such imageries of Mother Earth, only to inculcate a world view that included the earth as an integral part of human life, and to revere and love her. This view coincides with the Gaia, the primordial Greek deity and mother of all life and earth, before the advent of materialism, and the old pagan view of everything as interconnected and sacred.

The world view of an individual is essentially that of the society, and in Indian context, it can be said that society lost its Vedic values along the way. The country suffered many onslaughts by way of invasions from Mughals and the British for over two hundred years. Ever since Independence in 1947, India has been striving to eradicate poverty and contain population growth to ensure progress and prosperity for all people. Caught between a glorious Vedic tradition of the past and the stark reality of the present, where the Western civilization has been racing ahead. The country's leaders tried to adopt a middle path between democratic socialism. With globalization, the world has come closer and progress and development, and the focus on personal growth has come at the cost of abusing the earth and its natural resources. The individual world view, too, metamorphosed into selfishness and lack of consciousness for the environment, amplified by corruption, regional and communal outlooks.

We forgot the land as the basis of our life and remembered her only as something to be exploited. For the modern man god and goddesses became templates on their screens of life, the other pursuits include profit and unlimited growth. The exploitation of the earth goes on unabated, and ominous signs have appeared on the horizon—floods, droughts and wild forest fires, extinction of species, melting ice from the Arctic and the Antarctic, and global warming resulting in climate change.

What Climate Change Means Today

Climate change is a systemic and structural problem. The world has quietly slipped into complexity from linearity, and the solutions need to be addressing this shift. Ninety-eight per cent of scientists have affirmed climate change, as also the fact that this crisis is man-made. Climate change is not unusual for the planet. What is frightening now is the pace at which the change is happening. The rapid acceleration is taking us closer to the tipping points. The Paris Agreement has finally been reached with a containment of carbon emission and temperature rise to within 2°C this century.

Climate change is the alarming fallout of indiscriminate industrialization that has happened on a global scale. The rise of greenhouse gases, melting ice caps in the Arctic and Antarctic, ocean acidification, rising sea levels and the problem of waste management are all becoming severe. Land and maritime areas are inundated with waste and plastics, killing species, reefs and planktons. The Fukushima nuclear reactors disaster in 2011 following the tsunami in Japan, has resulted in radioactive waste being dumped into the Pacific, which is continuing even after five years, contaminating the ocean, and killing marine life on an unprecedented scale. Other effects include the danger of coastal towns and islands getting submerged and the movement of populations moving inland, creating security issues, as feared by the ex-president of the US, Obama.

The root of the problem is the world view of market fundamentalism driven by the idea of unlimited growth on a limited planet and globalization of trade. This idea created energy-intensive business needs leading to a fossil-fuel-based economy culminating in drilling and digging for coal, oil and gas. When reserves went down, and consumption climbed, the need arose for desperate measures such as fracking, shale gas, search for hydrocarbons and dangerously carbon-intensive Alberta tar sands in Canada. Capitalism and fuel-based economies were focused only on profit and encouraged negative behaviours like greed. Consider the huge pay packets of executives in the oil industry.

The three biggest industries based on fossil fuels are energy, food and packaging. The automobile industry is entirely dependent on oil. Next comes the farming industry manufacturing food for the rising population. The third and critical sector is packaging, which gives rise to enormous amounts of garbage and waste. (Documentary, *Inside the Garbage of the World*.) Population explosion is another cause, which is driving the manufacture of goods and services on an ever-increasing scale. Feeding and providing homes to billions has led to rapid deforestation on the global level, to grow food and provide employment, as well as provide food for cattle that are raised for meat. Due to lack of land for grazing, forests are cut down so that single crops like corn are grown to feed the animals. In addition to land, water is another resource going into animal farming, resulting in drinking water shortage. Large corporate with vested interests have driven many a farmer out of his land. Indonesia is systematically destroying forest areas for palm oil production, which is predominantly used in the fast-food industry. Overfishing has resulted in the collapse of fisheries and extinction of several species. (Documentary, *Revolution*, 2012). The rate of consumption of fish is much higher than the capacity of the ocean to regenerate them. Animal farming has thus resulted in deforestation, a single crop culture, food shortages, higher amount of methane being released by animal waste into the atmosphere, and spread of diseases like e-coli and diabetes (Documentary, *Food Inc.*, 2008).

We must start thinking of bringing a stop to this, and the very first step is to stop looking away. Joan Klein, in her book and the documentary, *This Changes Everything*, says people look away from the problem of climate change. We are reluctant to accept climate change as man-made. The belief in religion, which says God created everything, and therefore He will take care, sustains and justifies the 'I am so small, what can I do?' argument. This needs to change. We need to accept the fact that climate change is occurring because of our activities. Let's begin by reducing fossil fuel burning and lower greenhouse gas emissions, increase renewable energy production and explore free energy technologies.

Adequate monetary aid needs to be made available, especially to poorer countries, to smoothen the transition from fossil fuels to the wind, solar and water energy production. Implementation of a carbon tax could be another option to fund such activities. One important step is to declare plastic waste as hazardous. Long-term measures include effective town planning and urban design and to develop nature in urban environments (Documentary, *The Nature of Cities*, 2010). Some of the ways in which people can make a difference are effective implementation of the Paris Agreement. Governments have been dithering for over thirty years to reach the present level. There there is the fact that commitment is not built into the accord; the steps taken by the countries would be voluntary. The only option would be the uprising of people, which will exert pressure on governments to take practical measures. For this to happen, knowledge and awareness are required, and for that, world views need to change.

Another practical step would be to involve communities in environmental activities (Documentary, *In Transition 2.0'*, 2013). Curtail animal farming and destruction of forests and lands, and consume less of animal-based food, fast food, dairy, etc. (Documentary, *Cowspiracy*, 2014). Consume only food grown locally and in-season fruits and vegetables. Our obsession with accumulation of stuff needs a review, and we need to realize that unlimited growth on a limited planet is no longer possible. In the direction of population control, education and women's rights will go a long way.

There is a need to overcome the pervasive cultural conditioning of materialism and finding satisfaction and joy in human relationships and community. There is an urgent need to promote the values of conservation, cooperation and community. The ecological and feminist movements are both important in this regard, as they advocate the most profound value shifts through a redefinition of gender relationships and the redefinition of the relationship between humans and nature. Both these movements put together could contribute significantly to overcoming our culture's glorification of material consumption. We also need to understand the global network economy, arising out of knowledge generation and information processing.

A game changer could be identifying systemic solutions to the problems, for which the solutions include redesigning the governing rules and institutions of globalization, increasing the awareness of the climate crisis and catalyzing leadership for developing appropriate energy and climate policies. Resistance to genetically modified (GM) foods and promotion of sustainable agriculture and there needs to be a concerted effort to redesign our physical structures, cities, technologies, and industries to make them ecologically sustainable. The relentless pursuit of corporate and economic growth, built into the very structure and legal framework of companies, need to change. Reshaping global capitalism will not be possible without fundamental changes in organizational structures. At the very heart of the business model is the legal mandate to maximize the returns for the corporation's shareholders, which often happens at huge costs to the environment. Modern industrial society depends crucially on a continuous supply of abundant energy for its food production and manufacturing processes, lighting and heating of our homes and cities and the worldwide networks of transportation and communication, which is a relatively recent phenomenon.

During the centuries of the industrial revolution, wind, water and active power of humans and animals provided the energy to move carts and ships, operate mills and drive all other machines. In addition to declining supplies of fossil fuels, we are also depleting numerous other natural resources including water, copper, steel, rare minerals like scandium, terbium and yttrium, much required in aerospace and automotive industries. The other fallout of the 'peak oil' crisis is the increasing frequency and severity of accidents involving fossil fuel extraction. As conventional fuels supplies are getting depleted, oil companies are resorting to extreme extraction methods such as drilling ocean depths or Arctic and other technologies such as shale gas using fracking, which releases enormous amounts of methane and other toxins more harmful than carbon. Such toxicity has resulted in increasing number of cases of asthma, infertility and cancer. Nuclear energy is said to create significant greenhouse gasses and pollution, though interested parties project it as safe.

So, the urgent task is to develop systemic strategies to contain the risks: qualifying economic growth, redefining development, finding inner fulfilment in the community, changing the structure and legal framework of corporations and designing new forms of generative ownership. In the short run, we need to accelerate the transition towards a future without fossil fuels if we must survive the threat of global climate collapse.

Plan B, the book by Lester Brown offers a road map to save civilization. He suggests a three-pronged action plan—eradicating poverty, stabilizing population growth, stabilizing climate and restoring the earth's ecosystem. The programmes to be funded include universal primary education, eradication of adult illiteracy, school lunch programmes, universal basic healthcare, assistance to pregnant women and preschool children, reproductive health, and family planning. We do have the technology and resources to achieve these two goals.

For the second component of stabilizing climate, the goal is to cut carbon emissions by 80 per cent by 2030, which will stabilize atmospheric carbon dioxide at 350 ppm (currently, the emissions remain at over 410 ppm). He also suggests an expansion of forest cover, raising energy efficiency and developing renewable sources of energy.

In the third major component of restoring the earth's ecosystems, Brown suggests launching a major effort to protect and restore forests, conserve and rebuild soils, regenerate fisheries, protect animal and plant diversity and plant millions of trees to contain carbon. Recycling paper and going paperless will go a long way in this regard. To make this plan feasible, reorienting national budgets and economies will help restore the health of the ecology. The carbon tax is another factor in achieving this shift. Removal of hidden subsidies to industries that pollute must be considered. Armory Lovins suggests the 'reinventing fire' concept which means the business-led transition from oil, coal and ultimately gas to efficiency and renewable. Their key strategy is to redesign energy systems in such a way that their effectiveness is increased multifold, with massive savings that will be so attractive to industrialists that business will become the driving force of the entire process.

A variety of agricultural techniques—often based on traditional practices—is now emerging around the world in which healthy, organic food grows in decentralized, community-oriented, energy-efficient ways. The green revolution (chemical farming) has helped neither farmers, nor the land, nor the consumers. The practice of single-crop monoculture entailed high risks of large acreages being destroyed by a single pest and it also severely affected the health of farm workers and people living in agricultural areas, together with the heavy use of chemicals. Biotechnology in agriculture, in the form of genetically modified organisms (GMO) also proved to be more profit-driven than anything else, as illustrated by the Monsanto, who, for instance, produced cotton seeds containing an insecticide gene to boost seed sales. Technologies like these increase farmers' dependence on products that are patented and protected by intellectual property rights, which make the age-old farming practices of reproducing, storing and sharing seeds, illegal.

The hazards of genetic engineering and production of transgenic products are many. The gene-transfer vectors, a form of viruses, which help transplant genes into foreign DNA are used in this technology and these vectors are immensely hazardous because they are often in virulent forms, which combine with the existing ones to produce deadly varieties, which are antibiotic resistant. The trial-and-error approach of genetic engineering is also wasteful, with only about 1 per cent of the experiments succeeding. The cause of these problems is that the engineers of biotechnology concentrate more on molecular biology rather than ecology and remain ignorant of the biological processes of the entire ecosystem.

When farmers grow crops organically, they use their knowledge of ecology rather than the technologies of chemistry or geoengineering. A variety of crops is planted by the farmers, rotating them so that insects that are attracted to one disappear with the next. 'So, a fundamental principle of agro-ecology is the diversification of farming systems, mixtures of crop varieties grown through intercropping, agro-forestry, growing trees and shrubs with crops, and other such techniques. Livestock is integrated to support ecosystems. All these are labour-intensive, and thus lead to alleviating poverty and social exclusion. In the words of Miguel A. Altieri, 'Agroecology raises agricultural productivity in economically viable, environmentally benign, and socially uplifting ways.'

From an ecological perspective, the design should consist of shaping flows of energy and materials for human purposes. Environmental design is the careful meshing of human purposes with the larger patterns and flows of the natural world, and the study of the patterns and flows to inform human action. To practise design in such a context requires a fundamental shift in our attitude towards nature, from finding out not what we can extract from nature but what we can learn. One crucial difference is that when we speak of design, we are metaphorical since nature's designs emerged from self-organizing processes that are inherent in all living systems.

Ecological clustering of industries helps in the disposal of waste sustainably. The waste produced in one industry will be the raw material to produce the other. For instance, when we extract cellulose from wood to make paper, we use only 20–25 per cent of the trees, discarding the remaining 75–80 per cent of waste. Beer breweries derive only 8 per cent of the nutrients from barley or rice for fermentation; palm oil is only 4 per cent of the palm tree's biomass and coffee beans only 3.7 per cent of the coffee bush. This biomass contains valuable raw material for other industries. An organization called ZERI (Zero Emissions Research and Initiatives) helps businesses to organize themselves into ecological clusters, so that the waste of one is used as a resource for another, for the benefit of both.

A well-designed economic eco-structure will display a physical shape and orientation that takes full advantage of the Sun and wind, optimizing passive solar heating and cooling. That alone will save about 30 per cent of the energy use. Proper orientation along with other passive-solar design features, also provides glare-free natural light throughout the structure. Modern electric lighting systems, such as LED, save up to 80–90 per cent of energy. Even more impressive are the improvements in insulation and temperature regulation created by 'super windows', which keep people warm in winters and cool in summers without additional heating or cooling. Eco-friendly buildings can not only save energy but also produce energy, as in the case of photovoltaic electricity, which can be generated from wall panels, roofing shingles, and other structural elements. Similarly, cities can be designed not to depend on automobiles, but with the minimal role of public transportation, which will reduce usage of gasoline and prevent fog and air pollution.

Biomimicry means imitation of life. Many of our design problems have been solved by living organisms and ecological communities during billions of years of evolutionary tinkering in elegant, efficient and ecologically sustainable ways, and we can learn valuable lessons from this evolutionary wisdom of nature. Jenny Benyus, a naturalist and science writer, realized that developing bio-inspired technologies could provide exciting research programmes for scientists and engineers.

But the biggest hurdle is the attitude of the people. The vast majority lives in the same old ways expecting only leaders, governments and scientists to bring about change. Now is the time for all the humanity to take concerted action. Active and urgent individual participation is the call of the present times. Looking at the human activities and the consequences of the climate change, it is evident that everything comes back to the community and the individual.

Local communities need to take back control on issues such as renewable power, local economy and organic farming. In addition to all this, people need to cope with the situation. Joanna Macy in her book, *Active Hope: How to Face the Mess We're in Without Going Crazy*, gives some useful suggestions such as the following: Despair sets in when we learn that we are in a mess and there is uncertainty about the future and what role we can play as individuals. We don't know what to do and how to go about it, and we despair. The first signs of such a despair would be to turn away, avoid talking about it or hoping that something will happen on its own and it would all be okay. But it doesn't go away just like that. How are we going to deal with this despair at the back of our minds?

Our response could be either hopefulness or desire. The first, hopefulness, comes when we think the preferred outcome is likely to happen and when the obstacles appear insurmountable we become hopeless. In other words, it's a hope anticipating the result happening and not out of a firm commitment to an action plan. We also hope others do something about it or something happens, such as some new technology on the horizon, which will make climate woes vanish. But desire is different—when we express what we like to happen and how the question comes alive. This act of expression, which is action in one form, turns hope into an active force, instead of being a passive one. This 'activehope' requires us to have a clear view of reality, to identify the direction in which we would like things to move and take steps in that direction. Active hope is different from optimism, in the sense that the principle of 'activehope' can be applied even in pessimistic situations. The intention is the driving force of this approach.

According to Macy, there are three stories of the world and all of them are happening concurrently. The first one is 'business as usual', where people think everything is okay with the world and there is no need for any change, economic prosperity is essential, and getting ahead is good. The second one, 'the great unravelling', draws our attention to the disasters the first story has brought on us, and is a cautionary tale that there are more such crises to come if we continue our old path. The third story, 'the great turning', focuses on those who know that the first story is leading us into catastrophe, and who refuse to be intimidated by the second story, working instead, to put their energies behind good intentions of consciously overturn the consequences. From this, we feel empowered, and to this end, Macy offers the 'work that reconnects' humanity with the web of life and with one another, which, in turn, strengthens our capacity to face disturbing information.

What is astonishing is that Macy's ideas are applicable not only to climate change but also to a person and to society as well. It's not only about what to do about climate change but mainly, what to 'be' in the face of seemingly irreconcilable problems, to expand your capacity to respond creatively to the crisis of our time. This process of the work that reconnects moves through four stages of a spiral: coming from gratitude, honouring our pain for the world, seeing with new eyes and going forth.

I was unaware that the great unravelling was happening side by side. The economic meltdown of 2008 appeared to be happening far away in the US stock markets. I kept glancing and skipping reading about resource depletion, the unseasonal rains and unusually hot weather. Such conditions are 'normal' for India, mass extinctions were part of a 'grand' design of nature, and social tensions needed to be contained with an iron hand (I was earning a good salary, and the 'less deserving' communities were asking for more). The great unravelling, in short, were news items to be read and forgotten, while sipping morning coffee. All this sound like a belief system— either you believe God will take care of the mess or trust the scientists and hope that science and technology will take care of it. What is indigestible is that there is work for us to do personally.

Macy goes on to describe the three dimensions of the great turning; holding actions, life-sustaining systems and practices, and a shift in consciousness. It's interesting to see how the three of them are interconnected; how continued holding activities such as protests may end up in battle-weariness and the need to 'replace or transform' the systems that cause the harm, which is what it means to help organize life-sustaining systems and practices. To make these new structures well-rooted and sustainable, a deeply ingrained value system needs to be in place, and this is the essence of the third dimension of a 'shift in consciousness'. The other factors which helped to establish interconnection were the landing on the Moon in 1969, and the subsequent views of the planet from the Moon and space. It's true that during the past forty years, those earth photos, along with Gaia theory and environmental challenges, have provoked a new way of thinking about ourselves.

When we feel gratitude for life, we enhance our ability to look at, and not turn away from, bad news. When we honour the pain, we welcome the feeling instead of rejecting it, thereby bringing forth compassion and connection. Seeing with new eyes means understanding the actual context of things and we're not an isolated instance of only we facing the problem. This helps in finding our priorities for concrete action, says Macy.

It's interesting to note as to why information about bad news is not enough. The process goes through several stages; the first one is to accept it and not take it on a superficial level. The second stage is that of digestion, which mainly comprises taking awareness to a deeper level. Speaking out about what we already know helps us to reach this level of assimilation.

Nothing motivates an individual to change his old fossil-fuel-burning ways as an existing model. A good urban design could be one of them. Peter Calthorpe, in his book, *Urbanism in the Age of Climate Change*, defines urbanism broadly—by qualities, not quantities, by diversity, not size, by intensity, not density, by connectivity, not just location. He asserts that responding to climate change and energy challenge without a sustainable form of urbanism will be difficult. For instance, the average emission of carbon per person in the US is about 23 metric tonnes per person in a year, while that in Europe is 10 and the world average is 5.5. In other words, the world needs to reduce carbon levels by 80 per cent by 2050, which means an average person in 2050, must emit only about 12 per cent of what they emit today. The US urban carbon emissions consisting of buildings and transportations accounts for 62 per cent (global: 37 per cent), whereas all other forms such as industry, agriculture/waste and deforestation, put together account for only 38 per cent (global: 63 per cent). It's, therefore, evident that urbanization has a larger role to play in climate change. In the US, the per capita requirement of land for carbon emission has increased fivefold from 3 acres in 1961 to 15.83 acres in 2006, which is likely to be more in the last ten years of constant fossil-fuel burning.

According to Calthorpe, there are three interdependent approaches to climate change—lifestyle, conservation and clean energy. Lifestyle involves how we live, how much driving we do, the size of the house, the food and other goods we consume. All these factors depend on the types of communities we build and the culture we inhabit. Conservation revolves around efficiencies—in our buildings, cars, appliances and industrial systems. The third aspect of clean energy includes the new technologies for solar, wind, wave, geothermal, biomass, nuclear or fusion energy. Thus, says Calthorpe, lifestyle, urbanism and conservation are our most cost-effective tools to combat climate change. It's evident that our urban planning model is no longer viable. The population has outgrown the model of the 'one size fits all' housing market, rendering it ineffective in meeting the challenges of demographics, economic needs and climate questions. The time has come for affordable housing and walkable lifestyles.

In other words, the future market trends need to be towards smaller homes, higher-density communities and more walkable and transit-oriented environments. Calthorpe makes a comparison of combating climate change to the war on drugs; you go after the suppliers—coal-powered power plants in this case—or you can pursue the addicts, the inefficient buildings and suburban sprawls. He finds both as being equally necessary. On the one hand, we have specialization, standardization and mass production as our current standards; on the other, waiting in the wings are the principles rooted in ecology and not mechanics. These are diversity, conservation and human scale. The dictum of development and transit as co-evolving partners needs to modify in the light of climate change. Transportation is an opportunity for reduction of carbon emissions, which in turn depends on community design. To the contrary, we keep building alternate energy sources while allowing demand to increase exponentially.

As global population is likely to reach a whopping ten billion, sooner rather than later, much of it in mega cities, a new vision of urban development is long overdue. Thriving under these challenging circumstances will mean designs for sustainability; reducing carbon emissions and resource waste substantially, to balance long-term consumption with sustainable production and foster social forms of integrity, equity and durability. What Calthorpe states finally is ominous but real: 'We're at a critical juncture when energy, environmental, fiscal and national security challenges are converging at such a rapid pace that we can't afford another generation of unsustainable growth.'

I got up one morning, made a cup of tea for myself and opened the curtains to let in the light. It was a great morning with bright sunshine. The sky was a pure blue; the breeze was a little high, but still pleasant. I went to the beach, and the sea was again inviting. At the back of my mind, I was a little disturbed about climate change. But the beauty in front of my eyes made me forget about it; climate has always been changing, why not enjoy it when the going is good? I know this is the mindset of billions of people, while a few hundred thousand people keep suffering every minute of the day due to climate fury. The usual reasons all line up in my mind—God will take care; others will do something about it, governments need to rise to the occasion, karma has its way of working. The mind pulls out endless lists to pacify me. The question is, do I enjoy the sunshine and the beach or go to San Francisco to participate in the climate change rally organized by 350.org? Is climate change a bit like religion in demanding faith, only here, it is a question of belief in the scientists and their data? And the fact is that 98 per cent of the scientists agree that climate change is happening on an unprecedented scale and it's due to human actions. There is evidence all over.

And some people deny climate change. They project their arguments, facts and figures. The six-year drought in California has been wiped out by rains in a single season in 2016, so why bother? There is hardly anything exciting in climate consciousness compared to the thrill of constant growth, constant seeking of money, wealth and comforts. Likewise, women and children have been suffering; they have several needs to be met; equality of pay between genders, the right to food, education and health. Hence things continue in the same old way. The tectonic shift has not happened to bring about the tsunami of change. And life goes on. It's here that Joanna Macy's *Active Hope* brings light to otherwise a gloomy scenario. She is asking whether I am doing the right thing in my own, tiny, private life, and she suggests ways and means of doing it, irrespective of the scale and quantity.

Epilogue

The universe is made of stories, not of atoms.

−MURIEL RUKEYSER

Every human being, at some point in time, needs to develop a concept of life. Science rests on two principles— experimentation and repeatability—before accepting any hypothesis. I decided to employ the same method on spirituality. In a way, it is easy to accept something by faith, and all religions demand faith, to begin with.

My theory goes somewhat like this: the life of an individual is the story of his evolution towards full potential, which, in other words, can be defined as the purpose of their life. I might have had smaller objectives and aims within this framework, such as aiming for a good education, making a career, earning well and starting a family. However, life's purpose can be different things for different people; it can even just be an aim to be happy, whatever that happiness may mean. But a larger picture is essential to obtain a better perspective and to avoid certain complications and complexities. Chasing happiness may sometimes become tiring if you don't know what will make you happy or what happiness means.

This overarching view of life, as a process of self-evolution towards reaching one's full potential, opened many questions and possibilities. What exactly do the words 'self', 'evolution' and 'potential' mean and how am I supposed to attain this goal? I was born with certain things and I had no choice in the matter, such as a body, a mind and the environment into which I took birth. These are irreversible, and I could have done nothing about it. I needed to work from that point towards realizing my full potential. To that extent, these things which are given to me at birth become my tools for such a work; a body with all its limitations and potential, a psychology including my mind and its possibilities, and the cosmology, which includes the environment into which I was born.

When I say I am given my body and mind, that implies that I'm not them. If I have a car, I'm not the car. Then who am I? Shall I call that the self? The Bhagavad Gita calls it atman. My body has a name, Sampath, and address, some qualifications, family and possessions, and terabytes of impressions and experiences pouring out of all these things every second of my life and existence. If I'm not my body, then who enjoys the fruits of such experiences? My body can't because it's inert, it's driven like a car which can't enjoy the coastal ride. It's the occupant of the car who enjoys the journey or suffers injuries when met with an accident. Shall we then say it's me, myself or simply the 'self,' which enjoys or suffers the experiences?

So, I am here in this life to evolve and realize my full potential for which I have been given the tools of body, mind and an environment. The body is the primary instrument, in the sense that it houses my essential self. It comes equipped with its own set of subsidiary tools to help—the six senses, limbs, organs and everything else required to function effectively. Here I have a nagging question—if the body has the full capacity to process experiences such as these, then why is a corpse not able to eat food and digest? That only means there is something else, which is responsible for these things, including the signals sent by the senses. I suspected this to be the mind guiding the body through these experiences. I eat ice cream when I have the mood, and don't if I fall sick. That means the mind is not alone, but a whole lot of other things which decide what and when I eat, and the body follows mutely.

Another important point is about maintenance of the tools. If the devices are not used correctly, they go to waste. Similarly, the body and mind are subject to decay and need constant vigil and maintenance. The body needs to be nourished and used correctly to stay fit. Then comes the environment—both the outside world and an individual's inner world—that needs to be healthy for a person to thrive.

I have the responsibility of maintaining both inner and outer environments, mainly the external, as it is a shared environment. I can see the role that the law and societal rules play to ensure that the outer environment is conducive to all. Then comes the question of the people who inhabit this external environment. The community consists of people and what makes them all different from each other? Why is someone short and another tall? Why is someone rich and other poor or why do some believe in God and some others don't? Will all of them evolve to reach their potentiality? Is 'potentiality' the same for everyone or is it different for different people? G says everything depends on one's 'level of being'. This level is decided by the total of my internal environment including my thoughts, feelings, emotions and actions.

The 'level' of my being led me down the path that my life took. That explains why I was a police officer; someone else was an actor and someone the prime minister or president. The question is whether I would be able to influence my level of being and change it to attract a different kind of life or is it just a matter of chance, luck or accident? It occurs to me that it should be possible to reduce the role of chance in my life and change my level of being, provided I work on myself. To work on myself, I needed knowledge and understanding of how to go about doing that. Over several millennia, all masters, religions and philosophers and all the scriptures were trying to tell humanity one thing only: How to work on oneself. Sounds simple enough! But the question is with so many teachings available, whom to follow and what to do. To know the truth and to detect the underlying unity, I needed a key to understanding them.

Gurdjieff with his Fourth Way concepts provided such a key to me. With that, I could open the large treasure houses of scriptures from various religions. Remembering the original task of working on myself, with the help of the given tools and conditions, I needed to transform and evolve so that I uncover my real potential. The body and the mind were both necessary for the acquisition of knowledge, followed by understanding what I had imbibed. Or it's possible that both, knowledge and understanding occur simultaneously. Through the power of knowledge it should be possible, I speculated, to switch from instinctual to intellectual to intuitive planes of existence. Once intuition takes over, it should be possible to know the way to transformation. I also figured happiness and fulfilment occupied a place somewhere between intellectual and intuitive planes. It is the place that could be free of the urges of the instincts of hunger, sex, fear and other demands of life and free from the intellectual interferences of thoughts, logic and reason. This space is precious where your wants are met, and your logic takes a back seat as you realize the futility of words and expressions. Space stands created for higher influences to enter. That may be the reason why humans seek happiness by default.

I reflected on my theory of life for a long time. It was not perfect, and I could see gaps which needed to be filled. Nevertheless, it appeared to be a good starting point. Still, many issues needed to be resolved. The most important issue was that of God—whether He exists or doesn't. First, the answer required to come from inside and not outside. The world is largely divided between those who believe and those who don't, though the number of atheists far outnumbers those who don't. That doesn't mean by any measure, that those who believe necessarily got the answer from the depths of their being. Those who don't believe often take the route of rationalism and evolutionism that life evolved by itself. The other theory is called creationism, which maintains that God created life. For me though, the life process appeared too intricate and awe-inspiring to be a series of random processes. I believe that the universe was created by a single force, which can be understood provided we make efforts. Efforts, which help in finding ourselves before finding God. If we don't know ourselves, how could we possibly know another, let alone God?

Then there are the agnostics, who neither believe nor disbelieve in God. Osho says God is needed more by the poor than by the wealthy. You need the theory of God existing if you need to survive. Once you have money and other things in life, perhaps, you only have a God, who is waiting to punish you for your misdeeds, and who wants to be punished. There are other varieties of people who say work is God or that you see God in the innocent smile of a child, etc. To me, God is someone who needs to be discovered by working on oneself.

Once I accepted this theory, the next logical question was where I could find Him. Most of the organized religions, based on dualism insisted that God was external to oneself, far beyond, high in the skies. There are parts of Vedanta philosophy, such as monism, which talks about God as someone interior to all human beings, sarvantaryami. In other words, there is nothing except God in this universe. The Visishtadvaita, the basic philosophy of Vaishnavism, believes that God is both inside and outside. I take it that this means He is so high and far above that, I can't reach him quickly. At the same time, He is also deep within me, provided I make the effort to find him. I identify most with this theory because it means I needed to work on myself. Thus, I resolved the issue of God for myself.

Religious and spiritual traditions make the claims that through methods like yoga, meditation and devotional practices such as prayer will ultimately lead to Him. I believe that such practices may result in a point from where finding Him may become a little more feasible, like climbing a mountain to catch a glimpse of a glorious sunrise. There may still be issues though, such as a cloudy day. You may have to wait there until the clouds clear. It was evident that to think of God and find a path that led to Him, I needed to cross several stages and work through different layers, and despite that, I still was not sure of reaching where I wanted. In a state of clarity and calmness, one may get the next clue, like on a treasure hunt. You keep getting hints when you follow the arrow marks. Someone may know where the treasure is even without the clues. But I needed the clues. I also found that the philosophies of the East, particularly India, was related to the mind and the Western views worked primarily on the body. It appears they approach this concept from opposite ends. However, the Bhagavad Gita reconciles both, by saying that karma yoga done with a sense of non-attachment could be the way to go. Yoga includes physical postures, but I feel that most of the masters worked on their minds. The idea is that a sufficiently trained mind will take care of the physicality. I felt working on the mind to start with might be challenging and work on the body should precede work on the mind. Gita put karma yoga before dhyana yoga and bhakti yoga. I also realized the importance of selflessly serving society and the role it plays in one's evolution. Finding God in the process of finding one's potential, however, needs to be verified by one's experience. Who knows, finding one's potential might include finding one's God too.

Transcending one's identity is not the same as forgetting. In all these wanderings, I firmly had my identity in my heart. Without it, I would have been like a kite without a thread being held or like a climber without his rope. That identity has four parts: first (and foremost), I am a Hindu; second, I am a Tamizhan; third, I am a Brahmin; and fourth, I am a Srivaishnavan. I am aware that all four have been under siege for hundreds of years. I am confident that one day, all of them would triumph.

What I gained from this life are tonnes of experience, an estate of consciousness and vast acres of mind, which, I wish, remain with me forever.

I have wound up my life in India, sold and dispersed whatever assets I have gathered during my lifetime, booked a senior care home in the outskirts of Chennai, as I need a place to stay when I return from the US, and left some money in the bank in my wife's name. And I do have my pension from the government service.

My days in the US are fruitfully spent; in addition to going to the school twice or thrice a week, once in two or three weeks to the cyber security group meetings at Stanford University, helping my wife in household chores and gardening, reading books to my grandchildren, and, of course, a lot of reading. Going to the gym has been a regular habit. In the near future, I propose to explore the world of biohacking with the Bulletproof Labs in the beach town of Santa Monica in Southern California. This is about taking the health and fitness science to the next level. At the mind level, quantum consciousness is another field I would like to explore with Amit Goswami, a quantum science expert. I am also curious about what 'Siddha Veda', tells us about the meaning of human life.

If I get restless with my present life, what would I do? Perhaps reinvent myself all over again!

Acknowledgements

My special thanks to:

Debashish Banerji, the Haridas Chaudhuri Professor of Indian Philosophies and Cultures and the Doshi Professor of Asian Art at the California Institute of Integral Studies, for his invaluable suggestions.

Carolyn Cooke, Chair, Department of Writing and Consciousness and MFA Project Supervisor for her encouragement, guidance, valuable suggestions and showing immense patience in going through the manuscript and editing it several times.

Robert McDermott, Pireeni Sundaralingam and Elizabeth Jennings, for reading the manuscript and giving valuable suggestions.

Jaya, my wife, for enabling me in every way in writing this book.

Dhananjay and Kaushik, my sons, for lending a helping hand whenever I needed.

Bibliography

Agus, David B. *The End of Illness and The Lucky Years* (US: Simon & Schuster, 2016).

Brown, Lester. R. *Plan B* (W. W. Norton & Company, 2003).

Capra, Fritjof and Pier Luigi Luisi. *The Systems View of Life: A Unifying Vision* (Cambridge University Press, 2016).

Comite, Florence. *Keep It Up: The Power of Precision Medicine to Conquer Low T and Revitalize Your Life* (US: Rodale Books, 2013).

Fadiman, James. *The Psychedelic Explorer's Guide* (Park Street Press, 2011).

Goodman, Marc. *Future Crimes* (London: Random House, 2015).

Hesse, Hermann. *Journey to the East.*

Iyengar, B.K.S. *Light on Life* (US: Rodale Books, 2008).

James, William. *The Varieties of Religious Experiences.*

Johnson, Don. *The Protean Body* (Harper & Row Publishers, 1977).

King, C. Daly, *The Force of Gurdjieff.*

Lind-Kyle, Patt. *Heal Your Mind, Rewire Your Brain* (Energy Psychology Press, 2010).

Macy, Joanna and Chris Johnstone, *Active Hope: How to Face the Mess We're in Without Going Crazy* (New World Library, 2012).

Ouspensky, P.D. *In Search of the Miraculous* (Florida, US: Harcourt Inc., 1949).

Richard, William A. *Sacred Knowledge: Psychedelics and Religious Experiences* (Colombia: Columbia University Press, 2015).

Satguru Subramuniyaswami. *Merging with Siva* (Himalayan Academy Publications, 1999).

Swami Rama, Rudolf Ballentine and Swami Ajaya. *Yoga and Psychotherapy* (Himalayan Institute Press, 1976).